I0521757

Safely Abiding

Rosemary J. Fisher

Riverview Press

Safely Abiding
Copyright © 2022 by Rosemary J. Fisher

Author of the highly acclaimed romance novel
UNDER HIS WINGS

ISBN: Paperback: 979-8986772530
              Hardcover: 979-8986772547
              eBook: 979-8986772554

Printed in the United States of America

Riverview Press

THE WHITE DOVE SERIES

Under His Wings
Safely Abiding

CONTENTS

DEDICATION

Safely Abiding is dedicated to my mom, Wanda Gossell, who encouraged me to write more about Coop and Becky. She read the first half of the rough draft before her vision loss made reading impossible, even with a large font size. She gave me character name suggestions, plot ideas and just kept asking, "What's happening now?" She kept me going!

Mom prayed with me that my writing would touch the lives of readers, give them hope and bring them to a deeper understanding of God's love for his children. Sadly, mom passed away before I had completed the first draft. I believe she's smiling down from heaven, happy to see this novel come to publication. I can almost hear her say, "What's going to happen in the next book?"

ACKNOWLEDGEMENTS

Many people had a part in the completion of this book. The biggest help came from so many readers who supported my efforts with "Under His Wings," the first book in this series. Thank you for your encouragement!

I want to thank my friends Linda, who helped me with medical terminology, Tabby who shared her experiences and Aimee who answered my questions about cows.

Thanks also to Barb, Marilyn, and Lila for editing assistance and my sister Betty for cover ideas.

I also want to thank Pastor Tim DeVries for allowing me to use his thoughts presented in an inspired sermon on 'Abiding.'

A big thanks and lots of appreciation to my husband John for believing in me, even when I doubted myself. Your support means everything.

This book came about because so many of my readers requested a sequel. So friends, this book is for you! Enjoy the unfolding story of Coop, Becky and their family and friends. May you be blessed by the songs and scriptures within the pages. Abide safely under the comforting wings of our creator.

CHAPTER 1

———◆◆◆———

Built on the Rock

Marla Jean Smith entered the sanctuary of the Methodist church. The large room was empty and quiet, for now. Marla Jean knew that before long, the space would be filled with family and friends ready to witness the wedding of her son Coop to his sweetheart Becky Emerson. But for just a few minutes, Marla Jean wanted to sit quietly with her thoughts.

She hugged an 8x10 photo frame to her chest in a comforting embrace, and then pulled it out at arms length so she could see the photo inside. The smiling face of her husband looked back at her. Wearing his grey Sunday suit, with a deep red necktie, Walter Smith looked properly dressed to attend his son's wedding. Only Walter wasn't really here. His death just six months earlier meant that the seat next to Marla Jean would be empty.

Her heart ached. She missed her husband. She knew this was just one of many family gatherings where his absence would be felt by many, but most strongly by his wife of 31 years. She sighed deeply and placed a kiss on the cold glass covering his picture. 'If it weren't for the promise of heaven,' she thought, 'I don't know how I could go on.'

She knew Walter was proud of his son. As soon as Walter's health had started to fail, Coop had quit college and returned to the family farm. The last couple of years, Coop had taken on more and more responsibility with the farm work. Things were running smoothly, and Walter had often told Coop how much he appreciated his help.

Walter had met Becky just a short time before his death, and Marla Jean knew he liked her. He would have been so happy to see his son take this step with this young lady who seemed to love the Lord. He would surely have given his blessing to this union.

But he wasn't here. The empty chair would be filled with this framed photo. On the bride's side of the aisle, there was another photo, already in place. Becky's father was also missing from the ceremony. He had passed away many years before. On the seat, next to the photo, someone had placed a sprig of holly with red berries.

Marla Jean looked around and saw that the church, familiar to her on regular Sundays, was especially beautiful today. Winter sunlight was brightening the room as it filtered through the stained-glass windows that lined the sanctuary walls. The wooden cross on the front wall took on a special warm glow as the sunbeams hit it. The front of the sanctuary was decorated with poinsettias and holly branches. A wedding four days after Christmas made the choice of flowers pretty simple. In fact, most of the poinsettias had been here for the service at church last week. At the center of the altar table, an unlit Unity candle sat, with single green tapers on either side. The ushers would be in shortly to light the tapers before the service began. Then the guests would be seated, the mothers ushered down the aisles, and her son would be wed. He would begin a new chapter of his life.

'Dear Lord Jesus,' she prayed to herself. 'Bless them Lord. Guide them through the days ahead -- the joyful days, the uncertain days, the happy times, the frightening times, the angry times, the hurt that each may feel from time to time. Whatever lies ahead, cause them to remember to call on you. May they always remember to seek your wisdom. May they turn to you as they deal with whatever the future holds for them. These children are yours and are in your hands. Their days, whatever they may hold, are yours. Join Coop and Becky as one mind, to honor you, serve you, and be a united witness to your love and salvation. Bless their family with your constant care.'

Marla Jean wiped a tear from her eye and patted the photo frame. 'Wish you were here, Walter. But I feel you with me.' She rose and walked to the back of the sanctuary. People were already gathering outside in the foyer. She wanted to have a moment with Coop before he met with the pastor.

In the hall outside the bride's dressing room, she met Elizabeth Emerson, Becky's mother. She looked radiant, with a glowing smile on her face and eyes shimmering with happiness. The two women embraced warmly.

"Well, this is it," Elizabeth said. "Our children are fulfilling their dreams."

"True," said Marla Jean. "Or at least one of their dreams. I know there are lots more happy days to come."

"I know I couldn't be happier. Coop is certainly an answer to my prayers for Becky. And he's already shown what a great father he will be for Jenny." She took a deep breath. "But whew, what a whirlwind! I can't believe this day is here, and we got everything done in time. I think the Lord was watching over us, because everything fell into place smoothly. The weather couldn't be better, thank the Lord! I wasn't so sure a December wedding was a good idea, but it's all working out fine."

"The sanctuary looks beautiful," said Marla Jean. "And you do too! Is Becky almost ready?"

"She is," said Elizabeth. "I just have to run out to the car and get her boots. We forgot to bring them in."

"Boots," said Marla Jean with a chuckle. "She's getting married in cowboy boots! No wonder Coop loves her so much!" Elizabeth left to retrieve the boots, and Marla Jean went a little further down the hall to find her son. She needed to hug him once more.

The whole town seemed to be excited about this wedding. If Winslow, Kansas, had a newspaper, the headlines would have been "Local Hero to Wed." But since there was no newspaper in Winslow, Doc Larson and Jerry from the hardware store had taken it upon themselves to spread the news.

Doc had erected a large sign beside the entrance to the Animal Hospital. It read 'Becky's Gettin' Hitched'. It had a wooden cutout of two figures on horses, riding off into the sunset. He had a second sign that said 'The Happy Trails Begin In --- Days.' Every morning, when he unlocked the door to his veterinarian office, Doc would take a big black magic marker and change the number on the sign. He hadn't known Becky very long, only about a year, but he and his wife had grown to love her. He was pleased to announce to anyone and everyone that he was responsible for bringing the young couple together. He had introduced them, and knew right from the start that they were made for each other. Then Doc would puff out his chest and stand a little taller as he announced that HE would be walking Becky down the aisle. He even drove to Atkins and bought a new suit for the event.

There was also a sign out front of the hardware store. It was a big, professional sign, lighted at night, usually used to advertise new arrivals of farm and gardening supplies. But this was December, and there was no real need to sell farm equipment, so since the first of the month, the sign had read 'Emerson/Smith Wedding. Dec 29. Methodist Church. All invited. Pot-Luck reception to follow.' Jerry had been good friends with Walter Smith. Honoring Walter's son in this way was the least he could do for an old friend, God rest his soul.

The general consensus of the whole town was that these young kids deserved some happiness/ after all they'd been through. What with the lingering illness of Coop's father and his death last spring, and then that mess with the waitress and the drugs, and the drama around all that, well, it was certainly time for some joy. And what could be more joyful than a wedding? Especially one where the whole town was invited!

The newspaper in Atkins did run an engagement announcement. Lying in her hospital bed at Atkins General Hospital, Melissa Madison, otherwise know as Misty, read all about it. She gazed at the picture of two smiling faces, one she knew well, and one she had at one time hated with a jealous passion. But that was then, and now she had a new outlook on life. So much had changed. She sighed and, with no bitterness or anger, said, "Well, would you look at that! A happy ending!"

So as the townspeople got ready for the big day, spirits were high. December always brought joy because of the celebration of Christmas. But this year it would be even more joyful, because two of their friends were joining their lives as one. It was a new beginning, in many ways. And just one more reason to celebrate.

The women of Winslow had poured over their recipe books, wanting to choose just their very best items to contribute for the pot-luck. Grandma's special baking powder biscuits? The traditional chicken and rice casserole? Maybe scalloped potatoes and ham? So many decisions.

And what to wear? Something nice, but nothing to outshine the bride. Polish those shoes, press the dress, make sure the kids had matching socks. Maybe the hubby should get a new tie? There was so much to do!

Becky and her mother had a lot to do too, but everything had fallen into place easily. Despite the short timeframe – who gets married just four months after announcing their engagement? – they got everything done without any hiccups. Even the weather, sometimes unpredictable in Kansas in December, had cooperated. There had been a light dusting of snow the week before Christmas, only accumulating a couple of inches, but the streets had been plowed, sidewalks and parking lots cleared, and travel would be no problem. The cold temperatures were normal for Kansas folk. People traveling from out of state might shiver a bit, but hey, put on a sweater if you're cold. That's what we do in Kansas.

A To Do List had hung on Elizabeth's refrigerator for months, and everything on her list had been checked off. She had insisted on helping Becky plan this celebration (for that's how she saw it) and Becky had gladly given her the reins. Elizabeth had more free time, since Becky was planning to work until closer to Christmas. And of course, Becky had Jenny to care for and prepare for the many changes coming into her life. Elizabeth wanted Becky to relax and enjoy her special day. She really didn't mind dealing with all the little details.

Coop's mother, Marla Jean, had helped Becky pick out some music. Becky didn't want anything too contemporary; she preferred old hymns. So, they decided on a congregational song, "The Solid Rock" and "The Love of God" to be sung as a solo. Marla Jean thought Kaye Christianson would probably be a good choice for soloist, and volunteered to check with her. Becky loved the words to both of those songs and thought they would work perfectly into their ceremony. She and Coop both wanted the wedding to be a celebration, as well as an opportunity to spread the gospel. These songs would be perfect.

The detail of the dress, however, now that was all on Becky. She had a specific style in mind, and had searched the internet until she found just what she wanted. The dress had been ordered and, praise the Lord, fit perfectly without alterations. It was white satin, with a lace and pearl overlay. It hit just a little below the knees in the front, tapering to an ankle-length train in the back. The neckline was modest, with long sleeves topped with a puffy cap at the shoulders. She had debated whether to wear her white cowboy hat, or go with the traditional lace veil. It was a difficult choice, but Jenny, creative five-year-old that she was, had come up with the idea to blend the two styles. Viola! A white cowboy hat with a lacy veil! Perfect!

Becky decided to splurge and buy a new pair of white boots to complete the outfit. She had been wearing them around the house for weeks, to break them in without getting them scuffed up. Jenny also had a pair of white boots and she proudly paraded through the house, carrying a bouquet of artificial flowers and pretending to be a bride. This was a big day for Jenny too, and she was *so* excited!

Jenny would be the flower girl, wearing a forest green velvet dress. She would drop flower petals as she walked down the aisle ahead of her mother. She was so happy that Coop would soon be a real part of their family. In fact, just thinking about it made her want to skip for joy. Maybe she could skip down the aisle, instead of just walking. She'd have to practice skipping in her boots, to be sure she could do it. Jenny's cousin Danny, who was seven, would carry a pillow with rings. He'd have to be careful not to drop them. He couldn't skip down the aisle, but Jenny could!

Flowers for the church would be poinsettias and holly, left over from Christmas, but supplemented with fresh additions if needed.

Becky's bouquet – that was harder. Becky loved roses, but they were expensive, especially at this time of year. She was about to settle for carnations and other simple flowers, but her sister, Joyce, had offered to pay for Becky's dream bouquet of white roses with one red rose in the center. So that was settled. The ushers would have simple white rose boutonnières. The bridesmaids, wearing simple forest green knee-length dresses, would carry holly and white roses. Coop would have a more elaborate boutonnière with holly and one red rose.

Ladies from the church had volunteered to coordinate the potluck reception. They could use church tables and tableware. The tables could be decorated with candles and flowers and various Christmassy items. No problem there.

Janice Thomas was going to make the wedding cake. Becky had been so impressed with the cake Janice had made for Jenny's fifth birthday and had asked her to create something beautiful for this special day. Becky knew she could trust Janice to come up with the perfect cake, and didn't see any need to micromanage the creation. Since the guest list included the whole town, Janice was also going to make dozens of cupcakes to supplement the dessert table.

So everything was set. All the details had been attended to. It was time to get this show on the road. The bride and her attendants joined hands and were led in prayer by Pastor Green's wife. Becky held her daughter's hand on one side and her mother's on the other. Gathered around were her sister Joyce, Coop's sister Dana, Coop's sister-in-law Stacy, and Becky's friend Nancy. Coop's mother was there too, standing next to Dana. She had come in to give Becky one last wedding gift and was glad she was there for this time of prayer.

Mrs. Green prayed for the couple and for Becky in particular, as she was about to take on the role of wife. She prayed God's blessing on the family unit, the union of two becoming one, the home they would establish. At the conclusion of the prayer, both Marla Jean and Elizabeth had to dab tears out of their eyes. Memories of their own weddings, so long ago, were brought fresh to mind.

Before she left to find Michael, who would seat her at the front of the sanctuary, Marla Jean called Becky aside. She handed Becky a small sheet of parchment paper. Becky handled it carefully; it was easy to see that the paper was fragile. The edges were slightly frayed and the paper itself was yellowed with age. Written in a beautiful calligraphy style were verses from I Corinthians 13. Known as the Love Chapter, these verses were familiar to Becky and she teared up a little reading them. She gave her mother-in law-to-be a gentle hug and thanked her for the gift. "This hung in my parents' home, in their bedroom, when I was a child. When Walter and I were married, Momma gave it to me. Now I'm giving it to you. The frame it was in was old and brittle and came apart when I took it off of the wall to bring it to you today. But I thought we could make it part of your bouquet, if we're careful. Then you could carry it with you when you and Coop exchange your vows."

"What a thoughtful idea," said Becky. "I'd love to have it with me. And we'll get a new frame and hang it in our bedroom as soon as we can. Thank you so much."

Marla Jean took the parchment, rolled it gently like a scroll, and carefully tied a white ribbon around it. She tucked it inconspicuously into Becky's bouquet. She patted Becky's hand and turned to go.

The ushers and groomsmen were waiting in the hall. Most of the guests had been seated. Sounds of soft music drifted from the sanctuary, mingled with quiet voices that occasionally rose in muffled laughter. This was indeed a happy day. Michael, Marla Jean's first-born son, took her arm and together they stood outside the tall double doors of the sanctuary. Doc Larson and Elizabeth took their places, ready to follow at a distance.

The other groomsmen followed Coop and Pastor Green to the side entrance. The bridesmaids took one last peek in the mirror, and then took their places. Joyce checked to see that Danny still had the rings in place and Jenny was ready with her flower petals.

Then the doors opened wide, and Michael walked proudly down the aisle, with his mother on his arm. Marla Jean smiled widely, happy to see that so many of her friends had come to share this joyful day with her family. Michael seated her next to the chair that held Walter's picture. Marla Jean saw that someone had placed a sprig of holly on this chair too. Michael kissed his mother and left out the side entrance.

Doc Larson escorted Elizabeth down to her seat, where she sat beside her husband's picture. She clutched a tissue tightly in her hand, ready at any moment to wipe tears from her eyes. It was bound to happen. Weddings always made her cry, and this one was especially emotional. Her prayers had been answered. Her baby girl was marrying the man of her dreams.

Doc went back to wait with Becky. As the bridesmaids prepared to make their entrance, the men entered from the side door. Dressed in black jackets, blue jeans and white shirts, each man was wearing a black cowboy hat. As one, they removed their hats as they stood at attention. They turned and faced the back, where they watched the ladies walk down the aisle. First came Stacy, and Michael gazed lovingly at his wife. Next Dana entered and took her place. David Cole, Coop's friend from church, winked at her and she blushed a bit. Joyce walked down the aisle, her eyes misty as she remembered her own wedding to Stephen several years ago. She knew how Becky would be feeling right about now. The next to enter was Nancy Martin, Becky's maid of honor. She stood at the front, opposite her husband Greg, and smiled encouragingly at the children in the back of the sanctuary.

Jenny took a big breath and started skipping down the aisle, scattering rose petals as she went. Everyone chuckled, enjoying the joyful moment. Danny followed slowly, balancing the rings carefully on the satin pillow he carried formally in front of him. Jenny went to stand in front of Dana; Danny stood near his father.

The music changed, everyone stood and turned toward the back. Becky stood there, glowing with happiness. She held on to the arm of Doc Larson, who was happy to support her as she glided down the aisle. Cameras clicked and flashed. Becky smiled at her friends, old and new. The day she had thought might never come was here at last.

Then Becky caught sight of Coop. His eyes locked onto hers and she felt warm all over. There he was, waiting to become her husband. The Lord had surely blessed her beyond measure. Coop was a godly man, faithful and dependable, honest and thoughtful. They were prepared for whatever might come their way. Together, with God's help, they would face the future and serve Jesus. They would make a family that was dedicated to the Lord. Theirs would be a union that could not be broken, no matter what the future held.

As Doc turned to take his seat, Becky hugged him and whispered "Thank you." He gave her a quick kiss on the cheek and looked at Coop. "She's all yours now," he said softly.

Coop nodded and smiled at Becky. "Here we go!" he said to her.

Becky smiled back and said, "Let's do this!"

They turned to face Pastor Green, who had heard everything that they had whispered. "Okay, let's do this!" he said with a chuckle.

Pastor Green welcomed the friends and family of the couple and Greg Martin, Coop's best man, took his place at the podium, reading the love chapter from First Corinthians 13. Becky glanced over at the woman who would soon be her mother-in-law. They shared a knowing smile as Becky gently tapped her bouquet, where the precious parchment paper lay safely tucked away.

Next Kaye Christianson sang about the love of God. Becky's heart swelled when Kaye sang the last verse. "Could we with ink the oceans fill and were the skies of parchment made, were every stalk on earth a quill and every man a scribe by trade, to write the love of God above would drain the ocean dry, nor could the scroll contain the whole though stretched from sky to sky." Tears misted her eyes and Coop smiled down at her. He thought she had never looked more beautiful. The ceremony proceeded as normal, with one major exception. Becky and Coop had stressed to Pastor Green that they wanted to have a salvation message as part of their wedding sermon. They said that, since the whole town would be there, it was a perfect opportunity to present the gospel to everyone there, especially ones who might not have heard it before. So the pastor included passages from the book of Romans and encouraged listeners to turn from sin and give their lives to Jesus. He closed with the parable that Jesus had taught about the house built on sand and the house built on the rock. From Luke 6:49 he read, "The one who hears my words and does not put them into practice is like a man who built a house on the ground without foundation. The moment the torrent struck that house, it collapsed and its destruction was complete."

"Friends," he continued, "I admonish you today to turn from your sinful ways and build your house upon the rock. That rock, that firm foundation, is Jesus Christ, who gave his life on the cross for you. Without Christ as your foundation, your house will fail." He turned to the couple in front of him. "Becky, Coop," he said, "You have both given your lives to Christ. You are well on the way to building your marriage on the firm foundation. Storms may come, in fact, storms *will* come. That's just the nature of life. But Jesus promises that when the torrents hit, you will be safe on the solid Rock. When day-to-day circumstances make the ground feel shaky, you can stand squarely on Jesus' love and promises for you. He will never leave you or forsake you, whatever comes your way. Commit the words of Psalms 46:1 and 2 to your memory, and trust the promise. 'God is our refuge and strength, a very present help in trouble. Therefore, we will not fear though the earth gives way, though the mountains are moved into the heart of the sea.' Let us pray." Everyone bowed their heads and the pastor prayed for the couple standing so eagerly before him. At the end of the prayer, many in the congregation echoed the pastor's amen.

Pastor Green asked the congregation to stand and join in singing the first song. Becky and Coop knew the words and sang along while facing each other. The words of the chorus rang through the sanctuary. "On Christ, the solid Rock, I stand – All other ground is sinking sand. All other ground is sinking sand." Becky marveled at how well the song fit with the pastor's admonition to the congregation. God was certainly in this place.

Becky handed her bridal bouquet to Nancy, and Coop passed his cowboy hat to Greg. Coop and Becky went to the Unity candle, took their individual tapers, and lit the large candle in the middle. As they extinguished their individual candles and watched as the center candle glowed brightly, the pastor said, "Let no man tear apart what God has joined together."

Pastor Green asked for the rings, and Danny stepped forward on cue. Once the pastor was holding the rings, Danny was able to breathe a sigh of relief. He had done his duty. He could relax!

The vows were spoken, the rings exchanged, and Coop lifted the veil that was covering his bride's glowing face. "I love you Becky," he said, and kissed her sweetly.

"And I love you too, Coop," said Becky and they kissed again. A cheer rose from some of the people in the audience. Coop kissed her again, and Becky blushed but thoroughly enjoyed his embrace.

The pastor asked the newlyweds to turn and he said "Ladies and gentlemen, friends and family, I introduce to you, Mr. and Mrs. Benjamin Cooper Smith." The young couple stood beaming as the crowd burst into clapping and cheers. Becky gathered her flowers, Coop got his hat, and they started down the aisle as man and wife. Their new journey had begun.

When they were about half way down the aisle, Jenny called out, "Hey, wait for me!" and dashed towards the couple. Becky laughed and held out her hand for her daughter. Coop took Jenny's other hand and all three strolled towards the exit. "Swing me!" said Jenny, and to the delight of those in the audience, the newlyweds lifted the little girl off the ground and swung her back and forth a few times.

The family of three stood in the reception line as the groomsmen ushered the bridesmaids out of the sanctuary. Then Marla Jean and Elizabeth joined arms and walked together to greet their children. Both mothers had evidently been crying, yet had big smiles on their faces.

Mr. Simmons, the photographer they had hired, soon had the family pictures taken and was efficiently organizing the wedding party for pictures back in the sanctuary. That completed, the members of the wedding party headed off to the fellowship hall and Becky and Coop were left alone. Mr. Simmons took several pictures of just the two of them. He assured them that he had gotten many great photos during the ceremony, although the couple had not been aware of his presence. He was very discreet, which they appreciated. They thanked him for his work, he packed up his equipment and left.

Coop took Becky in his arms and kissed her again. "Mrs. Smith, I want to kiss you all night," he said, and Becky laughed.

"I can't think of anything I want more, Mr. Smith," she replied. Their lips met again and they shared another kiss. From the back of the sanctuary, someone cleared his throat loudly. It was Michael.

"Um, sorry to disturb you lovebirds, but your public awaits. Nobody wants to start eating until you get there, and everybody is hungry. So come on!" He motioned with his hand and held the door open as they headed for the fellowship hall.

Coop leaned down to whisper to Becky. "I guess we'll have to save most of our kisses for later. But I promise you, we are not done!"

"I'm gonna hold you to that promise," Becky whispered back. As the happy couple entered the fellowship hall, everyone burst into cheers. Becky, Coop and Jenny took their places at the front of the food line, filling their plates with all sorts of delicious looking pot luck items. They found their seats at the head table and were soon joined by Marla Jean, Elizabeth and other members of the wedding party.

The celebration lasted well into the evening. It was certainly the biggest social event ever held in Winslow. As the festivities wound down, Coop and Becky stood to thank their friends for coming and sharing in their special day. They were escorted outside, amidst well wishes and whistles, and Coop held the truck door for his bride. Becky sat in the truck, with her wedding dress gathered carefully around her, her bouquet on her lap, and waved happily to her friends. She blew a kiss to Jenny as Coop started the truck.

The newlyweds were on their way. The truck drove out of the church parking lot, tin cans tied on the back bumper rattling as they left.

CHAPTER 2

❖ ◆ ❖

A Cord of Three

Branson, Missouri, was beautifully decorated for the holiday season. Lights of every color brightened store fronts, doors and windows. Trees lining every street were aglow with white lights. Like a million stars, they blinked and twinkled, giving a festive spirit to the town. The air was cold and crisp, with a hint of coming snow.

Coop and Becky walked hand in hand down the sidewalk, enjoying the beauty and excitely taking in the sights together. 'Together,' thought Becky. 'Together forever.' She sighed with contentment.

Coop noticed and wrapped his arm around her waist, pulling her closer. "I love being here with you," he said. "Mostly because I love you."

Becky leaned into his embrace and sighed again. "It's really beautiful, isn't it? The lights and decorations, the feeling of happiness that is everywhere. It's a wonderful place. I'm so glad you picked this spot for our honeymoon."

"It's beautiful, all right," said Coop. "But it's made more beautiful because you are here."

"Oh Coop, you're making me blush. I love when you say sweet things like that to me."

"You're blushing? I can't tell. I thought it was just that your cheeks were red from the cold." He kissed her gently on each cheek.

Becky smiled up at him and said, "You can keep on saying nice things for the rest of our lives. That's fine with me."

"Fine with me too. I keep thinking about how beautiful you looked, walking down the aisle at the church, with your white dress and boots, and white cowboy hat. You took my breath away. I kept thinking about how lucky I am that I get to spend the rest of my life looking at you." He pulled her close again and said softly, "Of course, you look pretty good no matter what you're wearing, or not wearing!"

Becky giggled and lowered her eyes. "Now I really *am* blushing!" she said.

Coop led the way to a bench along the walkway to the Andy Williams Theater. They were early for the show, and had time to sit and enjoy the sights before entering the theater. A few people were making their way up the hill towards the building, chatting and laughing. Most of them were older adults, with a few young families as well. The children ran ahead of their parents, and then stopped to wait for them to catch up. Everyone seemed to be in a holiday spirit.

But the happiest spot along the walkway was the bench where Becky and Coop sat, comfortably cuddled together, oblivious of those passing by. They sat in silence for a few minutes, just enjoying being together. Then Coop sat up a little straighter and looked into Becky's eyes.

"I didn't mean to say that I was lucky to get to be with you…I really mean that I am *blessed* to be your husband. It's so good to feel, to *know*, that God has chosen you for my partner. I heard somebody say once that a cord of two strands is easily broken, but a cord of three strands is much stronger. If you think of the three strands as you, me, and God, then think how strong we can be together. Unbreakable! We should have put something like that into our wedding ceremony. Wish I would have remembered it sooner."

"Yes, that's a neat thought. I actually think I remember that it's a scripture verse, from somewhere in the Old Testament." She took out her phone, clicked on the Bible app, and found the verse. "Yes, here it is. Ecclesiastes 4:12. Though one may be overpowered, two can defend themselves. But a cord of three strands is not quickly broken." She closed up her phone and put it away. "But I thought our wedding was perfect. Pastor Green did a good job of sharing the gospel, and I believe some people were touched by the Holy Spirit. Your three strand cord idea can be something we meditate on together, just us, and remember that God is part of our union, and makes us strong enough to get through any difficulties that come our way."

"You're right, Becky." Coop thought for a minute. "Because I hate to say it, but difficulties *will* come along. That's just life. We don't know what's coming at us around the corner. Day to day, we'll turn to the Lord to help us handle whatever comes our way."

"I have a cross-stitch hanging in my bedroom. You haven't seen it yet, but you will. It says, 'A day hemmed in prayer will not unravel'. I bought it at a yard sale many years ago. It's helped me remember to start the day with prayer, asking for God's presence with me as I go about my work and parenting and whatever. And then I also end the day with prayer, thanking God for the blessings of the day."

"That's awesome. Is that something you want to continue on your own or would it be okay if we did it together? We haven't really talked about how our devotional life will look, now that we're married."

"I absolutely love that we are having this conversation," Becky said. "And I think we should each continue our own personal devotion time, like we are used to, but I really love the idea of having a set time every day that we can share scriptures and prayers together. What do you think?"

Coop nodded. "I think you're right. Having personal time with God is important. He can reveal things to us individually as we are dealing with our own spiritual battles. But I also think that we can discuss scripture together and build our home on that strong foundation like the pastor was talking about. And Jenny can be included in that family time. What do you think? Maybe every night after supper we could have a family Bible time."

"Perfect!" said Becky. "Jenny will love that. And I can continue to have prayer time with her before she goes to sleep."

"Um, do you think it would be okay if I sat in with that? Or maybe take turns doing it every other night with her?" Coop was a little hesitant, not wanting to upset the routines that Becky and Jenny had established. Yet he did want to be a strong god-head for his family, and that would include Jenny and any other children they might be blessed with in the future.

"Hmmmm," Becky thought about it and said, "Why don't we start out with you being in the room while we pray, and see how Jenny reacts. I'm pretty sure she will love having you there, but maybe we don't want to push too many changes on her at once."

"I know what you mean. We're throwing a lot of new things on her. A new dad, another person in her house, and a whole new family, and pretty soon a new house, and then kindergarten. It's a lot. But she's a pretty resilient little girl, I think, and that's thanks to you. I predict she'll do just fine." He kissed her again, and then said, "I think we better get inside. We are about to turn into popsicles!"

"Okay," Becky said. "But I don't feel cold at all. Whenever I'm with you, I feel warm all over."

"Love does that!" Coop laughed as he pulled her to her feet. "But let's go. We don't want to miss the show."

CHAPTER 3

---◆◆◆---

And the Two Shall Become One

As they drove out of town after the show, Becky sat in the middle of the seat, near Coop, leaning slightly against him. She felt so safe with him, so completely protected and cared for. She knew it was because she believed, without a shadow of a doubt, that Coop was God's gift to her. He was a wonderful man, kind and thoughtful, wise and strong. And Becky recognized that Coop relied on the strength of the Lord to give him direction and calm leadership. She sighed in contentment and started to hum one of the songs from the show they had just seen.

"I know I've said it before, but you really should think about joining the church choir," Coop said. "You have a really sweet voice. I love hearing you sing."

"Oh, thanks, but no, I don't think so. I could never stand up and sing in front of people."

"Never say never," Coop chuckled. "You don't know what the Lord has in store for you. And besides, if He leads you, He will strengthen you."

"That's funny," Becky said. "That's just what I was thinking about."

"What do you mean?"

"I was realizing that one of the reasons I feel so safe with you is because you get your strength from the Lord. And your decisions are God directed. And as long as you are following His leading, you will be taking the right path. And I'm safe with you."

"But you're forgetting one important thing, Becky." Coop turned off the main road and the truck began to climb up a steep hill. "You forgot that now WE are a team, and the decisions WE make are going to be God directed. With both of us listening to the Lord for direction, we can't go wrong."

"True. But I'll still be relying on your leadership. Like Paul says in Ephesians and Colossians, I will submit myself to you as I do to the Lord. But I also know that you will love me like Christ loves the church. So I feel protected and at peace. It's a good feeling. I mean, I know I was never alone, God was always with me. But now it feels wonderful, knowing that you and I will be making decisions together, and with both of us listening to the Lord, we are sure to be in His will."

Coop took her hand in his. "I love you Becky. I feel like God brought us together, and God will be with us, no matter what comes our way. We'll be a great team!"

He raised her hand to his lips and gave it a quick kiss. Then he took hold of the steering wheel and said, "Our turn should be up here soon. This road looks different in the dark, but I remember there was a big sign on the right just before the intersection. Ah, yep, there it is." He turned the truck right and they drove down a gravel road.

They were renting a cabin in the woods for a few days. The cabin had a fully stocked kitchen, with frozen meals in the freezer, plenty of fruit, drinks, and snacks. Milk and bread and sandwich makings were also provided, as well as a variety of breakfast cereals and eggs and bacon. They had everything they would need for meals, if they decided not to go into town. The cabin had a fireplace, a hot tub, and a screened porch with a swing. Coop thought it would be a great place for a honeymoon getaway, and Becky loved it.

"You getting hungry?" Coop asked as they turned into their driveway.

"Kinda. These leftovers from our supper at Mickey Gilley's smell really good. Should we save them for tomorrow, though? I could warm up that apple crisp that I took out of the freezer this morning. And there's ice cream."

"Sounds good. How about I make a fire in the fireplace, while you fix the apple crisp, and we'll eat in front of the fire?" Coop drove into the carport and parked the truck. He took the cabin key from his pocket and went to open the door for Becky. She carried the bag from Gilley's and their program from the theater. Before they entered the cabin, Coop looked up at the sky. "I think the temp's dropped 20 degrees since we left town. Feels like snow."

Becky stood on tiptoes as he held the door for her. She kissed him and said, "I think a fire would be wonderful. Warm this place up!"

An hour later, the couple was sitting in front of a roaring fire, eating warm apple crisp with ice cream. Becky playfully dabbed some ice cream on Coop's cheek and licked it off. She giggled as Coop scooped ice cream with his fingers and held them in front of her lips. Becky licked his fingers clean. "I love you," she said, and Coop took her in his arms. The fire crackled and the room was filled with warmth. Despite the falling temperatures outside, the cabin was delightfully comfortable. As their bodies joined as one, neither of them noticed any chill at all.

Hours later, Coop awoke when a half-burnt log gave way and fell into the embers. He gazed at his wife, sleeping on the couch, half wrapped in an afghan. "God, she's beautiful. May I be worthy of her. May I love and protect her always. Help me, God, to be a wise husband and father. Thank you." He walked quietly to the fireplace, careful to avoid tripping on a twisted heap of clothes on the floor. Coop put more logs on the fire. Then he bent over Becky, picked her up, and carried her to bed.

CHAPTER 4

◆◆◆

Surprises

Becky woke the next morning to the smell of coffee and bacon. She rubbed the sleep from her eyes and looked around. It took a little time to realize where she was, and why. Then she fell back onto her pillow, smiling and feeling a joy like she'd never known was possible. Her husband's side of the bed was cool to the touch, but the smell of him lingered on the pillow next to hers. She hugged the pillow to her face and inhaled deeply. With her eyes closed, she sighed deeply. "Thank you Jesus," she whispered.

Coop stood at the bedroom door, holding two cups of coffee. He had pulled on his jeans, but was wearing no shirt. The fireplace was warming the little cabin quite nicely, despite the falling temperatures outside. He smiled at his wife, noting the way her hair fell across the pillow and the bed sheet barely covered her leg. He softly whispered "Ditto," and stood watching her a moment longer.

"Good morning, Mrs. Smith," he said more loudly, and Becky opened her eyes. "Are you ready for breakfast?"

She sat up in the bed, modestly pulling the sheet up to her shoulders. "Um, yes, that sure smells good. But maybe I should get some clothes on first."

"If you insist," Coop said. "But you certainly don't have to on my account. I kinda like looking at you this way!"

"Well, let me at least brush my hair and wash my face and brush my teeth." She stood up and reached into the closet. Coop set the coffee cups down on the dresser and watched her. It was hard to take his gaze off her beautiful form. "Mom got me this pretty robe, and I haven't even worn it yet." Becky put her arms into the sleeves of her robe and walked to him with it hanging loosely. "Thanks for making breakfast." She kissed him, and he wrapped his arm around her. Then she padded into the bathroom and Coop looked after her.

He picked up the coffee cups and said, "Okay. Meet me in the kitchen when you're ready. I've got a surprise for you."

Becky was brushing her teeth, and mumbled something that sounded like, "Goody goody! I love surprises!" Before she went into the kitchen, she opened a dresser drawer and brought out a small box wrapped in pretty paper, tied with a deep green ribbon. She laid it on the kitchen table, which was laden with a delicious breakfast of scrambled eggs, bacon and toast. "I've got a surprise for you too."

"Let's eat, and then we'll open the surprises." Coop took her hand. "Let's pray."

Becky loved to hear Coop pray, and she also loved the way he squeezed her hand when he said "Amen." As she spooned orange marmalade onto her toast, Becky said, "You know, that hand squeeze is one of the things I first loved about you. It kinda felt like a secret club handshake, between you, God and me! I liked feeling included in your special club." She chewed thoughtfully. "It still feels special, after all these months."

"Then I'll never stop doing it!" Coop replied. He picked up a piece of bacon and said, "This turned out perfect, if I do say so myself. Nice and crispy, but not burnt." He took a bite and said, "I never asked you how you like your bacon cooked. Hope this is okay."

"It's perfect. Jenny likes it this way too, for future reference. Do you plan to fix us all breakfast every day?" Becky wiped her fingers and lips with a napkin.

Coop chuckled and said, "Sure, if you promise to always come to the table dressed in nothing but a robe!" He placed a kiss gently on the tip of her nose. "Probably not a good idea, though, since Jenny will be eating with us." He paused and took a sip of coffee. "Do you want to know the moment I started to fall in love with you?"

"Do tell," Becky said, and placed her hand under her chin. "I've been wondering."

"It was the very first day I saw you. You got out of Doc's truck and knelt down to pet Riley. I always knew that dogs were perceptive about people, but when Riley started licking your hand, I knew he liked you, and I figured I'd better check you out for myself!"

"I'm sure glad you did. I love you, Mr. Smith." Becky began stacking the dishes and pushed them to the center of the table. "Breakfast was terrific. Thank you." She nodded at the box sitting on the table close to Coop. "Now it's time for your surprise."

As Coop began unwrapping the gift, Becky continued, "Another thing I love about you is how good you are with Jenny. She feels so comfortable around you; in fact, I think she totally adores you. I love the relationship that's growing between you two. It's really important to me, you know, that we create a strong family. So I put this together, so you and Jenny would have these memories from the start of your relationship. I hope you like it."

Coop pulled a photo album out of the box. Turning the pages slowly, he looked at pictures of himself with Jenny, holding baby chicks, feeding carrots to the horses, swinging on the rope in the hay mow. He laughed when he saw the picture of himself milking Bessie. He had aimed the milk right into the mouth of one of the barn cats. Jenny was standing there, laughing with delight.

Coop turned the page and saw a picture of Jenny lying on the floor of the porch, snuggled up with Riley, who was asleep. Jenny was rubbing Riley between his ears. "This must have been just a few days before we had to put him down," Coop said softly, as he stroked the picture with his finger tips.

"Yes, it was." Becky stood behind Coop and put her hands on his shoulders. She began to massage his shoulders and neck, and his body relaxed as he leaned against her. "Do you think you'll want another collie pretty soon?"

"Oh, I *know* I want another collie. They are wonderful dogs to have on the farm. It's just a matter of timing. I don't think we should get a puppy while we're living at your house. We should probably wait until we're settled into the new house. And that will be the middle of summer probably."

"The new house, *our* house. I like the sounds of that." Becky took the breakfast dishes to the sink and began to run hot soapy water for washing. "We'll have a dishwasher, right?"

"You know it!" Coop laughed. "And even a stove, and indoor plumbing."

"Seriously, Coop, I feel so blessed. To think that your dad left you his life insurance money to be accessible *now*, if you needed to get right into it. It's like he knew what was ahead. He knew that you would need a house, so he made sure you could have one. And still he was providing for your mom and your sister too."

"And Michael," Coop added. "You know, Michael and Stacy are seriously thinking about adopting a baby from overseas. And that's expensive. Dad's insurance policy will really help them out."

"That's wonderful. There are so many children just longing for homes. I'm always glad to hear whenever a good family brings a needy child into their home." She drained the water from the sink and dried her hands. "It will be exciting to see how God answers their prayers for a baby."

"Speaking of babies...." Coop started. "I can't wait till we have one of our own. Just imagine the fantastic children we will create! Beautiful and smart and kind and sweet, just like their mother."

"And tall and handsome and honest and trustworthy, just like their father." Becky smiled up at him and said, "We'll have to get them all cowboy hats and boots. And we need to start saving for their college educations. There's a lot to consider."

"You're so right," said Coop. "We need to make a lot of plans, before we start making babies." He paused. "But, I really do like the baby-making process!" He grabbed Becky and kissed her, pulling her tight against his bare chest.

"Mmm, me too! Practice makes perfect! And we're getting pretty good at it!"

"Maybe we should practice some more," Coop said, kissing her neck and making her giggle.

"Oh no you don't! Not yet!" Becky said squirming out of his grasp. "You told me you had a surprise for me. So where is it?" She had already looked around the kitchen, but hadn't seen any packages.

"Just close your eyes, and hold my hand." Coop led her slowly through the kitchen to the back door of the cabin. "Keep you eyes shut till I tell you to open." He opened the door to the screened in porch and guided Becky outside.

"Whoa! It's cold out here," said Becky, but she kept her eyes closed as instructed.

"Now keep your eyes shut, and use all of your other senses. Tell me what you feel and hear."

Becky stood immobilized for several seconds. "It's so quiet. Like the whole world is asleep. I hear a blue jay call, but that's all. There's a little hum in the background, the hot tub I would guess. And there's a little warmth coming from that side of the porch. Hot water? It's cold on my other side, but not unbearable. I can smell chlorine. And I can still smell coffee. That's from your breath I think."

"Oh, sorry," Coop said. He kissed her and asked, "What do you taste?"

"Oh, definitely coffee!" she said. "And I also taste you."

"Okay, keep you eyes shut." He put his hands on her shoulders, turned her towards the back yard, and stood behind her. Coop unzipped his jeans and dropped them to the floor. "Take your robe off and then open your eyes."

Becky dropped her robe and opened her eyes. She stood facing the woods that surrounded the cabin, and she gasped at the sight before her. Snow had fallen in the night, and all of the trees in the forest were clothed in white. Branches were covered in snow several inches thick and the entire world was silent. The sun was shining through the trees, making each snowflake sparkle with an unearthly glow. "Oh my goodness, it's so beautiful! Like in the movie 'Dr. Zhiavago.' I feel like I'm in that snow house. I've never seen anything so beautiful."

Coop took a step to the side and turned so he was looking directly at Becky. "Neither have I," he said softly. Her body was mesmerizing, with sunlight highlighting the goose bumps on her flesh. He could barely take his eyes off her. He felt like the luckiest man in the universe.

Two blue jays began to chatter and bicker in a nearby tree, sending a miniature snowstorm cascading to the ground. Coop finally dropped his gaze and said, "The hot tub is ready. Let's get in and warm up." He helped Becky climb into the tub, then joined her. They spent the rest of the morning warming in the hot water, each enjoying the quiet companionship of the one they loved.

CHAPTER 5

---◆◆◆---

Snuggling in the Snow

Snow fell intermittently throughout the day. Late in the afternoon Coop and Becky took on the great outdoors. Bundled in winter coats, hats and gloves, they trudged through the snow, which at some points had drifted nearly knee deep. They were grateful for the snow boots they had put into the truck at the last minute. Becky had a knapsack draped around her back. Inside Coop had packed a flashlight and a blanket. Coop carried a thermos of hot chocolate. Two tin cups were laced onto his belt and bulged under his coat. They clanged together as the walked, muffled by the heavy winter coat.

The path leading to the lake was quite hidden, only visible because of the break in the trees. "I suppose this is the path," said Coop. "Can't really tell, but it must be."

"I trust you're right. Sure wouldn't want to get lost out here in the woods during a blizzard."

"Don't worry, Becky. Our body heat can get pretty high sometimes. I wouldn't let you freeze!"

"I'm counting on it!" said Becky, then stopped dead in her tracks. "Listen!" From the trees came the hoot of an owl, calling in solitude. There was no answering call, and he hooted again.

"What a mournful sound." Becky said. "He's all alone."

"Not for long, sweetheart. Spring will be here before we know it. Doesn't look like it now, but it's just a few months away. To everything there is a season. He'll find a mate, just like I did, and live happily ever after. Like us!"

They had reached the lake, which was frozen and covered with snow. There was a bench seat near the edge of the lake, where fishermen would sit in the summer. Now Coop scraped the snow away with the arm of his jacket and Becky spread a woolen blanket on the seat and back. They sat down, Coop poured cups of steaming hot chocolate, and they gathered the blanket around themselves.

"How wonderful to be here with you," Becky sighed. "My life has changed so much in just a few short months. A year ago, I never would have dreamed I'd be spending New Year's Eve like this."

"It isn't really the typical New Year's Eve, that's for sure! No parties, fancy clothes, merrymaking with a crowd. No countdown, or fireworks, or toasts at midnight. But we are together, and our coming year is filled with promise. That's what matters. When I kiss you at midnight, it will be our first kiss of the new year."

"The first of many, I hope!" Becky joked.

"You can count on it!" Coop said, and pulled her close. "I love kissing you. And other stuff."

Becky giggled and snuggled into him. "I love that other stuff too! It feels so perfect with you. Like we can read each other. Even after just a short time together, we've already learned so much. It's a miracle, how we are so in sync with each other."

"So, I'm doing it right?" Coop asked. "I just want you to be happy. I want you to know how much I love you. Completely. I want to make pleasing you my number one priority in life. Right behind serving the Lord, of course."

"Of course," Becky replied. "And you know, your desire to serve the Lord is just one more way you please me. I wouldn't have it any other way."

"Matthew 6:33," Coop quoted. "Seek ye first the kingdom of God and his righteousness, and all these things shall be added unto you."

Becky sang the verse softly, and Coop joined. "Allelu, Alleluia."

Together they sat, cuddled up and warmed by the presence of each other, and the love they felt. Darkness snuck up on them, and the stars blinked through the clouds. "Think we better head back?" asked Coop hesitantly.

"I don't want to leave, but I suppose we should. Good thing you brought a flashlight. Like the good Boy Scout you are. Always prepared."

"I'll have you know I was never a boy scout. But I do try to think one step ahead. You never know what may come your way."

"Lions, and tigers, and bears?"

"No, more like coyotes, and skunks, and deer." He laughed and said, "Just look over there." Coop pointed down towards the edge of the water on the other side of the lake. A deer was pawing at the snow, trying to break the ice to reach the water. It was a buck, with a large rack of antlers.

"So majestic!" Becky marveled. "I don't see how people can shoot them."

"Well, I understand if they are shot for food. But just for sport, no I don't get that."

Becky asked, "Do you like venison? I've had it a few times and don't really care for it. But I'll learn to fix it, if you really want me to."

"It's ok," said Coop. "But I'll be fine eating it just once in a while when somebody else fixes it. You don't need to worry about learning how to cook it. Leave that to someone who really likes it."

"Speaking of food," he said after they had watched the deer a few minutes, "I think we better get going. I'm getting hungry. Are you?"

"Hiking always makes me hungry. I took a tater tot casserole out of the freezer to have for our supper. Sound good?"

"It does!" Coop said. "You're a great cook!"

"I can't take credit for this supper, you know. But hopefully my real cooking will satisfy you."

Coop pulled her close. "You haven't disappointed me yet. And I know you never will."

"I love you more that words can tell," said Becky.

And Coop said, "Ditto."

CHAPTER 6

---◆◆◆---

A New Day – A New Year

New Year's Day dawned. Becky rolled over in bed and laid her head on her husband's chest. "Good morning, my love," she whispered. Coop raised his hand and stroked her head.

"Can we just stay in bed all day?" he mumbled sleepily. "That hike yesterday, and then staying up so late – man, I'm really tired."

Becky turned to look at the clock. "Good grief, it's almost noon already. We've been in bed half the day!" She pulled the pillow out from underneath Coop's head and said, "Get up, lazybones!"

Coop groaned and sat up. "Wow, you're like a slave driver. But if you insist.... What's for breakfast?"

"Let's have a big brunch. I'll fix it this morning. Or afternoon, or whatever it is. You do the dishes! Let's make a deal – whoever cooks, the other person does the dishes. Deal?"

"Deal," Coop said as he stood and stretched. "Extra incentive to get a dishwasher!" He headed towards the bathroom. "Okay if I take a shower before we eat?"

"Sure, it will take a while to get the food cooked, so that's probably good timing. And I usually like to take my shower at night anyway. So, you're a morning shower person, huh? That should work out well. I usually shower at night."

"I'm not opposed to night time showers. Actually, I usually get a quick shower before supper if I've been working in the fields. I'm usually so dirty I hate to sit down at the table until I've cleaned up. All depends on what I've been doing and how grimy I've gotten. Mornings are good, too, but wait! Maybe we should do joint showers. Now that sounds like a plan."

"Mmmmm, that sounds delightful! But I'll tell you what," Becky laughed. "We can do joint showers after we move into our house. Until then, we're sharing a bathroom with Jenny, and I don't think we want to expose her to family shower time!"

"You are absolutely right, my dear. Besides, I want you all to myself." Just then, Coop's cell phone rang. "Hmm, that's odd. I wonder who that could be." Becky stopped on her way to the kitchen to listen to one side of the conversation.

"Yes, Dale, Happy New Year to you too, sir."

"Really? I hadn't looked outside yet." Coop went to the window in the living room and pulled the curtain. "Oh wow, I see what you mean."

"Yes, we were planning on leaving tomorrow."

"I see."

"Well, we don't really have any choice, do we? And we're safe and warm here, so I don't see a problem with another day or two."

"I'm sure there's enough. You really had the freezer stocked up, so we'll be fine."

"I appreciate that."

"Thank you, sir. That's very kind of you. Stay safe. Goodbye."

Coop closed up his phone and turned to Becky. "Guess what? The roads are blocked with snow and Dale from the office says the snow plows won't get out this way for another day or two. So, we are snowbound. He said he can get to us by snowmobile if we need anything but otherwise, we get to stay here until they plow us out! And better yet, Dale said we don't have to pay for the extra days! How cool is that?"

"Incredible! What a blessing! Thank the Lord. We'll be safe, we have enough food, and we have each other. Perfect!"

"And I have two extra days of having you all to myself!"

Becky kissed him, then playfully pushed him off towards the bathroom. "I'll need to call mom after we eat, to let her know we won't be home when we planned. And I really want to talk to Jenny. I miss that girl!"

"Me too. And I'll call my mom. I wonder how much snow we got at home. I hope Dana won't have any trouble getting the cattle fed. But Michael and Stacy will be there for a few more days, so they can help her if needed. Though I don't think Stacy is much for the farm life. Michael either, for that matter. But he'll help Dana if she needs it."

"I'm sure she'll be fine. She's pretty resilient. And determined. Just like her brother."

When Coop returned from the shower, Becky had the table set with bacon, eggs and blueberry pancakes. She had prepared a half a grapefruit for each of them. Coffee was steaming in the cups. She had also managed to slip into some sweats and comb her hair.

"This looks amazing. And you do too!"

"Thanks. But don't get too used to big breakfasts. Jenny and I usually just have cereal before I drop her off at school. We save the pancakes for Saturdays."

"Not a problem. I will have to be up and out at the crack of dawn anyway. I'll just need some coffee, and maybe some to take with me. I'll head out to the farm, do the chores, and then hang out with mom. She'll feed me!"

"It's going to be hard on you, isn't it? Having to commute to work for a change?"

They had decided to live in Becky's rental house until their own new home could be built. That meant that Coop would have a lot of driving to do, out to the farm every morning, and back to town at night. Despite that, they figured it was the best way to manage things for now. Becky's lease would be up in a couple of months, and the landlord had agreed to go month by month until their new house was ready. By early summer, they hoped to be moved in.

As soon as they were engaged, they began making these plans. They looked at books of house plans, decided on one they both liked, chose the site for the house, and had the foundation dug and poured, all before the wedding. The builders were already at work, knowing that weather conditions might slow them down. They hoped to get it under roof before any major snow fell. It was a miracle, really, how quickly the house had come together. The crew was very efficient. Coop had hired a construction company from Atkins and was very confident that the general contractor would stay on top of things.

"I wonder how the house is coming. Hopefully there isn't enough snow there to slow them down much." Coop took Becky's hand as they sat at the table. He prayed, "Father God, we thank you for all these many blessings. This cabin and the warmth and safety it provides. The food we've been given and the beautiful hands that prepared this meal. We thank you for Dale and his willingness to share this space with us. We pray for those out plowing roads today. Keep them safe and warm. We ask a special blessing on our families back home. Be with Mom and Dana as they deal with the conditions at home. Be with Jenny and Grandma Elizabeth and bless their time together. And now Lord, we give this day to you. Whatever it holds, may we lean on you for our every need. Amen."

And of course, he squeezed Becky's hand.

"Building the house is exciting, that's for sure." Becky poured some syrup onto her stack of pancakes. "A once in a lifetime adventure! And I get to share it with you. Picking out the floor plan was fun, and it's the perfect house for us. Three bedrooms, one you can use as an office. Big kitchen with an eat-in area. I love having that big island. It'll be great when Jenny and I are baking together."

"Make lots of blueberry muffins," Coop said fondly, remembering the muffin Jenny had brought to him one day at church, not so long ago. "Before long, you'll get to pick out what kinds of cabinets and counter tops you want. Appliances, faucets, lighting. All that fun stuff."

"Lots of decisions. I hardly know where to begin."

"Well, when we get back home and settle in a bit, we'll drive over to Atkins and go to the Home Store. We'll look at lots of samples and be overwhelmed by the choices. Then we'll look at our budget, pray, and God will show us what's best for us."

"I'm sure He will," Becky said. "He showed me you, and you are certainly what's best for me! And Jenny too. She's pretty excited about moving to the farm, you know. She's already hoping Muffin will have more kittens, so she can claim them all. And she wants to learn how to ride the horses. She seems so little though."

"That girl is brave and adventurous. She'll have so much fun, being around the animals and learning about life on a farm. It's a good place to grow up. And who knows, maybe we'll get her a Shetland pony. They're small enough, she should be able to handle a horse that size. I can check around at farm auctions and see what's available."

"Not too soon, though, okay?" Becky asked. "I think we shouldn't just give her a pony. We could make it a goal, and have her work towards it. You know, chores around the house, showing responsibility to care for some of the animals, things like that. I don't want her to expect to get everything she wants. That's not preparing her for the real world. We all have to set goals, make plans, and work towards achieving the things we feel are important."

Coop looked at her intently. "You're a good mom. I can learn a lot from you about parenting. You'll help me, right? You've had more experience at it."

"Of course, I'll help, but you already know the basics. Look at life in your own family. You've had to work for the things you want. Nothing was just given to you. When you earn something, you value it more. You know that already."

"That's true," Coop admitted. "We have always had to work hard. Really, my parents set the example of hard work, and I guess us kids have just followed their example. So maybe our children will also learn by the examples we set."

"I'm sure they will. Jenny already has seen you busy on the farm. She knows that you value hard work, and she knows that living up to responsibilities is very important to you. Hopefully she's learning that from me too. I've tried to let her know that I go to work because I want to better our lives. We've never had a lot of money, but she knows that I'll do whatever I can to take care of her."

"That would describe us growing up too. Never had an abundance of money, but we had what we needed, and we knew mom and dad loved us and would take care of us.

Becky took his hand and leaned her head on his shoulder. With a soft sigh, she said, "Well, that's the key, isn't it? Love, I mean. We love our children and pray for them and set a good example by our own lives. And then we pray some more and do our best. Jenny needs to learn that life isn't always easy, that setting goals and working towards them is an important part of living productively. Goals, hard work, and God. That's what we all need."

Coop stroked Becky's hair and ran his thumb along her jaw line. He felt so good with Becky by his side. Complete. Whole. At peace. They sat together, feeling the magic of the moment. It was good, this feeling of oneness. Both Coop and Becky felt it.

Coop broke the silence. "I never saw a man work so hard as my dad. Sun up to sun down – he was always busy. Until he couldn't anymore." Coop paused a moment, reflecting on his father. "I really miss him," he said wistfully.

"I wish I had gotten to get to know him better. But I see similarities between the two of you. Honestly, you are a very hardworking man. To take on all the farm responsibilities, to throw yourself into all that requires." She looked at Coop and went on. "Your dad was proud of you. And so is your mom, I know. And me too!"

"I'm so glad I've earned your love," Coop said, and planted a kiss on the top of her head as he stood to take dishes to the sink. "I value it highly."

"That's so sweet. In fact, you are so nice to me; I'll be nice to you and dry the dishes. But you wash. I have to protect these beautiful hands!"

CHAPTER 7

◆◆◆

Daddy Coop

"But when, Mommy? When will you be home? I miss you." Jenny sounded disappointed.

"As soon as the snowplows clear the roads, honey. We have a lot of snow here. It will take a day or two before the trucks can come out on these country roads. But we'll be home as soon as we can. You can pray for our safe travel home, okay, Honey?"

"Okay Mommy. Daddy Coop is a good driver. He'll keep you safe."

Becky chuckled. "Yes, Sweetie, he will. But pray for everybody who has to be out driving on the roads. We love you, Jenny. Can you give the phone back to Grandma now?"

"Okay. Bye Mommy. I love you too."

When Elizabeth took the phone, Becky asked, "Daddy Coop? How did that come about?"

"It was her own idea! She came home from church saying that Hannah doesn't call her father 'Greg' and she didn't want to call Coop 'Coop' any more. So, she came up with 'Daddy Coop!' That girl! She's so creative. And funny. And head-strong."

"Oh oh. Does that mean she's been giving you trouble?"

"Oh, not really. She just got all excited when it started to snow, and was talking about sledding. She got her coat and boots out of the closet, and was starting to get all bundled up, but then the snow stopped and there really isn't enough for sledding. She was disappointed and insisted that she could go anyway. So, I let her try, to see for herself. Before long she was back in the house, pouting a bit. Hot chocolate brought her around. She's fine now."

"So, you don't have much snow there? We were wondering if the guys would be able to work on the house."

"Only an inch or so. And it's already starting to melt in the sun. I imagine the crew will be working."

"That's good. Well, I'll call you in a day or two. We must have gotten about ten inches here, but the road in front of the cabin has drifts at least two feet, I'd guess. And the man at the office says it will take a while for the snowplows to even get out to our road. We'll just have to stay until it gets clear. I'll let you know."

"Becky, don't worry about a thing. We're just fine here, and you just enjoy your time together. Oh, wait, don't hang up. Jenny wants to talk again."

Jenny's voice bubbled over the phone. "Mommy, Mommy, can I talk to Daddy Coop?"

"Sure Sweetie, just a minute." Becky motioned for Coop to take her phone. He said hello and broke into a big smile.

"Daddy Coop, when you come home, and when we get lots of snow and when I don't have to go to school, can you take me to the farm with you; and we can take my sled along and we can go sledding on the big big hill in the pasture? Please?" She finally ran out of breath and had to stop talking.

Coop laughed, "It sounds like you have this all planned out already! I think that would be lots of fun. Let's do it!"

"Oh good, I knew you would take me. Bye Daddy Coop. I love you." And with that, Jenny hung up the phone.

Coop turned to Becky with a grin. "She called me Daddy Coop! Isn't that cute? And she wants me to take her sledding in the pasture when we get more snow. And she said she loves me. I'm the luckiest man in the world!" He grabbed Becky around the waist and danced with her around the living room. They landed on the couch with a laugh.

"I'm going to bring in more firewood. Then I'll call my mom. Maybe after that we can each have our own devotional time. I have some journaling to do. I've missed a couple of days. Been kinda busy, I guess." He kissed Becky and said, "I've got a lot to thank the Lord for."

Coop pulled on his coat and headed for the door. He was smiling and shaking his head. "Daddy Coop!"

CHAPTER 8

───◆◆◆───

Truck Stop Memories

The interstate north of Atkins was totally closed. A dozen cars were in the ditch. /Several semis had jack-knifed and were blocking the roadway. Police were diverting traffic and expected the section of the highway would be closed for hours. Emergency vehicles and tow trucks were slowly making their way towards the scene.

The truck stop was bustling with weary travelers. Anxious to get off the road, to get something hot to eat or drink, to take their minds off the treacherous conditions outside, truck drivers and passenger car drivers alike had pulled into the truck stop for a break. Anyone going north northeast wouldn't be moving for a while anyway. Might as well get a meal, maybe find a hotel room for the night. Road conditions would surely improve by morning.

Craig Cashman sat in a booth, nursing a cup of hot coffee as he waited for his food to arrive. His fingers were freezing, and it felt good to wrap them around the big mug. It also felt good to be off the road. Even though he was an experienced truck driver, he disliked driving in these white-out conditions. It wasn't his driving he was worried about. It was the other idiots on the road. Cars that were traveling unnecessarily slow, vehicles that braked suddenly and for no reason other than fear, dummies who didn't know how to control their cars on ice. Well, it was good to get out of their way.

He had delivered his load earlier in the afternoon, and was on his way home with an empty trailer when the storm hit. Since he didn't have a schedule to keep, he figured he'd get a room and sleep comfortably tonight. The motel wasn't the best, but at least it would have heat and a TV. He could take a hot shower and feel fresh in the morning for the last leg of his journey home.

Nothing to rush home to anyway. Just an empty apartment over the tool shop on the outskirts of Catonsville. The rent was modest and the shop owners didn't mind him parking his rig out back. It wasn't a fancy place, but served its purpose. He was on the road most nights anyway, and didn't see a need for a bigger place, or a bigger rent.

Sitting in the truck stop diner, he remembered other times when he had been here. This was one of his regular stopping points on his cross-state runs. Most of the older waitresses knew him by sight, and a few of them called him by his nickname, Cash. He'd flirted with most of them, made a little progress with a couple, but generally just had a good time talking and kidding around. Driving a truck could be lonely, and he was always happy to have a little conversation with real people now and then.

An occasional release with a truck-stop lot lizard had usually proven unsatisfactory and left him with regrets. He'd become a trucker to make money, and hated himself when he threw his hard-earned cash away on prostitutes, no matter how desperate or needy he felt at the moment. He didn't really like that he was helping some woman support her drug habit, either. Not to mention the risk of disease. Craig had decided to stay away from the lizards, but wasn't opposed to finding companionship from other women from time to time He did try to choose cleaner, hopefully safer, women.

He remembered one time, last summer, when the conversation with another patron at the diner had led to a frisky romp in the sleeper compartment of his truck. He took a drink of his coffee and smiled to himself. That was his one claim to fame. That was the night he had helped the police capture a wanted criminal. And the sex wasn't bad, either!

True, he hadn't gotten his name in the paper, only the mention of a helpful truck driver who had notified the police of the location of the fugitive. But that was alright. He knew he was a hero, even if he wasn't mentioned by name.

He'd been following the story in the newspapers. Apparently, the girl, Melissa something, had nearly died in a motorcycle accident. She'd been taken to a hospital in Atkins, had several surgeries and was expected to live. A few months later, he read that she was recovering and all charges had been dropped. Not quite sure how that had come about, Cash had thought of her often recently. He'd like to know the story behind that whole escapade.

The waitress Charlene brought over his plate. Two thick slices of tender roast beef, mashed potatoes and gravy, and green beans, with an extra side of okra. Everything was hot - he could see the steam rising off the plate as she sat it in front of him. "Here ya' go honey. And I brought you an extra roll with that blackberry jam you like." Cash smiled up at her and reached for her hand before she moved away from the table.

"Thanks, Charlene. You got any apple pie tonight? You all know how to make some good pie."

"We do! I'll bring you by a big piece when you're done with your supper. You want ice cream with it, right?"

"Sure do! You're the best, Charlene. Oh, how about a refill on coffee, too?"

When Charlene returned with the coffee pot, Cash said, "Do you have to drive far tonight? To get home after work I mean. The roads are pretty bad. Wouldn't want you slipping into a ditch or anything."

"I'll be fine. I drive a jeep, and I'm used to this weather." She filled his cup up to the top.

"I got a room at the motel," Cash whispered. "You could always crash with me, if you're worried about getting home safely." It was a pretty standard joke between them. He was always making suggestions. She was always turning him down.

"Don't you worry about me, Cash, honey. Besides, I gotta get home and let the dog out."

"Stood up by a dog! Oh, that hurts!" Cash laughed. Charlene put her hand on his shoulder and leaned close to him.

"Nice try, though. Better luck next time!" she whispered in his ear. Cash patted her on the rear and she scooted away with a giggle.

Later that night, snug and warm in his motel room, Craig Cashman plugged in his laptop. He wanted to see if he could find out anything new about that girl on the motorcycle. He could look through newspaper archives and surely do a Google search. Maybe he could find her on FaceBook. Melissa something. He was just curious.

CHAPTER 9

Straight Paths

Becky sat on the couch, with her legs curled up under her. She had pulled the afghan down to cover herself, but then decided that the fireplace was keeping her warm enough. The blanket lay in a heap beside her. Her Bible, a devotional book and a notebook and pen were perched on top of the blanket.

It was New Year's Day. The devotional reading for the day logically focused on starting the year right by setting aside time with the Lord. The scripture verse was familiar to Becky already. Proverbs 3:5-6 in the NIV version said "Trust in the Lord with all your heart and lean not on your own understanding; in all your ways submit to him, and he will make your paths straight." Becky reached for her notebook and wrote down the verse. Then she prayed, "Lord Jesus, I want to let go of my own understanding. I want you to make my paths straight. Put me into places where I will have to rely on you, where it's clear that you are the only one who can get me through. As I take steps in this next year, lead me. I will be listening. Thank you for loving me enough. Amen."

She looked over at Coop, who was writing vigorously in his journal. He paused, tapped his pen against his chin, and gazed out the window. After a moment of thought, he wrote some more, then closed the notebook and sat it aside. When he realized that Becky was watching him, he smiled at her.

Becky moved her books and papers aside, picked up the afghan, and patted the couch seat beside her. Coop got up and joined her on the couch. "It's good to spend time with the Lord, isn't it?" she asked and Coop nodded in agreement.

"Yes, it is. I just started a new devotional book with an emphasis on being a Christian husband and father. I picked it out a few months ago, thinking it might help me understand the way a Christian family was meant to work. Today's verses were really good. Proverbs 3:5 and 6."

"Are you serious? Those were my verses today too." She started to quote the verses and Coop joined in with her. "My devotion dealt primarily with being in the place with God where I know I can trust him and rely on him to keep my paths straight. In other words, lead me in the right direction. What was your emphasis?"

"Almost the same. By putting my trust in God, leaning on his wisdom and his knowledge of the whole picture, by letting go of my own understanding of the circumstances, then God will be able to lead me, and thus my family, in paths of righteousness. And that's what I want: for my family to walk in paths of righteousness."

"Isn't that an awesome thought?" Becky asked in wonder. "God has a plan, a way, all mapped out for us. When we listen to him, and yield to him, instead of going our own way or demanding that we know what's best, he will lead us and guide us down straight paths. And if you think about it, the straight path is the easiest and most trouble-free road to take. No dangerous curves or sudden drop offs. It's God's way of protecting us along the way. Take God's path and it will be straight and easy."

"True. But it won't always seem easy. There are dangers along the way, even for the most devout follower of Christ. Satan is always out there, trying to trip us up," Coop said. "But I think the key is that as long as we are trying hard to listen to Christ and follow him, he will protect us and help us through whatever we have to deal with."

"Coop, I love talking with you about the scriptures. You really do have insight." She laid her head on his shoulder. "Jenny and I are blessed to have you leading our family."

"Isn't it great that, when we dig into the scriptures, we can often take away just what we need to hear? I mean, we both read the same verses. But our devotional writers took us down different roads with their applications. Neither interpretation was wrong. Each applied to specific situations." He paused and took a deep breath. "Man, there's power in the inspired word of God!"

The happy newlyweds sat together in silent contemplation for many minutes. Each felt the comfort of the other. Each appreciated the wisdom of the other. Each quietly prayed to the Lord, expressing thankfulness.

Becky broke the silence. "I've never envisioned my life as the wife of a pastor. But if you ever feel God calling you in that direction, I would go happily with you and serve as best I could." She took his hand in hers. "You really do have the gift of discernment. Your understanding of the scriptures and the way you can explain the meanings – Honey, you are so close to God. So many people can benefit under your teaching." She paused before going on. "Do you ever regret giving up your goal of going into the ministry?"

Coop didn't have to think. His answer came quickly. "Never. I'm convinced that God has me right where he wants me. I can lead my family, witness to those I come in contact with, maybe eventually teach a Sunday school class or lead a Bible study. There's lots of ways God can use me, from this side of the pulpit. Right now, my focus is my family. But I'll also be listening, to see where else God wants to take me."

Becky sighed. "And I'm convinced that my place is at you side, wherever that may be, and whatever I can do to be you helpmate. That's the word, isn't it?"

"Yes, my dear, that's the word. Helpmate. You are mine, and I am yours."

"Forever," Becky sighed again. "Together forever, working for the kingdom."

CHAPTER 10

—◆◆◆—

Homeward Bound

A snow plow finally made its way down the gravel road in front of the cabin, and an hour later Dale drove down in his truck with a snow blade attached to the front. He cleared out the snow in the driveway, then used a shovel to dig out the drifted snow around Coop's truck tires. When he was finished, he knocked on the door. Coop answered, with Becky standing a little behind.

"You should be able to get out now," Dale said. "The plow has cleared the gravel road enough to get through. Once you get to the highway, it will be much easier going. Just be careful on the gravel. The ditches have drifted and the snowplow pushed even more snow over to the side, so it's kinda like you're driving through a tunnel of snow. If you go off the road, you'll be stuck there a while. But you have a good truck. Should be fine. Just take it slow."

Coop held out his hand and shook Dale's. "Thanks so much sir. We really appreciate everything you've done for us."

"No problem," Dale said. "Hope to see you again." He turned and left.

An hour later, Becky scanned the rooms once more, checking to see that they weren't leaving anything behind. The truck was packed, the kitchen was cleaned up, and the hot tub was turned off. Coop came and stood beside her, putting his arm around her shoulders and pulling her close. "Ready?" he asked.

"Yes, we've got everything. All set." But she stood still, making no effort to move. "This has been a precious place. I'm so glad we got to spend these days together here. This place will always be special."

"Maybe we should plan to come back every year on our anniversary. Or maybe we should visit in the summer/ when the weather is better!"

"Oh, but it's so beautiful, with the snow. And summers are so busy for you, with all the work at the farm. I'd be satisfied with a couple days any time we could get away."

Coop looked at an envelope lying on the table. "What's that?"

"I left a note of thanks to Dale. He's been great, letting us stay here extra days. And I just wanted him to know how much we appreciated his generosity."

"You're an angel," he said. "Hey, let's pray before we get on the road." Coop took her hand. He prayed, expressing thanks for Dale, the cabin, their time of growing together, the beauty of God's creation, even the snow. And he asked for protection on the road as they traveled home. He squeezed Becky's hand and they joined in "Amen." Becky kissed his hand and said, "Let's go home, Mr. Smith."

"Yes, Mrs. Smith, let's go home."

The gravel road was partially cleared and the truck with its four-wheel drive had no difficulty maneuvering the hills. Few vehicles had been down this section of road, and the tracks of the snow plow were still fresh. The snow pushed by the plow was piled into high mounds along the roadside. It was very quiet and Coop reached over to turn on the radio. Praise music helped to lessen the tension caused by cautious driving. Becky looked over at him. "You doing ok?"

"Sure," he said with confidence. "I'm just not used to driving in this much snow. We'll be okay though. We should be on the main road in fifteen minutes or so."

Becky looked out the window at the white walls of snow surrounding them. "Guess what all this snow makes me think of," she said.

Coop shrugged his shoulders slightly and glanced over her way. "I'm not that good at reading your mind yet. You'll have to tell me, I think."

"It's a Bible verse. I bet you know it."

"Hmm, a verse about snow? Could it be Psalms 51:7? Wash me, and I shall be whiter than snow." Or maybe the verse in Isaiah that says "Though your sins are like scarlet, they shall be as white as snow."

"Smart alec!" laughed Becky. "I should have known you would know it. I didn't really know there were *two* verses! But of course, you did!"

"Okay, my turn," Coop said, playing along. "What song do you know that has those words?"

Becky didn't have to think long. She started singing an old hymn, "Whiter Than Snow." Coop joined in and they sang the first verse and chorus together. Before they could start the second verse, they both stopped and laughed. Neither of them could think of the words to the second verse.

"There's another song, too. Do you know "Jesus Paid It All?""

Becky shook her head. "No, I don't think so. How does it go?"

Coop cleared his voice and sang, "Jesus paid it all, all to Him I owe. Sin had left a crimson stain; He washed it white as snow."

"That's beautiful. Teach me. Sing it again."

The couple spent several minutes in joyful song, and the time passed quickly. Suddenly up ahead, Coop saw three black objects in the snow. Birds. Big birds. Turkey vultures. They were pulling at the flesh of some dead animal. Coop took his foot off the accelerator pedal and the truck slowed slightly. The three birds suddenly took to the air. One of them swooped up and over the truck, very near to the windshield. They could see a look of fear in the vulture's eyes. His wings touched the hood of the truck as he frantically pumped them to escape. His whole body blocked the view of the road. He was dangerously close to the windshield.

Fearing that the bird would hit them, Coop slammed on the brakes. This caused the truck to swerve wildly in the snow. When they finally stopped, the truck was facing a tall hill of snow in the ditch. The front bumper was buried in snow. Even the hood of the truck was embedded in the snow bank. They faced a wall of white. The vultures were nowhere to be seen.

Coop looked over at Becky. "You okay?" he asked.

"Yes," she nodded. "You?"

"I'm fine. Good thing no one else was coming." They sat a moment, waiting for their heart rates to calm down. "I'm thankful for seatbelts. Otherwise, we might be lying out there in the snow right now."

"Let's not think about that," Becky chuckled. "That would not be the best ending to our honeymoon, I'm afraid! Do you think the truck's okay?"

"Yeah, I think so. But let me just hop out and look around." He unhooked his seatbelt and grabbed the door handle.

"Wait," Becky called. "Put your gloves on. It's cold out there!"

Coop teased, "Yes mother," and kissed her. He dug the gloves out of his coat pocket and got out of the truck. Becky watched as he walked around the truck. She strained to see as he bent down and knelt beside each of the front tires. As he inspected each tire, he would disappear from view. Becky wondered what he had discovered.

Before long, Coop opened the back door of the truck and leaned in. "The tires are ok, and there's no damage anywhere that I can tell. But I'm going to have to dig out some of the snow, to get better traction. I've got a shovel back here behind the seat." He pulled the back cushions forward and retrieved a collapsible shovel.

"Once again, I'm glad I married a Boy Scout!" Becky chuckled, knowing full well what his answer would be.

"Never been a Boy Scout, Becky. Just always want to be prepared for whatever comes at me." He extended the handle of the shovel and turned back to the snow. Becky put on her own gloves and a knit hat and got out of the truck to stand beside him.

"Anything I can do to help, oh mighty Scout Master?"

"Well, you could get the ice scraper. It's under the front seat. You can clean the hood off with the brush. If you want, I mean."

"Of course, I want to. We're a team. I'm not going to sit in there and watch you do all the work while I stay all warm and cozy. What kind of a teammate would that be? We're in this together."

"That's my girl," Coop laughed. "Thanks. But be careful, the snow is pretty deep."

Cleaning the snow off the hood was pretty easy work. Becky tried not to send snow flying in Coop's direction, but occasionally some blew his way. "Sorry Coop. Didn't mean to do that!"

Coop rose up from his stooped position at the tire. He had a snowball packed and ready. He threw it towards Becky, aiming and hitting a spot near her on the hood of the truck. The snowball exploded, sending snow splattering all over Becky. "Oh, sorry Becky, I didn't mean to do that either!"

"I'll bet!" said Becky. "Now take that!" and she scooped a heavy shower of snow at him.

Coop dropped the shovel and ran around the back of the truck. Trapped by the wall of snow, Becky had nowhere to hide. Coop had his arms wrapped around her waist and tackled her, pushing her back against the snow wall. She tried to fight him off, grabbing snow and flinging it at him by the handful. Laughing and trying to fight him off at the same time, she slipped. Her feet flew out from under her. Coop struggled to keep her upright but it was useless. She landed with a plop in the snow, and Coop tumbled on top of her. Her laugh was subdued when Coop covered her face with kisses. Becky wrapped her arms around him, then her legs, and they embraced each other. Despite the snow and cold, Becky never felt warmer or happier.

They lay together there in the snow, cuddled and oblivious to anything around them. Coop stroked Becky's face, looked deep into her eyes, and said, "I love you so much Becky. Even here, in the snow, I want to make love to you. I want to express my deep love to you. I can't help myself. I get overcome with a desire for you." He kissed her again, slow and deep, and she responded with a moan of contentment.

When the kiss ended, Becky moved her head away slightly and said, "Coop, I love you dearly. But if you think I'm about to let you ravish me here, in the snow at ten degrees below zero, well, you've got another think coming!"

Coop pretended to be offended. "Oh yeah, well, I have needs, you know. And I need you." He tried to kiss her again but she pushed him away.

"Need me later!" she laughed. "We've gotta' get this truck out of the snow."

"Aww, you're no fun!" Coop murmured as he pulled himself off her. He stood, took her arm, and raised her to standing. "You owe me!" he laughed. "And I mean to collect."

"As long as we're not in waist deep snow, freezing cold and wearing winter coats," Becky said as she finished cleaning snow off the hood.

"Okay, I can promise you that. I think the tires are cleared, so how about you jump in and back up the truck? I'll stay out here and push."

"Sure, I'll try. Just you be careful."

"You will probably need to rock it back and forth to break it free. You know how to do that?" Coop was thinking maybe he should be driving, but he didn't want Becky to be doing the pushing. He'd have to hope she knew what she was doing.

"I do know how to rock it," Becky said with assurance. "We had to do it in Driver's Ed, back in high school. It's been a while, but I remember."

Becky put the truck in reverse and pushed the gas. Quickly she moved the lever to drive and went forward a bit. Back and forth she rocked it a few times. Coop pushed from the front and it finally pulled free of the snow bank. When the truck was totally back on the road again, Coop took over the driving.

"Whew. That got my heart going," he said.

"The vultures? Or the shoveling? Or the kissing?" Becky smiled coyly.

"A little of both, I guess. The vultures were scary. The shoveling was a workout. But the kissing, well, that was definitely the best boost to my heart rate!"

"We do make a pretty good team, don't we? I'm going to love working side by side with you for the rest of my life."

"Yep! Partners. Through the good and bad times. Side by side forever. Just like God planned it." Coop patted her hand.

"Thank you, Lord, for keeping us safe," Becky said.

"And continue to watch over us," Coop added.

"It's a good thing Jenny wasn't with us," Becky chuckled. "I can just imagine her saying 'That's fun. Let's do it again!'"

Coop laughed. "That girl! Always one for an adventure. Remember her in the swimming pool last summer? Once she got comfortable in the water, she had so much fun. I was tossing her up and she'd go down underwater, bouncing right up for more." Talking about those happier, warmer times helped Coop to relax, though he kept his eyes on the road, alert for any other wild obstacles that might suddenly appear.

Once they hit the main highway, the roads were fine. They made good time and were soon crossing the Kansas state line. "It's going to be late when we get home," Coop said. "Let's stop somewhere for supper, so we won't have to fix anything at home. This will be our last meal together before Jenny joins us and things get crazy with you getting back to work and me back to the farm."

Becky agreed. "This time with just the two of us has been precious. I love Jenny to death, of course, but I'm not sure I'm going to want to share you with her!"

"Don't be silly!" Coop laughed. "You'll always be my number one girl. But I've got plenty of room in my heart for Jenny too. And a dozen more, if the Lord so blesses us."

"Yikes! A dozen?" She giggled. "Let's think about this. That's a lot of mouths to feed. And we sure won't have room for all of them in our new house."

"No problem. We'll bunk some of them in the big house with Mom and Dana. And there's always the barn. I could insulate the haymow. All the boys can sleep there, so they are close to the cows and it's easy to do their chores." Coop turned the truck into the driveway of a truck stop. "Okay with you if we eat here? Wherever truckers eat, you can be sure the food's good."

Becky saw a dozen or more big rigs parked at the side of the building. "Sure. I'm getting really hungry, and I agree, if we don't eat till we get home, I'll be too tired to cook anything."

Over a supper of creamy broccoli and potato soup and fresh homemade bread, they continued the discussion about children. Both agreed that, at this point, they would concentrate of setting up their home and establishing the life of their little family. In time, they would want more children. But for now, they would enjoy their family of three.

"Speaking of babies," said Becky, "I can't wait to see Greg and Nancy's little boy. He was just born a couple weeks before our wedding, and I was so busy I didn't get to be with him much. Hopefully I can see him again soon." She spread some smooth butter on the bread. "Oh my, this bread smells so good." She took a bite and sighed happily, then went on with the conversation. "I was just so glad Nancy felt up to being my Maid of Honor. She's a wonderful friend. I can see our families growing together for years to come. And you know what? I bet she'll let you practice diaper changing on little Andy. It's very important that you learn to be a good diaper helper." She laughed. "So, in the night, when our baby wakes up, you can change him and bring him in to me, and I'll feed him. Teamwork, you know."

"Whatever you want, momma. Whatever you want." He reached across the table and took her hand. "I bet you will be extra beautiful when you're pregnant with my child. I can't wait to see your motherly glow."

"Don't romanticize it too much. There's also morning sickness, tiredness, aches and pains, and of course, that fat belly, swollen feet, and puffy face. It's not all a motherly glow!"

"Maybe so. But I still can't wait. I'll rub your back and massage your feet and even tend to you when you're throwing up. Teamwork, you know!"

"That'll be nice. Being pregnant with you at my side, well, that will be such a difference from when I was pregnant with Jenny. I was a mess back then. So many things have changed now, changed for the better. I have the Lord. I have you. I have a totally new outlook on my entire reason for living. I'm so thankful for how Jesus has brought me this big change."

"So, the verses we discussed on New Years Day can apply to this conversation, too. As we let go of our own understanding, Jesus can guide our steps, make our paths straight, and be with us, whatever comes our way. Pregnancy, morning sickness, labor pains, whatever."

"And we'll be together, with Jesus leading the way." Becky smiled at her husband. "I love you, Coop. Now let's get home and start living the rest of our lives as the Smith family!"

They paid the bill and walked through the gift shop area to reach the door. Suddenly Coop stopped and said, "Hey, look at this." He picked up a children's story book called "Five Minute Bible Stories for Boys and Girls."

"Do you think Jenny would like this? I'd love to get her a little present."

Becky took the book and browsed through it quickly. "Yes, this is nice. Maybe you could read a story to her every night. It could be your special time together." Coop carried the book to the counter to pay for it. Then they got back in the truck, and two hours later they were home.

Elizabeth's car was parked in front of the house. Jenny was standing at the window, waiting for them to drive up. Coop pulled his truck into the driveway behind Becky's car, which was parked in the car port. He barely got the truck engine shut off before Jenny came dashing out the door to greet them.

"Mommy! Mommy! Daddy Coop! You're home!" She ran to her mother first, and Becky picked her up with a big hug and twirled her around in a circle.

"I sure missed you, Baby Girl," she laughed. "But my goodness! I think you got bigger! We were gone less than a week and I think you grew six inches!"

"Grandma let me have macaroni and cheese two times!" Jenny whispered. Becky glanced up and saw that her mother was coming out of the house. She put Jenny down and went to hug Elizabeth.

"Hi Mom. It's good to see you. Good to be home, too." She looked up at the happy little house, which seemed to be aglow with a welcome to the newlyweds. Christmas lights framed the windows in the front of the house and Becky could just make out the shape of the Christmas tree in the living room. Yes, it was good to be home. "Thanks for taking such good care of Jenny."

Jenny had walked around to Coop's side of the truck, where he was opening the back door to remove their suitcases and packages. When he saw her, Coop stooped down and opened his arms wide. "Hello, Jenny! We missed you!" Jenny hurried to him for a hug.

"Daddy Coop," Jenny said, "Grandma told me you are going to live at our house now since you had the wedding. I made you a present."

Coop stood up and smiled down at her. "You did? Well, I can't wait to see it. Let's take these suitcases into the house and then you can show me." He turned to Elizabeth and gave her a hug. "It's good to be home. Sorry it took us a little longer than we planned. I hope it wasn't too much of an inconvenience for you."

"Oh of course not. I'm just happy to do it. And glad you got home safely. Here, let me help with that suitcase. It's cold out here." She took a suitcase and headed into the house. The others followed, everyone talking at once.

"Jenny made brownies to celebrate your homecoming," Elizabeth said. "I helped just a little. She's quite the cook." She poured cups of coffee for the grownups and hot cocoa for Jenny. Everyone settled in at the little table. Elizabeth offered a prayer of thanksgiving for safe travels. As soon as she said "Amen," Jenny jumped up from her seat.

"Here, Daddy Coop. This is for you. I made it." She handed Coop a drawing done in crayon. It showed the little house with three people outside in the yard. A tall man with a black cowboy hat, a much shorter woman with brown hair, and a little girl in the middle. The little girl had pony tails and a big smile. There was a yellow cat sitting by the door of the house, and a horse in the driveway. Along the bottom of the paper, in kindergarten penmanship, Jenny had written, "My Family".

Coop marveled and said, "Well, would you look at that! I see you, and Mommy and me!" Then he pointed to the horse and said, "And who's this?"

"That's my pony!" Jenny said proudly. "I'm going to ride him to school. His name is Benny. And here's my cat. My *real* cat. Muffin had babies, and this one is mine. He's a boy cat and I'm going to name him Mustard."

That brought a big laugh from Becky and Coop. "Mustard? That's sure a new name for a cat. Why did you choose that for his name? Coop was curious, and Becky was more that a little intrigued.

"Because he's yellow, like mustard, and I needed an "M" name. We have Muffin and Marmalade and Marshmallow. Now we'll have Mustard." Jenny was proud of herself.

"Interesting!" said Coop. "Very creative."

Becky looked at the drawing and smiled. "I think you have everything all figured out! I'm not so sure about riding your pony to school though. Where will he stay all day while you're in your classroom?"

Jenny thought a while and said, "I'll just send him home and he can come back and get me at the end of the day. He's a really smart pony. He won't get lost."

"Well, Daddy Coop," Becky said with a grin, "what do you think of all of this?"

"Hmmm," Coop said thoughtfully. "I think we should think about getting a pony when we live on the farm. This house doesn't have a barn or a pasture, and Benny wouldn't be too happy living in the carport. Can we wait till we move to our new house? Then we'll decide about the pony."

Jenny nodded in agreement. "What about Mustard?" she asked.

Becky answered that. "I'm sure if Muffin has kittens again, you can have one and name him Mustard."

"Jenny, I got you a present too," Coop said and reached for the bag from the truck stop. He handed it to Jenny, who pulled out the book and smiled.

"It's a book about Jesus," she said happily. "He's telling stories to the children." Jenny threw her arms around Coop in a big hug. "Thank you! Will you read it to me?"

"Every night at bedtime!" Coop answered. "Would you like that?"

Jenny nodded and started looking at the pictures in the book. Becky patted Jenny on the head and said, "Now, I think it's getting late and you better get to bed. Tell Grandma goodbye, then go brush your teeth. Daddy Coop and I will be in to tell you goodnight in a few minutes. Then he can read one of the stories in your new book."

Elizabeth had been cleaning up the dishes, smiling as she heard the conversation at the table. She turned from the sink, drying her hands and said, "I'm sure God is going to bless this family. He already is." She gave hugs all around, got her coat, and drove across town to her own house. It seemed very empty and way too quiet.

CHAPTER 11

---❖◆❖---

Best Part

Jenny, dressed in her flannel PJ's and fuzzy white slippers, ran across her bedroom and jumped onto the bed. She found her stuffed cat, Marshmallow, and hugged her tight. "It's time for bed," she said. "Where's your babies?" She looked under her pillow and found one of the little kittens. "Paul, there you are! Where's your brother?" Jenny scrounged around and found Silas and Mary under the bed sheet. When Becky and Coop came to the bedroom door a minute later, Jenny was hanging upside down, searching for the one missing kitten under her bed. "Martha, Martha, where are you?" she sang out, unaware that her parents were watching.

Coop stood behind Becky, resting his hands on her shoulders. He couldn't resist a chuckle. "So, this is part of the bedtime routine, I suppose?" he whispered to Becky.

Becky smiled and said, "You never really know. Every night can be a little different. You'll learn to roll with whatever!" To Jenny she said, "Ready for bed, Sweetie?"

"No, I have to find Martha. I can't sleep unless all the babies are with their mother." Jenny righted herself, flipping her hair out of her eyes. "Martha needs her mommy."

"Do you remember where you last saw her?" asked Coop. He was new at this daddy stuff, but was trying his best to be helpful.

He glanced around the room. It wasn't a large space, and there were only a few places where Martha could be hiding. The twin sized bed, a small bookcase, a desk, and a dresser lined the walls. On the desk, Coop spotted a kitten peaking out from under the new Bible stories book he had given Jenny earlier.

"Oh yeah!" Jenny said, and hopped off the bed. "I remember now. We were looking at my new book." She went to the desk, picked up both the kitten and the book, and said, "We were trying to find the story about Mary and Martha. But since I can't read, we just looked at the pictures. Can you read me that story before I go to sleep?" She handed the book to Coop, who looked over at Becky and smiled.

"Go for it, Daddy Coop!" she laughed. "I'll brush out her hair while you read." They settled on the bed, Coop with the book, Jenny with the cat and all four kittens, and Becky with the hair brush. Coop read the story from Luke chapter ten, showing Jenny the pictures of Martha working in the kitchen while Mary sat at Jesus' feet, listening to His teachings. When he was finished reading, Coop closed the book. Becky put down the hair brush and asked Jenny, "What did that story teach us?"

"It's good to cook food and clean the house, but it's better to sit and listen to Jesus!" Jenny answered quickly. "Eating will help us live, but listening to Jesus will help us live forever!"

Coop's jaw dropped and his eyes widened. He looked at Becky and said, "Wow! She got it!" He turned to Jenny and took her hands. "Jenny, you are so right! Listening to Jesus is the most important thing we can do. Of course, we have to eat and clean the house, and do our other responsibilities, but being close to Jesus is the only way we have eternal life. You've heard this story before, I bet?" he asked.

"I heard it in Sunday School." Jenny turned to her mother. "Prayer time?" she asked.

"Prayer time," said Becky. She looked at Coop and said, "We usually both pray, we take turns going first."

Jenny popped in, "Daddy Coop can be first tonight. It's his first night to do it."

They joined hands. Coop thanked the Lord for their new family. He thanked God for leading him to the Bible stories book, and prayed that they would all learn from the stories they would read together. He expressed thankfulness for Jenny's willingness to listen to Jesus.

Becky prayed that God would be close to each of them, as they learned every day to trust in the Lord and listen to him. She thanked God for their wonderful time at the cabin and safety on the way home in the snow. She expressed gratitude for her mother watching over Jenny while they were gone.

Then it was Jenny's turn. "God bless my two Grandmas. God bless my friends especially Hannah and her baby brother Andy. God bless my pony Benny and my new real kitty. And God bless Mommy and Daddy Coop. Amen."

Becky tucked the covers up around Jenny's chin and kissed her on the forehead. "Sweet dreams, Baby," she said softly. She stood and looked down on Jenny as Coop kissed the little girl's forehead and said, "Goodnight, Jenny."

They turned and walked together, holding hands, but before they could leave the bedroom, Jenny called out, "Wait Mommy. We didn't do best part."

"Oh, you're right. I'm sorry I forgot." Becky turned to Coop and explained, "Every night we think back and say what was the best part of our day."

"That's a great idea!" Coop said and turned to Jenny. "What was your best part?"

"That's easy!" said Jenny. "Mommy and Daddy Coop are home!"

Becky nodded in agreement. "That's my best part too! We are home!"

Coop beamed at his new little family. He looked from one to the other and nodded. "Yes. Home. We are all home. That's the best part for me too!"

Hand in hand, they quietly made their way across the hall to their own bedroom. While they had been away, Coop's mom and sister had brought some of his belongings over to Becky's house. Clothes were hanging in the closet and a suitcase of his more personal items was sitting at the foot of the bed. "Looks like I have some unpacking to do. Where should I put this stuff?"

"I made some room for you in the dresser," she said and opened an empty drawer. "Will this be enough?"

"Should be. I won't need to have all my things here. It won't be long until we are moved into the new house, and then I can get really settled in. This will be fine for now." They both unpacked things and put them away, trying to be fairly quiet, so as to not wake Jenny, whom they hoped had fallen asleep already.

Becky showed Coop where to put his dirty clothes and said, "I like to separate my clothes into laundry baskets like this. Darks go in this black basket, whites go in the white basket, and perma-pressed things go here, in pink."

"Pink, huh? Sounds pretty girly."

"Sorry sweetheart, that's they way I've been doing it for years. I'll get a blue basket, if you want me to. Don't want to rub against your manly sensitivities!"

He took her in his arms and said, "I'd like to rub my manly sensitivities up against you, any time, all the time!"

Becky laughed and said, "Oh Coop, sometimes I think you have a one-track mind. And sometimes I don't mind one bit!"

CHAPTER 12

❖ ◆ ❖

Day By Day

The little family slipped comfortably into a routine. Every morning at 5 a.m., Coop's alarm woke him. The coffee pot, prepped the night before, began to perk. By the time Coop was out of the shower, coffee was ready. He poured a cup and sat sipping it while having his morning devotions. Then he would fill a thermos, making sure to leave enough in the pot for Becky to have a cup later. By 6 he checked in on Jenny, went to Becky and kissed her goodbye, rousing her ever so slightly so that she was able to drift back to sleep after he left.

Becky rose at 7 and had her own devotion time over coffee. Then she woke Jenny, they had breakfast together, and left for school by 8:15. Becky got to the Animal Hospital to start her 9:00 shift. Usually around 10:30 she would get a text from Coop, or sometimes he would call.

Coop stayed at the farm most of the day. He worked with the animals, attended to chores around the yard and checked on the progress of their house. He had lunch with his mother, and sometimes Dana if she was home from her college classes. During the winter, he was able to drive home to Becky and Jenny for supper. They knew that when spring came and his farm workload increased, Coop would often be working at the farm until dark. On those evenings, he would probably eat supper with his mom. Driving back and forth to town added over half an hour to his day, time he'd rather spend with his family than on the road.

Becky usually worked till 5. Then she'd drive over to her mom's house and pick up Jenny, who went there after school. Most evenings they would go right home, to prepare supper for Coop. But on Wednesday, as had been their tradition, they ate supper with Elizabeth and then went to Wednesday night church activities. The only difference now was that Coop would drive from the farm to have supper with them at Elizabeth's, and they'd all go to church together.

Coop's mother, Marla Jean, had resumed her piano playing for choir practice. She would drive into town on Wednesday evenings for choir, and sometimes have supper with the family at Elizabeth's. If the weather was bad, Coop would drive her from the farm, they'd all have supper and go to church, and Marla Jean would stay overnight at the little house. On those nights, Jenny happily had a campout on the couch in the living room and Grammy Smith would take Jenny's bed. It wasn't ideal, but Jenny didn't mind. Camping in the living room was just one more big adventure for the little girl. And she was happy to share her bedroom with her new grammy.

Friday evenings were still special times for Becky and Jenny. Disney movies topped the list of Jenny's favorite things to do. Cuddled on the couch in front of the TV, they had time to talk extensively about how things were going in life. Coop usually let the girls have their time together, but sometimes Jenny asked him to join them. The evenings of three on the couch were becoming more and more frequent. A family was forming.

One day in late February, after Coop had his morning coffee and devotion time, he crawled back into bed with Becky. She was surprised and snuggled up against him. She was only half awake, but mumbled, "Hey, why are you here? Shouldn't you be going out to the farm? What time is it?"

Coop put his arms around her and kissed her neck. "I'm playing hooky. I wanna stay home with you." He nuzzled into her neck and kissed her ear and chin. Becky turned toward him and accepted his kisses. She moaned with pleasure, enjoying the feel of his body so close to her.

After a bit, Coop stopped his caresses and said, "It snowed. I had the TV on, and they say school is cancelled. Sounds like it's a good day to take Jenny out to the farm for some sledding. Think you can get the day off from work and come out with us?"

"Don't know. Guess I'll ask and see. It would be fun." Becky rolled away and sat up on the side of the bed. Coop reached over and pulled her back down onto the bed.

"Wait. Call later. Jenny's asleep and you and I are awake. I want you." He pulled her onto her back and kissed her again.

At 7, Becky's alarm rang and roused the couple from their special morning together. Becky moved to turn off the alarm, and then lay on her back, looking up at the ceiling. She sighed and said, "I wish every day could start like this."

Coop, also looking up, said "Me too. I love you so much Becky. I want to make you smile every morning." He took her hand in his. "Once we move into the new house, I won't have to get up and leave so early. We'll be able to stay in bed longer."

Becky laughed. "And Jenny's room will be on the other side of the house, so we won't have to be so quiet." She rolled over and let her hair hang down, tickling Coop's chest. She kissed him once more and said, "I don't need to get Jenny up so early, since there's no school. You want a big breakfast? We'll have time, but I guess I need to call Doc Larson first before we make plans for sure." She sat up and shivered, then pulled the blanket up over her bare shoulders. "Man, its cold. Wish we had a fireplace here, like we did in the cabin. That fire kept the whole place warm."

"That's why we are going to have a fireplace in the new house. It will save on fuel costs next winter. We have plenty of firewood at the farm."

"That'll be nice." Becky slid her feet into her slippers and grabbed her robe. She reached for her cell phone and called Doc Larson. After she hung up, she turned to Coop. "Well, that was easy," she said. "Doc said when there's a lot of snow like this, he usually has a lot of cancellations, so he's able to handle the few patients that make it in.

So, I'm free. I won't get paid for the day though." She stood to get dressed. "So, how about a big breakfast? We'll need a lot of energy for sledding."

"Sure. Pancakes, eggs and bacon?" Becky pulled a sweatshirt over her head and nodded yes. "And coffee. Lots of coffee!"

Coop called his mother to let her know they would all be coming out to the farm later. Then he went into Jenny's room, to wake her and tell her of the plans.

Jenny jumped out of bed and ran to the window. She pulled the curtain back and squealed with joy. "Snow! Snow! Yay, snow!" She danced around the room in her pajamas. Then she ran to the bed and jumped up on it. Bouncing up and down, laughing hysterically as her hands reached up and nearly touched the ceiling when her feet left the bed, Jenny sang out, "Snow! Snow! I love snow!"

Coop walked quickly to the side of the bed and said sternly, "Stop Jenny! We don't jump on the bed. Now get down."

Jenny looked at him. She was still standing on the bed, but her jumping had stopped. She put her hands on her hips and said belligerently, "I like to jump on my bed. Mommy lets me."

Coop was a little surprised at Jenny's attitude. He had never seen this side of her before. Her usually sweet compliance was replaced with a scowl and defiance he was not accustomed to. "Jumping on the bed could be dangerous. You could fall."

"I won't fall," Jenny said stubbornly, stomping her feet. She crouched, ready to jump again, but Coop reached out and stopped her.

"*Wait,*" he shouted. "I said to get down. We do not jump on the bed." He scooped Jenny off the bed and sat her down on the edge. She sat there, arms folded across her chest, pouting. Coop stood towering over the little girl, not sure what to do next.

Jenny's bottom lip began to quiver. "It's not fair," she mumbled, mostly under her breath. "Mommy lets me."

Coop decided to sit on the bed, closer to Jenny's level, and not so threatening. "Jenny," he began, "we need to work this out. I honestly don't know if your mommy lets you jump on the bed or not. But I'd be happy to ask her and see what she says."

Jenny's shoulders drooped and her head lowered. She knew what her mother would say. And she knew she hadn't told the truth. Coop noticed the change in her position and demeanor. He guessed what it meant.

Coop continued. "For now, though, I think we need to talk. We have a bigger problem to solve than just jumping on the bed." He took a big breath. This daddy business was all new to him, and he silently prayed to his Heavenly Father for guidance.

"First, I want you to know that I love you. You do know that, don't you?"

Jenny nodded but said nothing.

"And because I love you, I would never say or do anything to hurt you or upset you. I would only try to protect you and help you. Do you understand?

Jenny nodded again. Her eyes were starting to fill with tears.

"You and your mommy have been together for over five years, without me, and there are lots of things you guys know that I don't. Being Daddy Coop is new for me, and there's a lot I have to learn." He paused a bit. "But you can help me. When we have troubles, like we just did about the bed, we need to talk about it, and not get all angry and mad. Think we can do that?"

Jenny sniffed and wiped her hand across her eyes. She nodded.

"Good," Coop said, and hugged her. "And when I ask you to do something, even if it's something you don't want to do, or something different from what your mommy would have said, I want you to do it anyway. It might be very important for your safety. You need to do as I ask, and then we'll talk about it later. Does that make sense? Do you understand?"

Jenny laid her head against Coop's arm and said, "I understand. And I'm sorry I didn't stop jumping right away." She sat, leaning against Coop, for a quiet minute. "Can I tell you something?" she finally asked. Her voice was almost a whisper.

"Of course," said Coop. He turned to look directly at her.

Jenny took a deep breath. "Mommy doesn't let me jump on the bed. I just tried it and I wanted to do it some more."

"Thank you for telling me the truth, Jenny," Coop said. "It's very important for us to trust each other. I want you to trust me to always tell you the truth and do whatever I can to keep you safe and help you grow into a Christian woman. I want to always trust you too. Telling me the truth, like you just did, is very important. I hope I can always trust you, just like you can trust me, to tell the truth and be honest. Okay?"

"Okay," Jenny said.

In the hall, Becky stood just out of sight, listening to the conversation. Her initial disappointment in Jenny was replaced with a swelling pride as she owned up to her untruth, and promised to be truthful and obedient in the future. Becky was also happy with the way Coop had handled the issue. He was surely going to be a good father.

Becky cleared her throat to announce her presence and asked, "Who's hungry for pancakes?"

As they joined hands for prayer, Jenny said, "Me first," and started to pray immediately. "Dear Jesus. Thank you for our food. Thank you for Mommy and Daddy Coop. Help me to tell the truth and always obey my parents. Amen,"

As he prayed, Coop recalled a verse in Psalms. He included it in his prayer. "Help us, Lord, to remember to keep our tongues from evil and our lips from telling lies. Help us all to grow in honesty and trustworthiness."

Becky scooped some scrambled eggs onto Jenny's plate and asked, "How many pancakes do you want?"

"I can eat two," Jenny said, and reached for her plate. While she added butter and syrup, Becky continued the conversation about truthfulness.

"Was that a verse you quoted, Coop? About keeping our lips from telling lies?"

Coop nodded as he forked four pancakes onto his plate. "Psalms 34:13. Dad made me learn it when I was a kid. It was my punishment for telling a lie, but it's come back to my memory more than once. Dad meant it as a punishment, but I sure learned a good lesson from it."

Jenny nearly dropped her fork. "You told a lie? Really?"

Coop looked over at Becky and smiled. He saw this as an opportunity to teach an important lesson. "I did. And Dad found out about it. The truth always comes out eventually. Dad was not happy with me. But mostly he was disappointed."

"What happened?" What did you lie about?" Jenny still couldn't believe that her Daddy Coop had ever told a lie.

"I was supposed to milk the cow before I went out to swim at the pond with some friends that were coming over. When the guys came over, I hadn't done my chores yet, but I just went on with them to the pond anyway. I figured I could do the milking later. We had a great time. They left to go to their own houses and I forgot about the milking. Later that day, Dad asked me about it and I didn't want to admit that I had disobeyed him, so I lied and told him I had done it. But he knew."

"How did he know you were lying?"

"It's usually pretty hard to cover up lies. There were lots of clues. First, there was no pail of fresh milk. Second, the cow was down by the barn, crying and bellowing to beat the band. Her milk sack was so heavy she could barely move. She was in so much pain from so much milk, she was just miserable. Dad sent me off to the barn and, oh boy, I remember the way that cow looked at me. She was just as mad about it as Dad was."

Jenny giggled and said, "I guess you learned your lesson!"

"I did. And I learned that verse too. Dad stood over me, and with every pull of the cow's teats, he repeated the verse. One word for every squirt of milk into the bucket. And you better believe I will never forget it!"

"I should learn that verse too. But I don't have a cow to milk!"

Coop looked at Becky and winked. "Well, actually, before we go sledding, Bessie needs to be milked. We'll have to do it first when we get out to the farm, or she'll be complaining about a heavy milk sack."

"Then I'll help you. And I'll learn the verse like you did. And I'll learn my lesson!"

Becky began clearing dishes from the table. "That sounds like a good plan. You milk Bessie and learn the verse. I will have to do the dishes before we go. That's my chore!"

Jenny took her plate to the sink, and then went off to get ready for her sledding adventure. Coop stood up and started washing dishes. "I'll help," he said. "You fixed a great breakfast."

Becky put her arms around his waist and hugged him, laying her head against his back. "Thank you, Coop."

"I said I'd wash if you cooked," he said.

"No, I mean thank you for being such a good man. A leader for our family. I love you so much." She sighed. "You handled that with Jenny perfectly. Thank you."

"I pray every day for the wisdom to lead this family. But you've done a great job with her already. She was quick to own up to her lie and ask for forgiveness. She learned that from you, I'm sure."

"I've tried," Becky said. "Now let's go sledding."

"But first we have a cow to milk," laughed Coop.

CHAPTER 13

◆ ◆ ◆

House Plans

The trip out to the farm took a little longer than usual because of the snowy roads. As Coop was driving along, Becky joked, "Watch out for vultures!"

"What's a vulture?" Jenny asked from the back seat. Coop told the story of their adventure in the snow. Becky added that they knew God was watching over them, because no one was hurt, and they got the truck out of the snow bank without any trouble.

"It was even kinda fun!" Coop added with a teasing look at Becky.

"Well, I hope we don't get stuck," Jenny said. "I want to go sledding at the farm."

"Don't worry, honey. We're almost there. And Coop is a good driver. We'll be sledding before you know it."

Milking done and verse learned, the trio climbed the big hill in the pasture. Sledding had never been so much fun. The snow was perfect and after a few trips down, the hill was packed and slick. Standing at the top of the hill, Becky laughed as she watched her daughter and her husband rolling off the sled together, struggling to get up and climb the hill. "One more time," she called. "Then we need to get inside."

They climbed onto the four-wheeler for the ride back to the house. "Will Grammy have some hot chocolate for us when we get there?" Jenny asked Coop.

"Of course, she will. That's part of sledding, isn't it?" Coop laughed and made the four-wheeler go fast, bouncing off the little snow mounds in the pasture. Everyone was laughing when they finally got to the gate. Nell and Slick stomped their feet in the snow, curious about all the noise. Becky jumped down, opened the gate, and Coop drove through. Then Becky secured the gate again and climbed back on for the ride to the house.

Marla Jean was waiting on the porch, eager to help Jenny out of her wet clothes. Having that little girl around now and then was filling a void. Hearing laughter in the house again was refreshing. Sometimes the house seemed empty and lifeless. Walter's absence left a huge hole in her day. Dana was in and out of the house, depending on her class schedule at the community college. Even when she was home, she spent a lot of time in her room studying. Coop was around a lot, but not in the evenings. That's when the loneliness would settle over her like a cloud.

She tried to fill the evenings by making phone calls to church friends, playing the piano and writing cards to shut-ins. She'd been pretty busy getting ready for the wedding, but since then, she had starting crocheting again. There was already a scarf finished and wrapped for Jenny for next Christmas. It would be their first Christmas together as Grammy and granddaughter – and Marla Jean already knew it would be special. She just hoped she didn't forget where she put the scarf, come time to get presents around the tree!

But having Jenny in the house was such a pleasure. She was a good little girl, and full of curiosity about things on the farm. It would be fun having her living close by. Marla Jean looked across the yard at the shell of the new house. The roof was on, windows and doors in, and some of the dry wall had been put up before this cold snap and snowfall.

71

Jenny and Becky came into the kitchen, wearing dry clothes they had brought along to change into. Becky asked, "Can I help with the hot chocolate?"

"I think it's ready to pour," Marla Jean said as she took mugs from the cupboard. "Where's Coop?"

"He just got a phone call from Rod. Something about the drywall."

"I'll put in the marshmallows," Jenny said. "Three for everybody, right?"

Coop entered the kitchen, slipping his phone into his pocket. "Guess what?" he said. Everyone looked at him. "Rod says it's time to pick out paint colors. They should be ready to paint as soon as the weather warms up a little. They'll finish the drywall and then we paint!"

"Can I paint my room?" Jenny asked excitedly. "I want pink."

"We will leave the painting to the experts," said Coop. "But you can certainly have pink walls in your room. I'll bring some paint strips and let you pick out what kind of pink you want. Light pink, bright pink, cotton candy pink, flamingo pink, you pick."

"Let's go over and walk through the house when we finish our chocolate," Becky said. "I haven't been there in almost two weeks. Can't wait to see the progress."

A little later, Becky stood in front of the kitchen window at the new house, imagining washing dishes, looking out at the front yard. "This is perfect," she said. "I'll be able to watch Jenny walk down the driveway after the school bus drops her off." She looked around the room, noting the locations for the refrigerator and stove. "Yes, this is going to work just fine. I especially love that the dishwasher will be right here!"

"We'll go over to Atkins on Saturday, and make the final choices on cabinets. We have to pick out the appliances, too." Coop took a notepad from his pocket. "Oh, yeah, lighting too. We need to decide what ceiling light fixtures we want. I think we should have a fan in a couple of rooms. Do you?"

"Well, the bedroom for sure," Becky said. "I like to have air moving, especially in the summer. How about the living room too?"

"I agree. A ceiling fan for summer and the fireplace for winter." Coop looked around. "I can imagine this room all decorated for Christmas. The tree over here, and stockings hung on the mantel. A roaring fire and Christmas music, the smell of evergreen branches, and something yummy baking in the oven. Our first Christmas as a family." He put his arms around Becky and whispered, "We're going to make such wonderful memories here, Mrs. Smith. I love you."

Just then Jenny ran down the hall, happily calling, "I found my bedroom, and I have a bathroom too. Just for me!"

"Well, not *just* for you, honey. There's a doorway in the bathroom that goes into another bedroom. So, you will share the bathroom with whoever is in the other room," Becky explained.

"Who? My baby brother?" Jenny asked eagerly.

Becky laughed. "Well, yes, it might be a brother or sister, someday. Or maybe Grandma if she wants to come stay overnight sometime. It will be a room for guests until we need it for a sibling."

"I don't want a sibling." Jenny said. "I want a baby brother."

Coop laughed and said, "Sibling means your brother or sister. It's a good new word to learn. Someday you might have lots of siblings." He looked at Becky and said, "What do you think, Mommy? Five? Maybe six? The Bible talks about filling your quiver. I just don't know how many a quiver will hold."

"Guess we'll just have to wait and see what the Lord blesses us with. In the meantime, let's just concentrate on getting this house done." Becky looked around in contentment. "It's going to be lovely."

Jenny sang out "One sibling, two siblings, three siblings, four. Five or six or maybe more!" She danced around skipping and hopping on one foot. Coop joined her as they repeated the song several times, dancing and laughing till they were out of breath.

"Look what you've done now, Daddy Coop! She'll be singing that all night."

"I like my new song," Jenny said. "I made that song up by myself." She was really proud of herself, and happy that Daddy Coop enjoyed it too.

"Amazing! You are so precocious. You might be a famous song writer one day!"

"What's precocious?" Jenny asked. "Is it a good thing?"

"Oh yes, it's very good," Coop said. "It means you are really smart and creative and extra special."

Jenny continued to dance around, but her song had changed. She chanted "Precocious, precocious. I am precocious!"

As she danced and twirled, Jenny moved toward the back door. Suddenly Coop called out loudly, "Jenny! Stop!" Jenny obeyed immediately and stood frozen before a large gap in the wall. There was a drop off to the basement below.

Coop went to Jenny and touched her shoulders. "I'm so glad you stopped right away. This is a dangerous spot. That's where the basement stairs will be, but they aren't built yet. I wouldn't want you to fall down there. Thank you for freezing when I called out to you."

Becky came over too, and hugged her daughter. "You did the right thing, stopping when Daddy Coop called you. He always wants to keep you safe. Thanks for listening to him." She kissed Jenny's forehead.

"What's going to be down there?" Jenny asked.

"A big playroom, and some storage, and a room we might turn into a little bathroom later." Coop went on, "But mostly it will be our tornado shelter."

"Tornado? Like The Wizard of Oz?" Jenny asked. "When the house went into the sky?" She took her mother's hand and looked up at her. "Is our house going to spin in the sky?"

Coop bent down low to comfort Jenny face to face. "We do sometimes have tornados in Kansas, but the houses don't go flying through the sky. The wind blows a lot, and sometimes trees fall down, and houses can get damaged. But the safe place to be is in a basement or storm shelter. Down there, we will be protected."

"What about the animals? Do they have a basement?"

"No, they don't. But we will just have to trust that God will protect them."

"And Grammy and Aunt Dana? Do they have a basement?" Jenny was very concerned.

"They have an outside shelter, a big hole in the ground with a ladder to get down. But if there's a storm coming, we will invite them to come over here to our basement. It will be more comfortable here. But don't you worry, sweetie. We'll all take care of each other. And we'll be together, singing and praying and waiting for the storm to pass. Jesus will be with us too, even in the eye of the storm."

"Ok." Jenny looked down into the dark basement. "It's scary now. But I'm glad we have a basement."

Becky said, "Let's get back to the big house. I told Grandma Smith that I would help her fix supper."

Coop held the door and said, "I have some chores to do, but I'll be in before time to eat. I'll see you in a bit." He hugged Jenny and kissed Becky. As he crossed the driveway headed toward the barn, Coop zipped his coat against the cold wind. He looked up to the sky, where dark snowy clouds were moving in from the west. He thought "No tornadoes today, but looks like we might get more snow. Lord, we trust you to protect us through the storms of life, whatever kinds they may be. Keep my family safe and protected as we abide under your wings."

CHAPTER 14

Cashman Cousins

Craig Cashman was still on the road when his cell phone rang. He glanced at the caller ID and saw that the call was from his sister Pat. That was alarming, as she seldom ever called him. Something must be wrong. He pushed the buttons so he could talk hands-free. No sense taking risks while driving the big rig.

"Hey, sis, what's up?" he said, hoping to sound upbeat but preparing to hear bad news.

"Just got off the phone with JJ's wife Bev. She's hysterical."

"Why? What's going on?"

"Are you going to be around in the next few days? JJ had some tests done, and Bev says its cancer. She was in tears, she's so upset. And since their one and only kid is a total waste of space, she has nobody but us to talk to. I thought maybe we should go see them, you know, so they're not alone."

"Oh man," said Craig, thinking about his schedule and the routes he'd be running in the next week or so. "I'm going to be on the road the next few days. Won't be home again till Wednesday. Can you get over there before that?"

"I can, but I was hoping we could go together." Pat paused. "Well, I guess I could go see them a time or two before Wednesday. I sure hope Bev calms down. I couldn't get any real information out of her. I don't know what kind of cancer it is, or how bad. Bev was just a blubbering mess."

"Well, as soon as you know something, call me, okay? I'll be around on Wednesday afternoon, and can stay home a few days. So, I can go see them. Is he home? Or in the hospital? Do you know?"

Exasperated, Pat sighed, "I don't even know! Like I said, I couldn't get much out of Bev. I'll call you as soon as I know what's really going on." They said their goodbyes and Craig drove on down the highway, remembering better times with his cousin JJ.

Jonathan James was the oldest in a slew of cousins and the undisputed leader of the pack. They called themselves the Cashman Cousins. There were eight boys and six girls, all with family roots to Grandpa Joe Cashman. JJ had long ago given Craig the nickname of Cash. Most of the cousins still called him that. Craig didn't mind, though he usually used his real name with other people.

As happens in even the closest of families, the cousins had scattered far and wide. Craig and his sister Pat were the only ones who lived close to JJ and his wife Bev. But JJ, always the party planner, had tried to get the cousins all together every few years. Just last summer he had organized a fishing trip to northern Minnesota, where several cousins had met to do more drinking than fishing. They had a great time, despite a minor boating accident involving a submerged tree and a monster of a fish that got away.

Now, to imagine JJ with cancer, well, Craig was immediately reminded of his own mortality. 'You just never know what tomorrow may bring,' he thought. 'I hope he gets over this. It's hard to imagine JJ sick or slowing down.'

JJ had settled down, though, and Craig knew when it happened. Marriage. That had changed JJ. Bev was a teacher, a homebody, and not one for adventure. It was a wonder the two had ever met, much less decided to get married. Sure, she was pretty, but Craig had never expected his cousin to choose someone with such a sour personality to be stuck with for the rest of his life. 'Must be good in bed,' he thought. 'Or why else would he keep her?'

That thought lead Craig's mind back to the girl with the long legs and flowery tattoo. The best time he had ever had in the sleeper compartment of his truck. He had found himself thinking about her a lot lately. 'I sure would like to meet up with her again,' he thought, as his body began to tingle with the memory.

CHAPTER 15

———◆◆◆———

Sunday Visiting

Greg Martin hugged his wife. "I know you'd like to tell them, but you have to remember your position and what they taught you about confidentiality. You really shouldn't tell people's stories, at least not without getting their permission. And something as personal as salvation, and especially considering *whom* we're talking about, well, you definitely need to wait."

"Yes, I know you're right." Nancy replied. "It's just that, well, it's a great story. And since it was Coop who planted the seeds..." She trailed off, deep in thought.

"The time will come, I'm sure, when she'll want to share the story with others. And maybe especially with Coop. But until then, just leave it in God's hands." Greg picked up the baby's diaper bag and said, "I'm going to put this away in Andy's room, and pick up some of these toys in the living room. They should be here soon. You need any help in the kitchen?"

"No, I've got everything covered here. But thanks for picking up the toys. I don't know how all the kids' stuff takes over our living room!" She kicked off her Sunday dress shoes and slid her feet into fuzzy slippers. "Ahh, that feels much better." She turned back to the kitchen and checked on the food cooking in the crock-pot.

Nancy breathed a quick prayer. "Lord, help me keep my mouth shut. And give me the right words to say, when you *do* show me it's the right time."

Becky carefully balanced the chocolate sheet cake across her lap while Coop drove the truck. The aroma of chocolate filled the truck, and Jenny, sitting in the back seat, was anxious for dessert time. "I want a big piece," she said. "I could eat the whole thing!"

"I'm sure you could," replied Becky. "But let's be sure everyone gets a piece and then *maybe* you can have seconds."

"Does baby Andy get any?" Jenny asked. "Hannah told me he has a tooth now. So, he can eat cake."

"I think he's still eating baby food," Becky answered. "He is just learning to eat from a spoon. Would you like to help feed him?"

"Oh yuck! Hannah told me he spits his food out. One time she got green beans spit on her. Yuck! And Hannah doesn't even *like* green beans!"

Everyone laughed and Coop changed the subject. "What was your Sunday school lesson about today? Do you have a memory verse to learn?"

Jenny reached for the papers lying on the seat beside her. "Here," she said, thrusting them up to the front seat. "The story was when Jesus was sleeping in a boat and a tornado came and everybody was scared but not Jesus. He said 'Peace be still' and the wind stopped blowing. Everybody was safe."

Coop glanced over at Becky with a smile. "A tornado, huh?"

"Teacher said a big wind, but I know it's a tornado. But the boat didn't have a basement, so Jesus made the tornado stop."

"That's interesting. So, what is the memory verse? Oh, here it is." Becky found the highlighted verse on Jenny's paper. "Mark 4:39. Peace be still." She laughed. "Well, you already have it memorized!"

Coop added, "Now just remember it. When we are in a storm, we must remember that Jesus is with us and can calm all of our storms." He pulled the truck into the Martin's driveway. "We're here," he said. "And man, am I hungry."

"Don't eat everything, Daddy Coop. Make sure everybody gets enough before you get your seconds."

Becky just shook her head. 'Sometimes this girl is too much,' she thought as she stepped carefully from the truck, holding tightly to the cake pan. The front door opened and Greg welcomed them in. Becky took the cake to the kitchen and set it on the counter. Jenny was off to find Hannah and her cat Marmalade.

Nancy was trying to balance the baby on her hip while she took things from the refrigerator. Little Andy reached up and pulled her hair. Becky offered to help. "Here, let me take him," she said as she reached for the little boy. "He's getting so big! He's what, four months now?"

"Four months, and eating like a teenager already. He is hungry all the time. I've been giving him extra cereal at night to try and fill him up a little. Otherwise, he would be awake a dozen times in the night, wanting to nurse." She put the bowl of salad on the table, got some bottles of dressing from the refrigerator and walked over to the baby. Becky was holding him close and Nancy said, "You look like a natural, holding him. Being a mother is such a blessing." She looked over at Andy and planted a kiss on his cheek. "And babies are a blessing too."

"Your sheet cake looks delicious," Nancy went on. "I haven't had time to bake much lately. Thanks for offering to bring dessert. The crock pot was on all morning while we were at church. I think it should be done. I'm trying a new recipe – its pork chops with ranch dressing powder cooked with it. I hope it's good."

"Sure smells good. I love cooking in my crock pot. Especially on Sundays." Becky sat at the table and held the baby facing her. She leaned down and put her face close to him. "What do you think, Andy? Want some pork chops?"

"He probably would," said Greg, who was coming into the kitchen with Coop. "That boy can eat!"

"Nothing wrong with a healthy appetite!" laughed Coop. He looked over at Becky and smiled. She looked so happy, holding a baby. She caught him staring at her and smiled. "Want to hold him?"

Coop went close and leaned down a little. "Never done this before," he said, reaching out.

"Well, why don't you just sit down first? I'll give him to you." Becky stood and Coop took her chair. "Just remember, his neck muscles are still weak, so you have to help support his head. You can put you hand around the back of his head." She marveled at how naturally Coop took the baby and cradled his head.

Coop looked up at her, "Well, would you look at that! His head fits perfectly in the palm of my hand. I guess God planned that just right."

Becky nodded. "I guess God has planned a lot of things just right!"

The friends enjoyed their Sunday dinner together. It had been a while since they had been able to spend much time together outside of church. The first topic of conversation was the sermon they had heard that morning.

"I thought Pastor Green's message was right on today!" Greg said. That passage in Ephesians was one I haven't really studied much. But the comparison between knowing about God and really *knowing* God – that was really good."

"It really helped to clarify the meaning of 'abide,'" Coop said. "I've really only thought of abiding as meaning living. But it goes a lot deeper than that."

"I agree," Becky said. "And I love what he said about having a picture of God, versus a *relationship* with God. There's a big difference."

Nancy had been cutting Hannah's pork chop and slid the plate over to her daughter as she added, "He talked about how abiding in Christ gives us such hope. And when he said there is so much power in abiding in Christ, in really knowing him and trusting him, that was so encouraging. I'm going to try to remember that there's power and hope when we abide in Christ."

"And that he promises us riches. Meaning the riches of heaven, of course," Coop replied.

Becky paused for a minute and watched as Jenny carefully dipped gravy and poured it over her mashed potatoes. She smiled when Jenny took a big bite and licked her spoon. "I don't remember the reference. Ephesians something, I know."

"It was chapter one, near the end. Verse seventeen or eighteen maybe." Coop passed a bowl of peas and carrots to Becky and looked at her, smiling. "We can read it again this evening. Maybe memorize the verse about hope and riches and power."

Conversation flowed easily around the table. There was lots of talk about babies, siblings, house plans and ponies.

"My pony's name is Benny," said Jenny excitedly. 'But he isn't at our farm yet. He's coming when I show enough ponsibilty.' Maybe tomorrow."

Becky did her best to stifle a grin but Coop said, "Not tomorrow, but maybe soon. We need to get settled into the house, and you need to learn a little more about taking care of animals. But Benny is waiting for you, at Aunt Joyce's farm, and he'll be yours soon."

"That will be the best day ever. I'll ride all over the farm with him. You can come too, Hannah. I'll give you rides."

"I never rode a horse before." Hannah was a little hesitant.

"Me either. But it's easy. Daddy Coop will teach me. And then I'll teach you."

"How's your hospital work going?" Becky asked Nancy. It had been a while since they had had much chance to talk about anything. There was a lot to catch up on.

Nancy looked over at Greg and raised her eyebrows. He tilted his head and Nancy took that as a sign that she should proceed with caution.

"Oh, it's been great," she said with a smile. "I feel like the Lord is really using me there. So many people in the hospital have lost hope, or are drowning in fear. Sometimes I feel like Jesus is in the room with us as we share scripture and pray for the patients. And a few times, we've been able to share the plan of salvation. Those moments are really special." Greg smiled at his wife. She'd done well.

Becky and Nancy had just started clearing dishes from the table when a high-pitched baby wail came from the nursery down the hall. Greg stood up to go get his son. "Sounds like his hungry cry. I'll change him and bring him to you. Wanna' come Coop? I can give you a diaper changing lesson."

"Sounds like a lot of fun!" Coop joked. "Let's go!"

Jenny got up and went with them. "I want to learn too."

Hannah laughed, "No you don't! It's gross!"

"Maybe your sibling is gross. But my sibling won't be gross. My sibling will be precocious, like me." The grown-ups looked at each other and broke into laughter.

Jenny looked to her mother and asked, "Why are you laughing? Did I say it wrong?"

Becky shook her head. "Oh honey, you said it just right. We were laughing because you surprised us with those new words. But you certainly are right. You are quite precocious."

Hannah piped up, "Then I want to be precocious too!"

Nancy hugged her daughter and said, "Hang around with Jenny and I'm sure you'll be precocious in no time!"

"These girls!" Greg laughed. "Come on Coop, we've got some diapering to do!"

CHAPTER 16

---◆◆◆---

Mercy and Grace

Only a few people were gathered in the chapel of Atkins General Hospital. Barb Olsen, the hospital Chaplin, had organized the baptism. Standing at the altar at the front of the room, she smiled reassuringly at the baptismal candidate. Pastor JD Green, from the Winslow Methodist Church, was ready to perform the ceremony. He was dressed in a navy blue suit and looked very official. Mrs. Green was there too, wearing a pink blouse and black dress pants. She was a large woman, short and stocky. The first thing everyone noticed about her was the smile that lit up her face. She was free with her hugs, and everyone at church loved her.

Nancy Martin was there, too. She had been counseling with Melissa since the beginning, and was actually the one who had led the young woman to the Lord. It was an amazing conversion story, and Chaplin Olsen was thrilled to see how the Lord had moved. Just one more example of God's mercy and grace.

Titus 3:5 came to her mind. "Not by works of righteousness which we have done, but according to his mercy he saved us." She smiled and slowly shook her head. Once again God had amazed her with his unconditional love. Only he would have considered this woman worthy of his plan of salvation. Lots of people would have turned their backs on Melissa, who was considered a criminal by many, and certainly a woman of ill repute by most everyone who knew her. Yet Jesus died for her sins, took the punishment of the cross, and accepted her into his kingdom.

Nancy had laid out the plan of salvation clearly to the girl as she laid in her hospital bed, recovering from life-threatening injuries sustained in a motorcycle accident. She used verses from Romans to show her that everyone has sinned, all have fallen short of God's intended glory, and salvation was freely offered by Jesus.

It took a while before Melissa was ready to make the decision to follow Christ. She knew she didn't want to go to hell. That was made clear when she had her near-death experience. The fear of hell had driven Melissa to seek someone to talk to. She needed to tell her story, get some answers, and decide what it all meant. When Chaplin Barb knew that Melissa was ready to talk, and really listen, she had contacted Pastor Green and his team of compassion workers. The Pastor, and especially Nancy Martin, had been an answer to prayer. Nancy seemed to have a heart for the lost, and knew just what to say to bring the gospel to Melissa in a loving, non-threatening way.

Barb remembered a conversation she had had with Nancy after an especially moving visit. Nancy had come to the Chaplin's office, smiling with happiness. She said Melissa was getting close to accepting Jesus. She had admitted she had done many terrible things in her life, had even used the word 'sin'. She said she deserved punishment and probably should go to hell for all the trouble and hurt she had caused. But the vision she had had, that night months earlier, when she lay in a ditch at death's door, had frightened her. She felt the flames of hell, and knew she was doomed. Weeks later, when she came out of her medically induced coma, Melissa could still smell the fire and brimstone and knew she never wanted to get any closer to hell than that vision. Somehow, she knew, if hell was real, so was heaven. And she knew she didn't want hell.

So, she had asked the doctors to find someone she could talk to. One thing led to another, and now she and Nancy were working through salvation scriptures together. Nancy had cautioned Melissa that trusting in Jesus was not just an insurance policy. It was much more than simply a way to avoid punishment in hell. It was a life change, a promise of dedication to the Savior, a commitment to put Jesus first.

In the Chaplin's office, Nancy and Barb prayed once more for Melissa. And at Nancy's very next visit, Melissa was ready. Barb was so glad she was in the room as Nancy led Melissa in the sinner's prayer.

Melissa's face had taken on a glow of pure joy when she had asked for forgiveness and accepted Jesus as her Savior. It was a scene Barb would never forget. And what a story of redemption! 'Somebody ought to write this all down' she had thought. 'What a testimony!'

And now here she was, ready to take the step of baptism. The young woman, once considered a criminal, one of the worst of the worst, had become a new creature in Christ. She was ready to publicly declare her desire to follow Christ.

Only a few were here to witness the event. Melissa clearly didn't have many friends. Her father was here, silent and skeptical, but here nonetheless. He had been reluctant at first, but when he saw how important this was to his daughter, he had decided to come. He did have to admit that a change had come over her. In the past few years, they had barely spoken to each other. But now, Melissa was making a real effort to spend time with him and build a relationship. So, he was here, and despite his worn jeans and crumpled shirt, he had been welcomed. These people seemed genuinely happy to get to know him and include him in this ceremony. He sat stiffly and quietly watched the proceedings.

A couple of nurses had come down to the chapel to watch. They sat discreetly in the second row. Nancy's husband Greg was also there to witness the ceremony. He was smiling proudly at his wife.

Pastor Green called Melissa up to the baptismal font. Nancy stood with her as support and mentor. Barb took a seat next to Greg. She had her camera ready to document the special day.

When the service was over, Nancy and Greg and Pastor and Mrs. Green took Melissa out for lunch in the hospital cafeteria. They had asked Melissa's father to come with them, but he had declined. He wasn't quite comfortable with these people and their ways. Melissa hugged him and thanked him for coming. He turned and slowly walked out of the hospital and found his car in the parking lot. Sitting behind the wheel, he lit a cigarette and inhaled deeply. There were things he needed to think about. Things were happening, and he didn't really understand it all.

Over soup and salad, Nancy asked Melissa if it was okay to tell others about the happenings of the day. Melissa assured her that it would be fine.

Greg looked at Melissa intently and asked, "How about Coop and Becky? They are good friends of ours, you know, and we think they would like to know."

Melissa hesitated a little but said, "Well, yes, it's okay to tell them. I have nothing to hide from anyone. In fact, I want the world to know how Jesus has changed me. But I don't think it would be appropriate for me to talk to them about my salvation. I probably better not talk to them about anything at all, considering everything I've put them through."

"You could be right. But I know Coop like a brother and I know he's forgiven you and moved on. Obviously, he holds no grudge. He dropped all the charges against you, after all. I'm sure Becky supported him in that decision, but we haven't talked to her about it. I'm sure they would both be glad to hear about your conversion."

"I'm so lucky he dropped the charges." Melissa glanced at Nancy sheepishly, remembering a conversation they had had a few weeks before. "No, I mean, I'm not lucky. I'm blessed." Nancy nodded her head, happy that Melissa was learning new ways of thinking.

Melissa went on, "I feel like a new person. It's a slow process, and I know I've got a lot to learn. But the old life, the old me, is put away. I don't want to be that person any more. That's why I dropped the name I've used for the last few years. That's not me anymore. I'm Melissa now, and never want to be called Misty again. Those days, that life, it's in the past. I'm new in Christ."

She paused and looked at Greg. "Would you tell Coop that I'm thankful he dropped the charges? I mean, I could still serve Christ from jail, I guess. That guy Paul did, right?" Greg nodded and Melissa went on, "But I see clearly that I have a place at the hospital now.

I'm so lucky – blessed, I mean, that I was ordered to do community service here. Volunteering and serving others, that has given me an opportunity to comfort and care for people. A chance I probably wouldn't have gotten if I were in jail."

"Sure, I'll tell him. And maybe you will get a chance to tell him yourself."

Nancy piped in, "But yes, Melissa, I think you're right. To keep proper appearances, I think you shouldn't make the first move to talk to them, especially to Coop. You wouldn't want to slip into any kind of perception of ungodliness. And whatever you do or whenever you talk with them, be sure to approach the conversation with prayer. God will give you the words to say."

"Of course. I'm learning to approach everything with prayer. And I sure wouldn't want to do anything to cast doubt on my salvation. I'm a child of the King now! And he will walk by me and guide me and draw me closer to himself. I trust him."

"Look how far you've already come," Pastor Green said. "Not too long ago, you were running to God as an escape from the fires of hell. And now, here you are, inviting him to walk with you and help you live for him."

Melissa checked the time and announced, "It looks like it's time for me to get going. I have therapy in a few minutes, and then I need to get to an appointment with my Probation Officer. Thank you, everyone, for coming and supporting me and walking this walk with me."

Pastor Green offered a prayer before they departed and went their separate ways. Melissa walked slowly down the hall toward physical therapy. She had a smile on her face and a new song in her heart.

Craig Cashman, at the hospital to visit his cousin who was having surgery, walked down the hall too. He noticed the tall thin woman walking toward him. She seemed self-confident and strong, despite her obvious limp. He liked her smile.

She stopped in front of the elevators and reached out her arm to press the up button. As she did so, her full arm was exposed. Craig caught sight of the tattoo. Vines and flowers, all up and down her right arm.

He stopped short. It couldn't be. But yet it had to be. The elevator door opened, a small crowd of people filed out and the inked woman entered with a middle-aged man and a woman pushing a baby stroller. The door closed.

Craig stood staring as the elevator climbed upward.

He had read everything he could find about her in the newspapers and online. He knew about her attempted escape and near fatal accident. He knew that Cooper Smith had dropped the extortion changes against her. He knew that she had gotten off with just probation and community service. He didn't understand how that had happened, seemed to him that she deserved jail time, but he wasn't a judge, so who knows.

Nothing in the media gave her address, but he figured she had to live somewhere locally, so she could meet with her probation officer. That could be anywhere in the county, but probably pretty close to Atkins.

He had checked Facebook, trying to locate her. He found her or at least thought he did. It was confusing! The pictures she posted were not what he would have expected. He was figuring she'd have skimpy clothing and be drinking with friends, partying and acting in a loose manner. But her profile pictures showed a smiling woman, nicely dressed, neat and clean and, well, nice looking. Not what he had expected.

Her face did look a little familiar, although he hadn't taken much notice of it the first time they met. He had been more interested in other parts of her body. The flowery tattoo showed up in a few pictures, so he was pretty sure he had the right Melissa. How many Melissa's could have that tattoo anyway?

Craig had known her first as 'Misty' but had since discovered that her real name was Melissa, and she was going by that now. All the newspaper articles had used her real name, not Misty. So, she had changed her name, and seemingly changed a lot of other things about herself as well.

The things she posted on her timeline – that had him really stumped. There were a lot of Bible verses and inspirational sayings. The music videos she posted were of Christian groups. She didn't seem like the praise and worship type, but here it was, posted on Facebook! And if it was on Facebook, it must be real! Craig chuckled at the thought.

Interesting. Had to be the same girl, but this was so unlike the wild sexy woman he had played with in the sleeper compartment of his rig just last year. 'There's got to be a story here,' he thought. 'Unless it's some kind of con.'

When Craig saw that the elevator had stopped on the second floor, he took off running for the stairs. He made it to the second-floor landing and opened the door of the stairwell just in time to see her go through the doorway to the physical therapy clinic. He walked slowly past the clinic and watched as she checked in at the registration desk.

After several trips up and down the hall, he saw that she had been called back into the therapy room. He walked into the clinic and took a seat in the waiting room. After waiting over half an hour, she emerged from therapy and stood at the registration desk making her next appointment. Craig made a mental note of the date and time, watched as she left the clinic, and then took the elevator up to the surgery floor. He hoped his cousin would still be in the hospital next Tuesday.

He found his cousin's wife, Bev, sitting in the waiting room. She had a magazine on her lap, but seemed to be dozing off. Craig approached carefully, so as not to scare her. He was actually relieved that she was asleep. The last time he had seen her, she had been a hysterical basket case. He sat beside her, glanced up at the monitor that listed patient numbers and information, and wondered what was happening with his cousin.

JJ was older than Craig and had always been the ring-leader at family get-togethers. Always the first to dream up something risky to do, always getting the younger kids to do things their parents would have been shocked to know about, always pushing Cash to try cigarettes or booze. JJ had introduced Craig to pornography and had even taken him to some parties where there were rumors of lots of fun things happening in the basement, the room they called 'the playroom.' Craig never went down there, but did always wish he had been invited.

JJ was working in road construction and made a good living. Bev was a teacher and a real good bread maker. It was her one asset, Craig felt. She always brought fresh baked bread to any family gatherings. JJ and Bev had one son, but he'd moved out when he was eighteen and nobody knew where he went. He had always been trouble.

Craig didn't like to think about illness or death. Who did? But here was JJ, the fun loving cousin, with kidney cancer. A sobering thought, for sure.

Craig was glad that his sister Pat had been able to visit with JJ and Bev at their home. But unfortunately, she wasn't able to get away to be waiting at the hospital. Pat had told him that it sounded pretty serious, but she couldn't take time off from her nursing home job. So Craig volunteered to stop by. And he was sure glad he did. Seeing Misty/Melissa was a big bonus.

Craig cleared this throat and Bev stirred and woke. "Oh, hi Cash," she said, as she stretched and readjusted in her seat. She ran her fingers through her graying hair and leaned over to give him a hug. "So nice of you to come by. I don't want to be alone."

"No problem. I told you I'd be here." He fumbled with his words. "It's good to see you. Well, maybe not so good to see you *here*!

"It's just terrible, Cash. Terrible." Bev answered and went on with a shudder. "It's cancer, Cash! Cancer!" and she burst into tears. He awkwardly put his arm over her shoulder and patted her comfortingly.

"Cancer? Oh man. I'm sorry to hear that." The truth was, he had heard it all before, first from Pat and then from Bev herself. But she had forgotten, and he didn't see the point in confusing or upsetting her more. So, he played along, pretending that it was all news to him.

"It's in his kidney. A tumor. They did a biopsy last week and as soon as the doctor got the report from the pathologist, he recommended this surgery to take it out." She dug a tissue out of her purse and blew her nose.

"They are taking out his kidney?"

"No, Cash, they are taking out the tumor and *part* of his kidney. It's called a partial nephrectomy. I'm learning new words – not that I really wanted to learn them. But they said he's only at stage one, so that's good. And it hasn't spread to the lymph nodes or any other place that they can tell."

"Well, that sounds good. Better than loosing the whole kidney." Craig was surprised that Bev seemed to be a wreck one minute, but then the next minute she seemed completely lucid. He looked up at the monitor on the wall. "What number is he? What's happening?"

Bev looked up and said, "Still in surgery. Progressing well. He's number 621."

"Did they say how long the surgery should take?"

"The nephrologist said about three or four hours. It's already been over two."

"Nephrologist, huh? Another new word?"

"Oh yes. I learned that 'nephr' is Latin for kidney. 'Ectomy' means taking it out. 'Ologist' is for the surgeon who does the nephrectomy. Makes perfect sense, once you know the Latin roots."

Craig patted her hand. "Always the teacher!" he laughed. "Well, I've learned something new today. What's this nephrologist's name?"

Bev sat up and leaned forward. "Dr. Spollen. Dr. Marion Spollen. She's a woman!" Bev nodded her head for emphasis. "And she's supposed to be the best there is!"

"A woman, huh? Interesting." Craig looked up at the screen again, nervously wondering what to say next. "How about recovery time? Will he be here in the hospital long?"

"Four or five days, if all goes well. They plan to do the tumor removal laproscopically, so there should be less pain and a quicker recovery time. If all goes well," she repeated.

Craig mentally counted the days. Good. JJ would still be here Tuesday. Then he felt bad for being happy that his cousin was in the hospital. But it did make following Melissa easier.

As time dragged on, Bev began to get agitated and concerned. "It's taking lots longer than it's supposed to." She got up and paced in front of the monitors, staring at the screen as if willing the update to change. Finally, she went up to the registration desk to see if they knew what was taking so long. When she came back to Craig, she was obviously frazzled.

"They can't tell me anything. Just that he's still in surgery. There must be something wrong. It shouldn't be taking this long. It's probably worse than they thought. He's probably going to lose that kidney, and then what? Live the rest of his life with just one kidney? It's possible, of course, I mean, I've heard about it. But there are risks. And how will we cope? Will he have to quit work? All the expenses, and our insurance isn't that great. Oh, this is going to be awful. I just know it." She was spiraling again.

Craig wished he had words to comfort her, but there wasn't anything he could say. He didn't have any answers. All he could do was sit with her and wait. Not his idea of a fun afternoon, but well, he'd stay for a while.

CHAPTER 17

House Blessings

Several dozen people were gathered outside the new house. A spring breeze was blowing, and the air was warming nicely. A circle had been formed with Becky, Coop and Jenny in the center. Marla Jean, Dana and Elizabeth stood nearby. Becky's sister Joyce and husband Stephen had driven over for this special day. Their son Daniel was digging in the mud with the toe of his boot. All the family members joined hands in a close circle around Becky and Coop. The others in attendance held hands in a larger circle and surrounded the young family.

Doc Larson and his wife Lila smiled on Becky. They had come to love her as a part of their own family. This was a special day for them all. Greg and Nancy Martin were there too, trying to keep six-year-old Hannah out of the mud while holding tightly to little Andy, protecting his head from the wind. Janice Thomas stood near a couple of other ladies from Becky's Wednesday night Bible study group. She smiled at Becky, happy for her young friend, whose life had taken such a joyous turn.

Pastor JD Green and his wife were there, and many of the people from the young people's Sunday school class. Dave Cole, the class leader, led them in a scripture reading from Proverbs 3:33 – 'The Lord blesses the home of the righteous." Greg Martin read Proverbs

12:7 – "The house of the righteous stands firm." Then Pastor Green spoke up. He preached a short sermon on Matthew 7:24-27, the verses that talked about the house built on the rock. Becky and Coop smiled at each other, remembering their wedding and their discussion about these verses just a few months ago. And now they had their own home, built on the firm foundation of trust in the Lord. It was a wonderful new beginning.

The ground, softened and muddy, gave way to footprints as the little congregation circled the newly constructed home. Coop, as leader of his family led the parade, with Becky at his side. Jenny held her mother's hand and marched around the house. As they walked around the exterior of the house, members of the church choir raised their voices in songs of praise. They sang "Rock of Ages" and "Blessed Assurance." Then Janice and her friends started singing a new favorite, "I Can Sing of Your Love Forever." Becky and Jenny sang out on that one.

As the house was totally encircled, they all bowed for a moment of silent prayer. After a little, Pastor Green called out loudly "And all the people said…" and from all around the house, north, south, east, and west, came dozens of voices shouting joyfully *"Amen!"*

The circle broke and many friends came to congratulate Coop and Becky and wish them many years of happiness in their new home. Mr. Simmons took pictures, intending to give them to the Smiths as a way to remember this special day. As Becky stood on her new front porch and smiled at her husband, she couldn't believe how blessed she felt. God had been so good to her, so faithful to give her the desires of her heart. She squeezed Coop's hand with joy. How could her life get any better? Was it possible that she just met Coop a year ago? So many wonderful things had happened to her in such a short time. Becky folded her hands over her tummy, raised her head toward the heavens, and said a soft "Thank you Lord." Mr. Simmons snapped the picture and smiled. It was a perfect capture of the moment.

Elizabeth looked at her daughter and smiled. "She's practically glowing," she thought. "I've never seen her look so happy. Even on her wedding day. God is good."

Marla Jean had prepared a table full of snacks and drinks. Janice had supplied the party with some of her famous cupcakes. Several gaily wrapped gifts sat on a separate table, house warming presents for the family. Under the table were several boxes of canned goods and staples. The ladies of the church had decided to gift Becky with an old fashioned 'pounding.' The pantry shelves of the new kitchen would soon be filled with the generous offerings of friends and neighbors.

As the friends filled plates with cheese, crackers, and fruit, they milled around chatting happily. It was a beautiful day, and everyone was happy for a reason to be outside. Celebrating a new home was as good a reason as any! The men stood talking about the crops that were being planted soon. Coop had gotten the fields tilled and was ready for planting corn and soy beans. The winter wheat was ready to be harvested in a few weeks. Life was busy this time of year, but it was good to spend some time with friends.

Friends, family and farm life. Coop sighed with contentment. He looked over at Jenny who was running with Hannah and a couple of other little girls, chasing after the barn cats. He laughed a little when he saw the cat named Muffin. It was obvious that she would soon be delivering kittens. That would make Jenny happy for sure. A terrific house warming present for a little girl.

Several of the women asked Becky to give them a tour of the house, so they walked across the yard and entered the screened in porch. Coop had really wanted this porch, reminisant of the porch on the big house where he had grown up. Becky loved the idea too. There was a screened door, too, just like at the big house. Marla Jean had warned her about it. She said Coop had a tendency to let that screened door slam every time he came into the house. Becky would have to keep on him about that.

The ladies took their wet shoes off and left them on the front porch. They wandered with Becky from room to room. There was no furniture in the house yet, that would happen next weekend. Most of the furniture would be coming from Becky's rental house. They had decided to hold off on any major furniture purchases for now.

The front door opened and Dana stuck her head in. "People are starting to get ready to leave, Becky. They want you and Coop to open some presents before everyone has to leave."

"Presents? People weren't supposed to bring presents," Becky said in surprise.

One of the older ladies, Marilyn Hennessey, said, "Honey, you should know us farm folk love to shower young families with blessings. It's our way of sharing God's love and getting you young people off to a good start. Think of it as a way we can bless you, and it's our honor to do it." She tucked a wisp of gray hair behind her ear. "Someday down the road, you will have the chance to be a giver too. But right now, accept these gifts for what they are – a way of showing love. That's what God wants us to do, you know. Love your neighbor as yourself."

Laura Richards, who was nearly ninety years old, softly laid her wrinkled hand on Becky's arm. "When you allow others to give to you, whether it's gifts or time or just a listening ear, it not only helps you, it is a blessing to the giver as well. I get such joy from knowing that God has used my generosity to help others. See, that in turn blesses me! It's a wonderful circle of compassion."

Marilyn added, "The world needs more compassion. And it starts right here, at home."

Becky nodded her thanks and they all put their shoes back on and went over to the big house. Coop was there, waiting. Together they opened the packages. Pastor and Mrs. Green had given them a ceramic plaque that read "As for me and my house, we shall serve the Lord."

"We'll hang this right by the front door," Coop said.

"Thank you," Becky said to the Green's. "This is perfect."

The Martin's gift was a door knocker, engraved 'Smith'. Other gifts were kitchen towels, candles, a pretty tablecloth, and other decorative household things. When the boxes filled with canned goods were pulled out from under the table, Becky burst into tears. "You all! You have done so much for us. Thank you so much. Really!" She looked around at so many friends gathered on the porch and in the yard. "We appreciate all this so much. Your friendship is such a blessing."

Members of the young adult Sunday school class had pooled their money and gotten them a framed painting of a white dove with wings wide-spread. The words "Under His Wings I Am Safely Abiding" decorated the painting, and musical notes were scattered throughout. The background was a watercolor farm scene, with green fields, a red barn and white farmhouse.

"It's a dove!" Jenny exclaimed. "Oh, so pretty," she cooed. "It looks so real. Can I touch the feathers?"

Coop leaned the painting close and Jenny gently rubbed her fingers over the bird. "What do the words say?" she asked. Becky read them to her.

Jenny looked up at Coop and asked, "Abiding? What does that mean?"

Coop explained, "Abiding means living, or staying, or resting. If we abide with Jesus, he will protect us and we'll be safe. No matter what happens, Jesus will love us and care for us." Jenny let the words sink in, then her eyes widened. "You mean like the chicken, how she keeps her babies safe under her wings?"

"Yes, exactly like that. You *are* precocious!"

Jenny beamed. She liked learning new words. And she felt the pride the word precocious stirred within her, especially when Daddy Coop said it.

Coop smiled at his friends and neighbors. "Having friends like you is truly a gift from God. These physical gifts are wonderful, but the best gifts today were your fellowship, friendship and prayers. Becky, Jenny and I are honored to know you all."

As the party broke up and people started to leave, Becky's sister Joyce came up to them carrying an envelope. "There's one more gift for you," she said. "This one is from Stephen and me, and mom too."

As she opened the envelope, Becky said, "Whatever it is, you shouldn't have. We're just so happy you and Stephen and Danny could come over and be with us today." She withdrew a gift card from the envelope and looked at it, puzzled. "The furniture store in Atkins? What's this for?"

Elizabeth answered. "We wanted you and Coop to go and pick out a new bedroom set for yourselves. That old bed you're using now can go into your guest room. You really should have new furniture in your new bedroom. What you're using now is just odds and ends from thrift stores. You need some nice new furniture in your nice new room."

Tears welled up in Becky's eyes. "I don't know what to say. Thank you isn't enough. I love you guys!" She called to Coop, who was out in the yard saying goodbye to the Martins. "Coop, you need to see this."

Coop listened as Becky explained the purpose of the gift card, and then he hugged Joyce and Elizabeth. "We can't thank you enough," he said. He looked at Becky. "Maybe we can go furniture shopping as soon as I get the corn planted. Might be a week or two, but we can use the old furniture until then."

"Sure, we can put the old bed in the guest room, and use it until we get the new set." Becky smiled happily. So many wonderful things were happening in their lives. God was indeed very good.

Stephen came over and put his hands on his wife's shoulders. "Now," he said, "about Jenny's gift. Just let us know when you're ready. We'll keep him on our farm until you say, and then drive him over here in the trailer some weekend. That is, if Danny is willing to let him go!"

"Danny has his own pony, Summer. I know he's getting attached to Benny, but he'll be willing to give him to Jenny, I'm sure," Joyce said. "I have a feeling we will be over visiting a lot anyway. We'll get to try out your new guestroom!"

Coop said, "You are welcome any time. It's always good to have family around." He looked at Becky and said, "We just want to give Jenny a little time to get settled in, and acquaint her with the idea of farm chores and responsibilities."

Becky nodded in agreement. "We want to make sure she understands how important it is to follow through with obligations. Having a pony is a lot of work. We want to be sure she's ready for the responsibility."

"A couple months maybe. We'll let you know. I'll want to talk to you about a collie, too, in a couple of months. There's a big hole at the farm since Riley's been gone. I'm thinking it's almost time to get another good farm dog."

"We've had several litters already this spring, and a couple more due soon. We have a few older dogs too, if you don't want a puppy. Just let us know." Joyce took care of most of the collie business, while Stephen tended to the farm crops and animals.

Becky and Joyce had grown up on that farm, while their parents ran the businesses. After their dad passed away, the farm had gone to Joyce and Stephen, and Elizabeth had moved into Winslow, where Becky joined her after she had gotten pregnant. The relationship between the girls had been strained for a few years, but they were both hoping things would be better, now that they had more in common. Elizabeth was praying for that also. She wanted her daughters to be close. After all, one of these days, they wouldn't have their mom, and would need to rely on each other.

Jenny and Danny ran over to their parents, gasping and all out of breath. "Daddy Coop," Jenny said between gulps of air, "Can we swing on the rope in the haymow? I want to show Danny how to do it."

Danny said indignantly, "You don't have to show me how to. I already know. I do that at my own barn."

"Okay well, anyway, can we swing, Daddy Coop? Can we?"

"I'm glad you asked me before trying it on your own. It's always good to have a grown-up with you." Coop looked over at Stephen. "What do you say? Do we have time for a few rope swings?"

Stephen glanced at his watch and nodded. "I'd like to get going in half an hour or so. But that's time for a few good rides. Let's go!"

As the group moved toward the barn, Coop noticed his sister Dana standing near the pasture fence, stroking the nose of her horse Nell. With her was Dave Cole, the teacher of their young adult Sunday school class. They seemed to be deep in conversation. "Hmmm. I wonder what that's all about," Coop thought. He caught Dave's eye and waved. Dave waved back and Dana turned to smile and wave. When Jenny saw her aunt Dana, she took off on the run.

"Dana, Dana!" she called. "Did you bring carrots for the horses? Can I feed them?"

"As a matter of fact, I did," Dana said, reaching into a back pack that was hung over her shoulder. "Here ya' go!" Jenny took one carrot and fed it to Nell. Danny joined them at the fence and said, "Come on Jenny. Let's go swing. We don't have much time. Come on!"

Jenny took another carrot from the bag and handed it to Dave. "You feed Slick. Hold it like this," and she demonstrated the proper way to feed carrots to a horse. "Let him take it out of your hand. Keep your hand flat." She turned and ran with Danny back to the barn.

Dana chuckled and said, "That girl! She's quite the character. I think she's going to be just fine living on the farm."

"Seems like Becky has done a great job raising her so far. And Coop's fitting right in as dad. Do you and Becky get along?"

"Oh sure! She's like the sister I never had." Dana turned to lean her back against the fence. "But the best thing about her is how happy she makes Coop."

"They do really seem to be in love." Dave wiped his hands against his jeans and leaned on the fence beside Dana. "They make a great team. That's special; you don't see it every day. A family built on the love of Jesus. That should be the goal of every marriage, don't you think?"

"I guess I do. I try not to think about marriage much, to tell you the truth. My goal right now is school, and figuring out what I want to do in my life. I wish God would speak to me loud and clear some day, and tell me what I'm supposed to do. Coop seems to get messages directly from God, but I never have. Sometimes I wonder why."

"Keep asking, and then make sure you take time to listen. Sometimes the answers to our questions come from other people, speaking as God directs them. You don't necessarily have to hear the voice of God himself, to still hear his words."

"I guess," Dana said thoughtfully. "I'll try to be a good listener."

Amidst the peels of laughter in the haymow, Coop turned to Stephen and said, "I like having you around. Ever since my brother left the farm, I've felt like something was missing. We used to swing up here for hours. It was nice having the two of us working and doing chores together. I know he never really liked farm work, but we did have some fun. It's good to have you here, even for just a little while."

"I know what you mean about having a brother around. My brother Todd and his family bought the farm next to us about eight years ago. It's been great having them so close. We help each other out. Todd and his oldest son Tucker have been great help with our crops."

The men stood watching the children frolic in the hay. Swinging on the rope and dropping to the hay covered floor below brought them squeals of delight. The men couldn't help but smile at their joy.

"We need to make sure the girls get to spend more time together, too," said Stephen. "Joyce doesn't say much about it, but I think she would like to be close with Becky again." He gave Danny another big push on the rope swing.

"Yeah, let's try to get together more often. That's what family is all about. Spending time together."

"Deal." Stephen looked around. "Danny, one more push and then we have to go. It's a long drive home."

Joyce and Becky were coming out of the new house as the kids ran across the front yard. "Do they ever slow down?" laughed Becky.

"Oh, Danny will be asleep as soon at the tires start rolling. He'll sleep the whole way home. I may take a little nap myself. It's been a busy day."

"Thanks so much for coming to be with us today. And thanks for your help with getting the canned goods in the pantry." Becky gave her sister a hug. "We really need to get together more often. Mom would like that."

"I know, and I agree. We have to try to do better."

From the porch of the farmhouse, Elizabeth watched her two daughters. She smiled to see them getting along so well. It hadn't always been so.

They all made a final stop at the bathroom and then the families gathered at the car, ready to say their goodbyes. After hugs and tears and promises to see each other soon, they were off.

Becky and Coop stood in the driveway, waving as the car disappeared down the road. "We better be getting on home, too,"

Coop said. "We've got a lot to do there before the trucks come for the first load of stuff tomorrow afternoon." He turned to Marla Jean and said, "I'll see you in the morning, mom. Thanks for everything you did to make this a special day."

"Yes, thank you," Becky added. "It was a wonderful day."

Elizabeth said, "I'm going to stay a bit and help Marla Jean get things cleaned up. Jenny can stay here with us grandmas. I'll bring her home later. That might help you get a little more done."

"Okay, good," said Jenny. "I've been looking for Muffin. I need to talk to her."

"Talk to her? Whatever for?" asked Becky.

"We have to talk about kittens. I have to tell her what kind I want." Jenny skipped off toward the barn. "I'm going to check in the barn first. I gotta find her."

"Remember," said Coop. "You don't go up into the haymow without a grown up."

"I remember." She called over her shoulder, "Don't worry Daddy Coop. I remember."

Becky sighed contentedly as she fastened the seatbelt across her chest. She felt an odd twinge as the belt settled between her breasts. Not for the first time, she wondered if it could be true. There had been so many changes in the last year, especially the last few months. Were they about to be facing another big change? Were they ready?

She settled back into her seat and thought to herself, 'Ready or not, here we come.'

CHAPTER 18

---◆◆◆---

A Hope and a Future

Becky lay in her bed thinking. Coop was sleeping beside her, breathing rhythmically. It was comforting, listening to him sleep. In the last four months she had gotten very used to sleeping beside him. She enjoyed his passion and his desire to please her. And she also enjoyed just lying close to him, sharing hopes and dreams as they drifted off to sleep. Marriage was still new. Love making was still new. There was still a magic to living together.

Would their lives change? Of course, everything would be different. But change isn't necessarily bad. Just different. Are they ready? Is any couple ever truly ready?

Jeremiah 29:11 came to her mind. "For I know the plans I have for you" declares the Lord, "plans to prosper you and not to harm you, plans to give you hope and a future."

"Lord Jesus, I put this all into your hands. I know you have wonderful plans for us. And I know you will be with us, whatever comes our way. I just trust you." Becky prayed, "Thy will be done."

While Coop had been in the shower, Becky had looked carefully at her calendar, trying to remember dates and counting back to the last time she could remember having her period. The thing is, she'd been so busy with moving and working and packing and finalizing purchases for the new house, she had not been faithful to mark the date on her calendar. So everything was a guess. All she knew for sure was that it seemed like surely she was late.

But then, stress could sometimes make a woman skip her period. It had happened to her a few times in the past, when she had gone though a couple of job losses and was feeling very insecure about her life, and that of her baby daughter. But those days were long past. What did she have to be stressed or worried about now? Things were busy, true, but she was not stressed out. There was only one logical explanation.

Well, she would pick up a pregnancy test on her way into work tomorrow. Meanwhile, a good night's sleep was called for. Packing with Coop for a couple of hours, then getting Jenny ready for bed, then devotion time - well, she had almost fallen asleep while Coop read from the Bible story book. Fortunately, Jenny was pretty worn out from the business of the day and had fallen right to sleep.

Tired as she was, Becky couldn't stop thinking. She debated waking Coop and telling him of her suspicions. But no, he needed his sleep too. He had worked so hard today. Well, every day, actually. He had a lot of responsibilities on his shoulders. No sense giving him anything else to feel responsible about. Not just yet, anyway. Not until she was sure. And to start this conversation now, well, waiting a day or two really wouldn't make any difference. In the mean time, she would keep this little secret to herself. Time would tell.

She placed one hand on her stomach and one hand on Coop's back. She closed her eyes and visualized the connection that would grow between the three of them. She could almost feel the blood of life circulating from Coop, moving up her arm, across her chest, down her other arm, and to the little life growing within her. Maybe growing there. Maybe.

'Let's not jump to conclusions. It's so early, if at all.' But she couldn't shake the feeling. She smiled and prayed for the little one they could call their own. If not now, then sometime in the future.

Still she couldn't sleep. 'I wonder if it's a girl or a boy. I wonder which Coop would prefer. I think he would like a son. A name sake. A future farmer. Or maybe he'll be a preacher. That would bring Coop's dreams full circle.'

Becky rolled over and fluffed up her pillow. 'But no, he'd love to have a little girl to spoil. His little princess. I can see it now. She'd have him wrapped around her little finger.' Becky smiled and closed her eyes. As she finally drifted off to sleep, she repeated the Jeremiah verse over and over. Her last thoughts were 'a hope and a future.'

CHAPTER 19

Tuesday

About twenty minutes before her appointment time, Craig took a seat in the waiting room and pretended to be reading a magazine. Melissa came in just a few minutes later. She signed in, sat down and stretched out her legs. She flexed her foot and made circles with her toes. 'Warming up for therapy I guess,' thought Craig. He watched her as she lifted her leg up slightly attempting to tighten her thigh muscle.

'I'd love to help her with her exercises,' he thought. 'We'd use a lot more muscles than just the legs.' He shuddered slightly, remembering their time together in his truck. She'd been a willing participant; in fact it was all her idea. She wanted a favor, a ride, but had no money. They'd made a deal – she offered herself in trade for a ride out of the state. Little did she know, he wasn't planning to hold up his end of the bargain. As soon as they were done, he turned her in to the cops.

He remembered how it felt to have those long legs wrapped around him. He remembered her lips, her tongue. He remembered how he almost exploded when her teeth scrapped along him. He remembered wishing he had taken her down the road a few days, so he could have enjoyed her body a few more times. It would have made that trip a lot more fun.

Oh well, that was then and this is now. And now he had another chance with her. Who would have imagined that he'd ever see her again, much less have an opportunity like this?

As soon as Melissa went back into the therapy room, Craig hustled upstairs to visit with his cousin JJ. Just as Bev had predicted, the surgery had taking longer than expected because of complications. The tumor was bigger than they thought, and attached more deeply than Dr. Spollen had anticipated. They had had to remove more of the kidney, and recovery time would be lengthened. JJ would be all right, given time, pain medications and antibiotics. He would be hospitalized for another several more days. Craig just had time for a quick visit; he wanted to be down at the therapy clinic when Melissa came out.

He had it all planned. He would be waiting for her in the hallway when she finished her therapy. He'd walk with her down the hall and ask if she knew who he was. He'd remind her of the good time they had enjoyed last year and he'd apologize for getting the cops involved. He'd tell her he had been following her case and was glad she got off easy. Then he'd ask her if she'd like to get a drink and talk some more. And hopefully things would move on from there.

But things didn't quite turn out like he planned. She did remember him, seemed happy to run into him again, and accepted his apology without hesitation. But she turned down his invitation for a drink. She said she had to get to her volunteer job in the hospital gift shop.

As they walked together to the gift shop near the hospital entrance, Craig was already planning his next move. Somehow he had to get her to agree to spend some more time with him. A little food and drink, some conversation (otherwise known as suggestive flirting) and then, off to bed. He was already picturing it. But how to get there, that was his first obstacle.

That's when she surprised him. She suggested that he come by later, when she was off work, and they could maybe go get a pizza and have time to talk. She spoke with an inviting smile and it seemed like she was already really into him.

Walking out of the hospital, his step was light and joyful. He would drive over to Catonsville, clean up his place some, take a shower and be back in a few hours to get her. He sighed as he unlocked his car door. She was practically offering herself up on a silver platter.

CHAPTER 20

---◆◆◆---

Surprises of a Different Kind

Melissa stood in front of the mirror and took a deep breath. This was going to be tough, but she had a confidence in herself and her God. She knew she wasn't facing this alone. She closed her eyes and tried to remember the verse she'd been memorizing. "Trust in the lord with all your heart and...." she couldn't remember the rest.

"Well, I guess that's the most important part anyway. I will trust in the Lord. I can't do this on my own." She took a look at herself in the mirror and dug her hairbrush out of her purse. A quick brush through and she was ready to go. "Lord, help me," she said. I trust you." She walked out of the staff restroom with a determination that surprised her and brought her assurance and peace.

Craig was waiting for her in the gift shop. He was wearing jeans and a Dallas Cowboys T-shirt. His black hair was clean and combed, and it looked like he was freshly shaved. She liked that he had cleaned up for her. Made her feel special.

He turned toward her and smiled. "Hi. You ready to go?" She nodded and he went on, "Do you have a favorite pizza place in town? I'm not familiar with Atkins so you pick the place. What kind of pizza do you like?"

"Hawaiian is my favorite. Ham and pineapple, lots of cheese, yum!" She started out the door. "I know just the place."

Before they started eating, Craig got his first surprise. Melissa said, "I would like to pray before we eat. Okay?" He nodded and lowered his gaze. She spoke softly but with confidence. She thanked God for the food and the people who prepared it. And she thanked God for the opportunity to catch up with a friend. She asked that the Lord bless their time together.

Craig didn't know what to think. So he quickly dived into conversation. He told her about his truck driving job, which took him on long hauls across country. He told her about some of his adventures, mostly weather related accidents he'd seen, or some antics of drunk drivers. He told of long lonely drives, when he wished for a passenger to keep him company. He talked about truck stops and waitresses and good places to eat.

She was easy to talk to. She paid attention, responded to his stories, asked questions, and laughed at his attempts at jokes. Craig reached for another slice of pizza and said, "But enough about me. Tell me what's been going on with you. I read about your accident. How's your therapy going?"

"Therapy can be rough, but I'm seeing improvement, so I'm grateful for that. I go three times a week, and do exercises at home every day." Melissa licked her tongue over her lips to catch some melted cheese that was dangling there. Craig could hardly take his eyes off her. She noticed his leering stare and picked up her napkin to completely wipe her lips.

"Speaking of home, where are you living? Here in Atkins?"

Melissa nodded as she took another bite. "I'm actually living in housing appointed by the courts. They wanted me close to keep an eye on me. I have to meet with my PO once a week."

Craig reached across the table and took Melissa's hand. He looked her in the eye and said, "Hey, I'm really sorry about calling the cops on you. I feel real bad that this all happened to you. It's kinda my fault."

"Thanks, I appreciate that. But I'm certainly not blaming you. It was all my own fault. And now I'm dealing with the consequences."

She pulled her hand away to reach for her soda glass. After a drink she said "And actually, I should probably thank you. It was the best thing that has ever happened to me."

That was Craig's second surprise. "Huh? How could that accident have been the best thing to happen to you? It nearly killed you!"

"It's really an amazing story, and I'd love to tell you about it. It was the end of one life and the beginning of another." She was sitting on the edge of her seat, eager to tell this man about the changes Jesus had brought into her life. But where to begin? 'Lord Jesus, please help me,' she prayed quietly.

"Sounds interesting. Go on." Craig took another drink of his soda and settled back in his chair.

"See, I crashed the motorcycle when a deer ran out in front of me. I lay there in the ditch, with the bike on me, and the deer kicking me all over, trying to get away. And I thought for sure I was going to die. Everything hurt, and truthfully, I just *wanted* to die. My life was a mess. I had nobody who really cared about me. Nobody would care if I lived or died. And the pain – I just wanted it over. I knew I was in big trouble with the law, and I didn't want to think about going to jail. I just wanted my life to be over. I sorta gave up."

She shook her head as if to shake off the memory. "I guess I blacked out, or maybe I even died for a few minutes. I had this vision, or a dream or something." She looked at Craig intently. "You may not believe this, but I had like an out of body experience."

"You mean, like you were floating above your body? I've heard about people who have flat-lined during surgery and then are revived, and they say they saw the Doctors working on them. Was that what happened?" He seemed really interested.

"Well, yes and no. It wasn't exactly like that. It was more like I felt myself being pulled into the after-life. Like I was being lead, or ushered into eternity."

"Oh, I've hear about that too!" Craig was excited. "But I've never actually known anyone who experienced it! So, did you see a bright light, and see God reaching his hand to you, and did you feel yourself floating down a tunnel with the bright light at the end? What was it like?"

"Actually, it was just the opposite. I wasn't being pulled toward heaven; I was going down to the pit of hell. I was spinning uncontrollably downward, closer and closer to the most evil feeling place. Worse than I could ever imagine. I saw flames and darkness. I smelled the fire and brimstone. There were horrible looking faces pulling at me, frightening beings with leering smiles. It was terrible. I knew right then and there that I was going to hell to be punished for the way I had been living my life. And I knew I deserved it. I was so scared."

"Whew, sounds awful. Then what happened? Obviously you didn't die. You didn't go into that pit. What saved you?"

"I prayed!" Melissa said. She smiled in remembrance. Her whole countenance changed as she spoke. "I hadn't ever really prayed before then, but somebody had tried to show me how once and I just took his lead and asked God to save me and give me another chance. Next thing I remember, I was getting unloaded from the ambulance, and Doctors were everywhere. I hurt all over, and I know now that they put me into a medically induced coma because the pain was so intense. They had to do surgery on my brain to relieve some swelling, and on my leg, and I had some broken ribs and other internal injuries. My kidney was damaged. I was a mess. I didn't come to for almost eight days. And when I did, I was hooked up to all sorts of machines, and could hardly move a muscle. A nurse had to feed me, it was that bad. But I still had that memory of being pulled into hell, and I wanted to never experience that again."

She paused to catch a breath. Retelling this story always made her so appreciative for the people who had walked with her through this journey. Where would she be now without them? Chaplin Olsen, Pastor Green, Nancy, and yes, even Coop Smith. Maybe even Coop the most, he had started this whole thing. She owed a lot to them all. She went on, "The hospital Chaplin brought some people in to talk to me and eventually I prayed to God, asking him for forgiveness for all the evil things I'd done, and I gave my life to him. Everything changed after that. I'm a new person."

"You do really seem like a different person from the girl I met at the truck stop. I sure have never known anyone who has talked about

God like you do." Craig had a lot to think about. He'd really been hoping to hook up with the wild woman from the truck stop. This turn of events posed a new problem.

"I can't help but talk about God. He saved me. Saved me from my wicked ways, saved me from a derelict life, saved me from the very pit of hell. I came so close, and he saved me. Of course I want to tell people about it. And I want to live the rest of my life, showing my appreciation for what he's done for me."

Craig thought a moment before replying. "I've never been a religious person. Never saw a need for it. I mean, I do alright on my own. Don't see why I should get bogged down with rules and rights and wrongs and trying to live by some doctrine or other."

"Haven't you ever wondered what happens after you die?" Melissa asked, leaning forward for emphasis. "Well, I saw what would happen to me, and I didn't like it! I am at peace now, knowing that my eternal home is in heaven. I wouldn't wish hell on my worst enemy."

Craig shrugged. "No, I don't think about things like that. I figure - I live, I die, and that's the end of it."

"But what if you're wrong?" she asked.

"Ya, well," he shrugged. "I guess I just don't think I am."

"Well, listen Craig; I was a lot like you. I didn't think about God, ever, except to swear in his name. I went about my life doing whatever I wanted, not concerned about eternity, not caring about who I may hurt or what the consequences of my behavior might be. As long as I was getting what I wanted, that's all I cared about. But that experience of seeing hell, well, I guess you could say it scared the hell *out* of me! I believe it was real, and I never want to get that close again."

Craig could think of nothing to say. Melissa went on, "My friend Nancy, the lady who came to the hospital to talk with me, she told me about this verse in Romans. I know I was a sinner, and I know I still have sins in my life every day. But the thing is, I know my Savior forgives sin, and I feel drawn to him and compelled to live closer to him every day. Not saying it's easy. I have a lot to learn, and thank goodness I have some new friends who are helping me understand the Bible and showing me how much Jesus loves me, despite my unworthiness."

"And this all happened just a few months ago?" he asked. "You're already talking like a church lady. How'd you learn all that in just a little while?"

"It's mostly because of my friend Nancy. She comes twice a week to do Bible Study with me. And I talk with the Chaplin here too. She's always here, so if I have a question, or I'm having a hard time with remembering that Jesus really truly loves me, I go talk with her."

"Humph," Craig mumbled. "Well, you sure talk different, and act different, than you used to. Not what I was expecting, when I ran into you."

"I heard a song the other day on the Christian radio station. It said something about 'the man I am now is not who I used to be.' That's not exactly the right words, but the right idea. It's like that with me. I've changed. I'm not the girl you met in the truck stop. I'm not the girl that caused a lot of trouble and heartache for people. That girl is gone. Nancy taught me a verse "Old things are passed away, everything has become new." That's me! I'm new!"

He could see that she was sincere and it confused him some. Could a person really change that much? Was there really something to this God stuff? It was worth thinking about.

CHAPTER 21

Moving Day

All the furniture was in place, or at least close enough. The box with dishes was sitting in the kitchen. The garage was piled high with boxes that would eventually be emptied, but for now they could do without books on the bookshelf or knickknacks on the end tables. They had unpacked enough clothes for the next few days. Their toothbrushes were in the holder in the bathroom. That was good enough for now.

The little family gathered on the front porch. Elizabeth, Marla Jean and Dana were there, standing a little off to the side. Dana had her camera ready to document this special moment.

Jenny stood proudly and spoke clearly. She had memorized her part and practiced with her grandmas. "Bless this house O Lord we pray. Make it safe by night and day." She smiled up at Elizabeth and Marla Jean, who clapped their fingertips in silent praise.

Becky quoted, "Bless the walls so firm and stout. Keeping want and trouble out."

Coop took up the poem, "Bless its roof and chimney tall. Let His peace be over all."

The whole family said "Amen."

Coop nodded to Jenny, who knew her next responsibility. She opened the door and held it for her parents. Coop scooped

Becky into his arms, lifting her feet off the ground, and carried her over the threshold. Becky was giggling. This was unexpected. She gripped her hands tightly around Coop's neck. He was so strong. She felt safe.

"Welcome home, Mrs. Smith." Coop kissed her before he set her carefully down in the living room. Once firmly established on the floor, Becky said, "Welcome home, Mr. Smith," and she kissed him back. Dana snapped pictures.

Jenny was super-excited. Getting her to bed was difficult. Her special bedmates were cuddled in next to her, and prayers had been said. Still Jenny wanted to talk about her new room, her new house, living on the farm, and getting Benny, the pony. Coop and Becky shared her excitement, but finally convinced her that sleep was required. "Best part is the new house!" Jenny exclaimed, and the grownups had to agree. "Now go to sleep," Becky instructed and kissed her forehead. "Goodnight Jenny," added Coop. "Tomorrow will be another day."

Eventually Coop and Becky left her room and went to sit on the living room couch. They cuddled together, surrounded by half-emptied boxes and wrapped in the comfort and security of their new home "What a day, huh?" said Coop, gently stroking her hair. "We couldn't have done it all in one day without help from the guys from church."

"Don't forget Dana's friend Marco. He's a little guy, but he sure can hustle."

Coop laughed. "Yeah, I noticed. I think he was showing off for her. How strong he is, how fast he can move. And how organized. Did you see all those boxes in the garage? Marco stacked them pretty much all by himself."

"I did notice him smiling at her a lot. Ahh, young love."

"Have you also noticed that Dave Cole has been paying Dana a lot of attention? I saw them talking together at the house blessing, and today, whenever she was carrying something, there was Dave, taking it from her. My little sister is being pursued by two men."

"Dave's a great guy. That would be a nice match."

"He's quite a bit older than her. But I agree, a great guy."

They sat in silence for a few minutes. "I'm going to love this house. It's already filled with love. Thank you," Becky said.

A sense of euphoric peace settled over Becky. She was experiencing the last few minutes of her secret, and she wanted to treasure each second. Once she revealed the hidden mystery, she would have to share the special knowledge with Coop and the world. Not that that was a bad thing, but for now, she liked knowing what was happening inside her body. It was kind of mystical, knowing that she knew something no one else anywhere knew. It was just between herself and God, and this little being growing inside her womb. She sighed and put her hand lovingly on her belly. 'Just our secret, for a minute more,' she thought.

It was time. And really, she couldn't wait. She wondered how he would react. Becky took a deep breath. She was so comfortable, cuddled up in Coop's arms, but she wiggled to sit up and look at him. "I have a housewarming gift for you."

"What? You shouldn't have done that. I didn't think to get you anything." Coop sat up and looked around. "I don't see anything. Where is my present?"

Becky stood up. "Oh, you have already gotten me something. You just don't know it. Yet." She reached into the back pocket of her jeans and pulled out a thin white plastic tube. She handed it to Coop, who took it from her but looked puzzled.

"What's this?" he asked. He studied it, trying to figure out what this thing was. He'd never seen anything like it before. The tube was about five inches long, with a little window-like opening. Inside the window, there were two little pink lines. He looked over to Becky. "Really," he said. "What is this?"

"That, Mr. Smith, is a home pregnancy test. And those two little pink lines? That means we are pregnant!"

"What?" Stunned, Coop looked closely at the pink lines. "Seriously? Really?" he stuttered. "We're having a baby? What?"

Becky was beaming from ear to ear. "Yes. It's true. I'm pregnant. You're going to be a father."

Coop jumped up from the couch and took her in his arms. He held her tight and danced her around the room. "A baby? Are you sure? I mean, how did this happen? No, I know how, I just mean... Oh I don't even know *what* I mean. A baby!"

He placed his hand gently on Becky's tummy and said, "Our baby. We're going to have a baby." When he looked up at Becky, she saw tears shimmering in his eyes. Becky took his face in her hands and said, "So, you're happy?"

"Happy? Well of course I'm happy. I've never been happier! And I've never loved you more!" He bent his head to kiss her, while one hand lovingly rubbed over Becky's belly. "I can't believe it! We're having a baby."

"Shhhh," Becky whispered. "You'll wake Jenny."

"We should. We should wake her up and tell her the news right now. And I should call mom! She'll be over the moon. Oh, there are so many people to tell. Greg and Nancy will be thrilled."

Becky put her fingers lightly over Coop's mouth. "Wait. Let's just keep this between us for a little while. It's early yet, and things could happen. Besides, it'll be nice knowing we have a little secret, for a few weeks anyway. Okay?"

"Well, sure, if that's what you want. Here, sit down. You need to rest. Put your feet up. Do you want anything? Some tea? Can you drink tea? Maybe you should have some milk. How about a backrub? What can I do?"

"Coop! I'm not helpless. I'm fine." She laughed, but sat down and put her feet up. "We do probably need to get to bed though. I'm pretty tired. It's been an amazing day."

"Best day ever," Coop said and sat down beside her. "Absolutely the best day ever." He pulled Becky over close to him and she laid her head on his chest.

"We can bring Jenny's old crib in from Mom's garage. There'll be room in our bedroom for the crib, until he gets a little older and sleeps through the night. Then we can move him to the bedroom next to Jenny." Becky was talking groggily, sleep was creeping ever closer. "I guess that means we don't have a guest room. Oh well. It'll be fine." Becky closed her eyes and drifted toward sleep.

"He?" Coop repeated. "You said he? Do you already know we're having a boy?"

"No, of course not silly. We won't know that for several months. I just said 'he' as a generalization. We don't want to call our baby 'it' do we?"

"We'll have to pick out names. What do you think? How about Matthew? I've always liked that. A good Biblical name." He paused a second to think. "And girl's names, I don't know why, but for some reason I've always liked the name Holly. Hey, when do you think he or she will be born? We've got lots to do."

He looked down at Becky, who was sound asleep. Coop gave a contented sigh and prayed softly, "Thank you Lord Jesus. You have granted me one of the desires of my heart. I know you have formed this child within my wife's body. I know you have planned for this and you already know this child. Thank you for your gift. Keep our child safe. Help me to be a godly father, to lead this family in paths of righteousness. Oh God! Thank you."

Coop sat on the couch, holding his sleeping wife, with their child nestled deep within her. He knew he should wake her, take her to bed, and get some good sleep. But sleep was elusive. He kept counting his blessings, marveling at the goodness of God and the generosity of his gifts. Was it only a year ago he had been single, praying for God to lead him to the right woman, a woman who would be a teammate, who would work side by side with him to further the kingdom? Well, here she was, right here in his arms. His partner, his teammate and the mother of his child. Together they would bring up their children in the ways of the Lord. They would lead them and teach them and work hard to make sure the circle would not be broken. The whole family, on the pathway to heaven. Oh indeed, God was good.

CHAPTER 22

❖ ◆ ❖

The Cat is Out of the Bag

Jenny raced in from the barn calling, "Mommy, Mommy, Daddy Coop! You gotta come quick. I need you." The screen door slammed as she rushed into the kitchen. Becky rolled her eyes. Evidently Jenny had learned the slamming door habit from Coop.

"We gotta go to the barn. I found Muffin. I need to go in the haymow. Come with me. Quick!" She impatiently pulled on her mother's arm.

"Slow down a bit, will ya?" Becky said, turning from the cabinet where she was organizing dishes and cups. Elizabeth came in from the hallway, holding a stack of kitchen dish towels. She bent to put them in a drawer while Becky said, "Daddy Coop is out in the field planting. And as you can see, Grammy and I are in the middle of something here."

"But I followed her, and she climbed up the ladder to the haymow. I just know the babies are up there. I need to find them. I need to get my kitten."

"I'm glad you didn't climb up there by yourself. You remembered the rule about taking a grown-up with you. But if Muffin has her kittens up there, you really need to leave her along until they grow a little. You can't hold them yet, you can't take any of the babies away

122

from their mother. She'll feed them and protect them and keep them warm. You have to leave them alone until she thinks they are big enough to come down and play with you."

"But Mommy, I need to *see* them at least." Jenny looked disappointed but hopeful at the same time.

There was a little knock at the door and Dana stuck her head in. "Mom said to bring this bookshelf over to you. I guess it goes downstairs in the office?"

"Yes, that will work perfectly. We just need a little space for some books and folders. Tell her thanks." Becky turned back to the dishes she was stacking in the cabinet.

"I'll take that downstairs," Elizabeth said. "It doesn't look heavy."

"You sure?" Dana asked. "I could take it down."

"No, I'll do it. I think Jenny might have something to ask you." Elizabeth headed for the basement steps.

"Aunt Dana, do you want to go with me to the barn? I need to go up in the haymow. I saw Muffin go up there." She lowered her voice to a whisper. "I think she has babies up there." Jenny tugged on Dana's arm and her heart as well. Dana already loved her new title of Aunt.

"I'm not surprised. That's where she usually hides her kittens. Sure, we can go look, if it's okay with your mom."

Becky shrugged and nodded her permission. "Thanks Dana. I really wanted to get these dishes put away and have one more box outa' here." To Jenny she said, "You be sure and listen to Aunt Dana. And if you find the kittens, you just look. No touching."

"Okay Mommy. I'll just look. I want to see my Mustard. He's all yellow. I told Muffin that's what I want." She turned to Dana and said, "Let's go now."

Becky finished her chore with a glad feeling of accomplishment. She went into the living room to sit a while. 'Yep, I'm pregnant,' she thought to herself. 'I get tired so quickly, just doing the simplest things. I remember when I was carrying Jenny. I was tired all the time.' She sat back on the couch and closed her eyes. 'You just grow, little fella'. Mommy's going to take good care of you.' And just like that, Becky was asleep.

Elizabeth returned from the basement and saw her daughter sleeping there on the couch. "She's been working non-stop. Poor girl, she's dead tired." She found a light blanket and covered Becky. Then suddenly she stooped and kissed her daughter on the forehead. She was overwhelmed with love and joy. "Thank you, Lord, for this young woman you have given me. Bless her in the years ahead. Make her an instrument of your peace." She went into the kitchen, gathered up the empty boxes and took them to the garage. Then she went over to the big house to see if Marla Jean needed help with supper preparations.

It took a little searching, but eventually Dana and Jenny found Muffin and her kittens nested safely in the notch between two hay bales. "Oh!" Jenny said in awe. "They're so tiny."

"They are! I think they can only be a couple of days old." Dana sat on a hay bale and Jenny sat beside her, watching as Muffin nursed her babies. "I see four, but there might be more lying under her."

"She won't squish them?" asked Jenny.

"Oh no, she's a very good mommy. She's had lots of kittens. She knows how to take care of them. She would never squish them!" Dana rubbed Jenny's back. "Did you know that baby kittens are born with their eyes shut, and they won't open for a few weeks? They are helpless. Muffin has to do everything for them. She's a good mommy. She feeds them and cleans them and protects them. Just like your mommy takes care of you."

Jenny looked closely at the furry little babies. She said, "I wish Muffin would move over, so I can see Mustard under there. There's no yellow kitten up here, so I think he's hiding under her."

"Well, next time we come up to look, maybe we can see more kittens. But for now, let's just watch a little more and then go back to the house to tell Grammy what we found."

"Okay, but can we come back tomorrow?"

"We can come back in a day or two. The babies need to sleep a lot, so they can grow. We don't want to bother them too much."

"Okay. But I hope we see Mustard."

Jenny couldn't stop talking about the kittens. All during supper, gathered around the big table in the big house, she went on and on about the cute little babies in the haymow. She was determined to find her yellow Mustard. She was convinced that there really would be a little yellow kitten in the litter, since she had put her order in with Muffin weeks ago. Coop had to explain.

"Honey, there might not be a yellow kitten. We can't tell our animals what colors of babies they have to have. We just take what we get, and learn to be satisfied. Just like when we pray. We tell God what we would like to happen, but we are not in charge, *he* is. And sometimes his plans don't match exactly with what we hope for. But he knows best. And he will help us remember that he is with us, even when we are disappointed. We can trust him to make things work out for our best."

"But I really want a yellow kitty," Jenny said, with a slight quiver in her voice.

"Well, let's just wait and see. And let's keep watching for how God is going to work. He always has a plan. Always."

Coop looked over at Becky and smiled. "Ready?" he asked. She nodded and took his hand. "We have an announcement," Coop stated, and every eye turned to him. He had a little speech rehearsed in his head, but at this moment it all left his mind. He looked around at his family, sitting expectantly, waiting somewhat impatiently to hear what he had to say. Coop blurted out, "Becky's pregnant! We're going to have a baby!"

The table erupted into shouts, cheers, hand clapping and tears. Elizabeth rose immediately and hugged her daughter. "I knew it! I thought so weeks ago. I just knew it!"

Marla Jean asked, "Oh honey! Congratulations! When are you due?"

Becky answered. "I haven't been to the doctor yet. I have an appointment next week. But I'm guessing probably November or maybe December."

Jenny quietly crawled up onto her mother's lap and put her arms around her neck. "Mommy, can I have a brother, like Hannah does?"

"We just have to wait and see, honey. God will decide whatever is best for us. And I'm sure you will love your brother or your sister, whichever we get. You will be a wonderful big sister." She gave Jenny a reassuring hug.

"You mean like with Muffin?" Jenny asked. Becky was a little confused.

Coop understood what she meant and answered. "Yes, Jenny, it's like that. God has a plan, he knows what's best. We will wait and see and we will be happy with his choice for us."

Dana was all smiles as she congratulated her brother and sister-in-law. "I'll baby sit whenever you want. I'll spoil that baby so much!"

"You can't spoil a baby," Marla Jean said. "You love a baby and cuddle a baby and respond to his needs. Then he'll trust you and love you back. Parenting is such a blessing. One of the best gifts God can ever give us is a child. Second only to the gift of his own son."

The evening ended with prayer and happy hugs all around. As everyone headed home to sleep in their own beds, there were many prayers offered through out the night. Lying in her bed, unable to sleep, Jenny prayed, "Thank you for my brother or my sister. But please make it a brother."

In her parent's bedroom, Becky and Coop were praying too. They prayed with thankful hearts. They prayed for wisdom and patience. They prayed for health and safety. And they prayed that they would lead their children to salvation. They fell asleep wrapped in each other's arms.

CHAPTER 23

Holy Plans

Becky dismounted and Coop, standing right near the horse, ready to stabilize her as she landed. He had his arms ready to catch her if necessary. Her balance was a little off these days, with the growing width around her middle. It took a little getting used to. Even getting up out of a chair took a little thought and extra coordination.

But Becky landed softly and firmly, not the least off balance this time. "I'm fine, honey. You worry too much. I've done this before, remember. It takes a little getting used to, but I'm fine." She turned to rub Nell's nose and spoke to her. "You are such a good girl. Let's take this saddle off and get you rubbed down."

She spoke to Coop as she unfastened the saddle. "I'm so happy to be riding again. I just can't believe I let so many years go by without riding. I guess that's an extra benefit to being married to you!"

"Oh, is that how it is?" Coop teased. "You only love me for my horses!"

"You know what I mean," Becky laughed. "I love you for who you are. The horses are just a bonus!" Coop carried the saddle to the tack room and Becky led Nell into her stall. She tethered Nell securely and reached for the grooming brush.

Coop came and stood near her. "You really are turning into the perfect farmer's wife. I don't know how I got so lucky!"

"Lucky? Luck had nothing to do with it. It was all in God's plan. He was preparing me for you, and you for me, from before we even knew each other."

"Before we were even born," Coop said. "Jeremiah chapter one."

"I was reading that this morning, as a matter of fact." Becky said. "It was part of my devotions today. I compared some versions. Did you know that the Message says, 'Before you saw the light of day, I had holy plans for you.'? I like the way that's worded. Holy plans. I wonder what holy plans he has for our little peanut."

"Guess we'll find out." Coop smiled and said. "It is pretty amazing to think about, isn't it? He knows all about that baby. He knows all about each of us. What tomorrow holds. What is coming our way. And how he will be with us whatever comes along. We can rest in that, trust that his ways are higher than our ways. He loves us and will always be beside us."

Just then they heard the door to the side of the barn open and waited to see who would be coming in. But no one entered the barn stall area, and Coop and Becky caught the sound of crying. It was Jenny. They found her sitting in the corner of the tack room, leaning against a pile of horse blankets. Tears streamed down her face. When she saw her mom, Jenny tried to stifle her sobs. Coop sat on the floor beside her and took her on his lap.

"What's the matter, sweetheart? Are you hurt?" He looked her over quickly but saw that she wasn't bleeding. He looked up at Becky, unsure of what to do next.

Becky asked, "What happened, Jenny? Why are you crying?"

Jenny didn't even try to control her sobbing. "It's my Mustard," she said, burying her face into Coop's shoulder. "I saw Muffin's kittens. She didn't give me a yellow one. I asker her for it, and I prayed and I need a yellow kitten to call Mustard and now I don't have one. It's not fair. It's all I ever wanted." Her body shook with sobs and Coop patted her back.

"Oh sweetie, I know you're disappointed. But remember what I told you? We can't tell animals what kinds of babies to have. It is just a part of nature. We never really know. We accept what God has given us. We know it's his plan."

Jenny howled, "But I want a yellow kitty. Why didn't God even listen to me? He should have been able to make me a yellow kitty. Maybe Muffin couldn't do it, but I thought God could do anything. Doesn't he love me? It's not good that he didn't listen to me."

Becky pulled a saddle blanket from its place on the wooden railing and somehow managed to get comfortable sitting on the floor. She stroked Jenny's hair and used the tail of her shirt to dry her tears. "Jenny, of course God loves you. Never doubt that. He made you, he loves you. He has a plan for you. You know that, don't you?"

Jenny nodded and sniffed, trying to get her crying under control. "I do. You told me before. But what about my kitty?"

"Well," said Coop, "let's think of our choices."

"What do you mean?" Jenny was calmer now, and listening carefully to Coop.

"Well, we could cry or get angry at God. But would that really do any good?" He didn't wait for an answer. "We could choose a different color of kitty to name Mustard." He paused as Jenny considered this. "We could wait for Muffin to have more kittens and then she might have a yellow one for you. Maybe."

Becky added, "There are other barn cats besides Muffin. Maybe one of the other momma cats will have a yellow kitten."

Jenny was quiet for a very long time. She twirled her pony tail hair around her index finger while she thought. "I guess I'll just wait. God will tell me his plan." Becky and Coop smiled at each other over Jenny's head.

Coop said, "Lord, please show us your plan. And help us be patient while we wait."

Becky and Jenny chorused, "Amen."

CHAPTER 24

─────◆ ◆ ◆─────

Revelations

Coop and Becky sat in the diner, drinking iced tea and waiting for Greg and Nancy to arrive. They were having Sunday dinner together, just the four of them. No kids allowed this time, just grown-up talk. Marla Jean and Dana had agreed to baby-sit all three children after church. The little girls would have a great time playing together at the farm, while Marla Jean taught Dana the fine points of infant care.

It was a rare time out for the two couples, and they were all looking forward to adult conversation. They each had a lot to talk about. After making their meal choices, Becky jumped right in. "We've got news!" she said and reached over the table to take Coop's hand. She didn't wait for effect; she blurted it right out. "We're pregnant!"

Nancy was quick to congratulate them, hugging Becky while she said, "Oh that's just wonderful! I thought you looked especially radiant. Now I know why! When are you due?" Greg slapped Coop on the back and said, "Congratulations. Oh boy, your world is about to change."

Coop answered him, "I know, and I'm ready. So excited about this new journey. God is good!"

"I'm thinking it'll be in November. I have an appointment next week." Becky looked at Nancy, "So our babies will be about eleven months apart. Not quite as close as the girls, but still close."

"It was a surprise to us, that's for sure. We don't quite know how this happened!" exclaimed Coop, which made everyone laugh. "Well, we know *how* it happened," Coop ducked his head in embarrassment. "What I mean is, we weren't planning to have a baby quite this soon, but I guess God had other plans."

"And we're overjoyed, as I know you can imagine! We told our mothers the other day, and Dana is excited to spoil this baby. Jenny knows too, and she's already talking about her sibling. She's sure it's a boy, so that he and Andy can be friends, like she and Hannah are."

"I'm so happy for you!" Nancy exclaimed again. "Wonderful news!"

The food arrived and Greg prayed, being sure to thank God for this special blessing. Holding hands across the table, Becky and Coop echoed Greg's "Amen" and squeezed each other's hand. As they began to eat, Greg said, "Nancy has some good news too."

All eyes turned to Nancy, who understood their expectant look immediately. She held up her hands as if in surrender and said, "No! No! I'm not pregnant again! It's not that!" Everyone laughed and Nancy went on. "You know I've been working at the hospital, and I've had opportunities to meet with Misty, the woman who caused you so much heartache last year." She paused and looked especially at Coop. He nodded and Nancy went on.

"Not long ago, I was able to witness with her, and explain the way of salvation. She prayed the sinner's prayer of forgiveness. She's accepted Christ into her heart and she's born again! She's a new child of the King."

Greg added, "We attended her baptism a few weeks ago. She has an amazing testimony. She's a totally changed woman."

"Really? That *is* great news." Coop put down his fork and looked at Becky. "Isn't it, Becky?" There was a pause before she answered.

Becky wasn't so sure. That woman, that Misty, she'd brought a lot of trouble into the Smith family. Becky knew it wasn't godly to hold a grudge, but to accept that woman, and love her as another child of God, well, that was asking a lot. "But do you think you can really trust her? Is it for real? Or is she maybe using a relationship with God as a way of getting out of the consequences of her actions?" She looked around at her friends at the table and went on. "I mean, Coop's already dropped the charges against her. Which was a very generous thing to do. And now, she's confessing sins and says she's born again. Well, maybe, but maybe it's all an act. She's been devious in the past, to manipulate people and get what she wants. What's to say she isn't pulling a fast one on us now?"

The more Becky talked, the more worked up she became. Coop noticed that she was clenching her fists and trying to hold back her anger. Greg spoke up and broke the tension. "Melissa asked me to tell you how grateful she is that you dropped the charges. She's serving several months of probation, and meeting with her parole officer every week."

"Melissa?" Becky echoed. "I thought her name was Misty."

Nancy explained, "Her real name is Melissa. Misty was just a nickname. She's going by Melissa now. Another way to show how she has changed. And I believe she really has, Becky. She is studying Scripture, praying, and has really cleaned up her life. It's an amazing testimony, actually."

"I want to believe it, but it's such a stretch. I guess I'd have to see it for myself. I mean, I believe in miracles, and I believe God changes lives, but trusting her?" She shrugged her shoulders and looked questioningly at Coop. "It's a lot to ask."

Coop understood her hesitation. It was quite a lot to take in. Then Greg said, "You remember how God met Saul on the road to Damascus? After his conversion, Saul was a completely changed man. I'm sure there were people who didn't believe it could be possible, and were skeptical like you are. But look what happened! Saul became Paul, and what an impact he had on the world! Back then, and even today, people are brought to Christ because of Paul's words."

Becky nodded in understanding. She looked directly at Coop and said, "Then I won't say it's impossible. I won't pass judgment. I'll wait and see. And if it's really true, that this Melissa is now a new woman in Christ, then I will trust her." She smiled and said, "But she just better keep her hands off my husband!"

CHAPTER 25

───◆◆◆───

Another Name Change

Coop spread papers across the kitchen table. "There's sure a lot of forms to fill out. This is going to take some time."

Becky came up behind him and put her arms around him. She leaned her head against his back and inhaled deeply. "You smell good."

He turned toward her and put his hand over her growing baby bump. "How are you feeling today? Tired?"

"Not too bad. I took a nap this afternoon. I'm sure glad I have reduced my hours at work. It was nice of Doc to find some extra help so I could have some time off." She picked up a stack of papers and looked them over. "Can I help with any of this?"

"You can, but most of it we have to do together. One thing we need to do is try to track down her biological father. Do you have any idea how to do that? He has to sign a release form. Either that or we have to document his abandonment of care."

"Well, he abandoned us, that's for sure. But I don't really have any documentation. No letters or legal papers. He just never spoke to me again. How to prove that though, I wouldn't know."

"We'll figure it out. So, we are going to need a home visit too. Not right away, but before we are finished. No worries there though. And they want to observe me interacting with Jenny, to see what kind of relationship we have."

"You're right, that won't be a problem. You have a fabulous relationship with her. She loves you to the moon. That's easy to see." She kissed him. "Thank you for doing this."

"I love her. I want her to know I'll be her daddy forever. Do you think she'll be okay with changing her last name?"

"Absolutely. She loves you too, you know. You're the only dad she has ever known. She'll be happy to have your last name. Then we will be the Smith family for sure."

Coop stacked the papers and slipped them back into the large manila envelope. "Let's tackle this tomorrow. It's late, and I want to take you to bed."

"I like the sounds of that," she said.

"As long as you say it's okay, and if you're not uncomfortable." Coop looked at her with concern.

"The Doctor says it will be fine for a few more months. No harm to the baby. But pretty soon I'll be so big I'll hardly be able to move. And I sure won't be able to participate much. So I guess that means we better do it while we can."

Coop laughed. "In farmer language, we call that making hay while the sun shines. And I support that philosophy whole heartedly." He reached for her and they walked together toward their bedroom, entwined and kissing as they went.

Later, lying exhausted and satisfied, Becky gazed up at the ceiling. Suddenly all of her senses were alerted. It seemed that she was in touch with every nerve and synapse in her body. Her toes and fingertips tingled. Her heartbeat pounded in her ears. She inhaled quickly and widened her eyes. Was it real? Did she really feel that? She lay still and waited, hoping for more.

The waiting seemed eternal. Maybe she had just imagined it. Maybe the lovemaking was still pulsing through her. She laid her hand softly on her belly and willed to feel it again.

There! Again! A slight wave, a little wiggle, the soft flutter of butterfly wings. It *was* real! She smiled and whispered "Hello, little one."

Coop rolled over and said, "What did you say? I was almost asleep and didn't really hear you."

"I wasn't talking to you!" she giggled. "I was talking to our little peanut. I just felt him moving for the first time."

"Really?" Wide awake now, Coop sat up and reached his hand towards the little baby bump. "Can I feel him too?"

"You can try. But it's still more of an internal flutter. I doubt you can feel it. I wasn't even sure I was really feeling it."

They laid still and quiet for several minutes. Then Coop placed his face close to the bump and said, "Alright little one. You just keep your secrets with your mommy for a little longer. Keep growing and pretty soon I'll feel you kicking too. For now, your mommy and daddy need to get some sleep."

As sleep settled over the couple, a little tear trickled down Becky's cheek. She sniffed and dabbed at her eyes. Coop was alerted and asked, "What's the matter? Are you crying?"

"I'm just so happy. God has given me so much to be thankful for. And I love you so much."

"I love you too. And our peanut. But don't cry. Everything's good."

"Get used to it, honey. My hormones are about to go crazy. I'll be laughing, singing and happy one minute, but then *bam* I'll switch to tears. Don't worry though. It's all part of pregnancy. I'll be fine."

Coop laughed. "Just think of all I have learned in the last year! Who would have thought that I would ever know about your body and hormones and cycles and stuff? What an adventure you are bringing to my life!"

"Just count your blessings. You haven't had to learn about morning sickness. I haven't had more that a twinge of nausea with this pregnancy. With Jenny I was throwing up every morning for months. It's so different this time. Maybe that means we're having a boy."

"A boy would be great. A girl would be great. I don't care, as long as you are both healthy. Now let's get to sleep. We both have work tomorrow. Goodnight. I love you."

They fell asleep, with whispered prayers of thanksgiving on their lips.

CHAPTER 26

---◆◆◆---

Dog Days

"If you're ready, I think I have the perfect dog for you." Joyce said. "She's four years old, crate trained and potty trained, and best of all, she's a herder. She lived on a farm in Iowa until the man had a medical problem and they had to move into assisted living. Now the woman has been diagnosed with Alzheimer's and with all that going on they've decided to re-home their collie. We got her back a couple of weeks ago, and she's doing great. She's really good with Danny, and she likes cats. She'd be a good fit for your family."

Becky cradled the phone against her shoulder while she stirred the tomato sauce she was getting ready to can. The garden was producing well, and Marla Jean had taught her the basics of canning. She'd already put up some bread and butter pickles. Now, with tomato sauce and chili base made from the tomatoes Jenny had picked yesterday, the pantry shelves were filling up. Beets and carrots would be next.

Becky turned off the heat and stretched. Her back had been hurting more lately, which was understandable, considering the growing weight she was carrying in her womb. She was beginning to feel a little front heavy. The doctor said she was about 16 weeks along. He was a little surprised when she told him she had felt the flutters of movement, but said that sometimes occurs with a second pregnancy. The mom is more aware of the movement because she knows what to expect.

She sat at the table to rest. "Tell me more. Color, personality, health, all that."

"She's a tricolor. I know you like that. And she's pretty mellow. Not mischievous at all. We've left her in the house alone some, just to see, and she never gets into the trash, or counter-surfs, or destroys stuff. She's really calm and easy going. She likes to sleep near me, for some reason. But she doesn't jump on the bed, just sleeps on the floor on my side of the bed."

"I do like tris," said Becky. "And she's good with kids?"

"Sure is," said Joyce. "Course, I think that's true of any well bred collie. Oh, she has lines that trace back to King. Remember him, the tri male we had when we were little?"

"I do remember King. He was a great dog."

"She's up to date with all shots. She has been taking a joint supplement because she has some arthritis in one shoulder. But other than that, she's fine. It sure doesn't slow her down when she's herding. She excellent with our goats and sheep. We haven't tried her with chickens though, but I'm sure she'll catch on quick. She seems really smart."

"She does sound perfect. I'll have to talk to Coop of course. He's out in the wheat field, driving the combine. They're trying to get it all in today since it's supposed to rain tomorrow. It's going to be a long night."

Joyce was familiar with wheat harvest. "Does he have help?"

"Yes, he hires some guys to help. He has another combine in, and a tractor-trailer to haul it into the grain house. Marla Jean and Dana fixed lunch for half a dozen guys today. Apparently they can put away some food!" She laughed. "I had to work all day at the animal hospital, so I missed out on the lunch crew. Coop says one of the guys is sweet on Dana. I think his name is Marco."

Becky got up to stir the tomatoes again and said, "Well, I'll talk to Coop when he gets in later. And I'll get back to you as soon as I can. Hey, what's the dog's name?"

"It's Holly. Holly the collie – isn't that cute?"

Becky couldn't help but chuckle. "That's funny!" she told her sister. "Coop told me he likes that name. He would like Holly to be the name of our baby, if it's a girl!"

"Perfect!" Joyce laughed. "Then you have a boy, and Coop can have his Holly collie! Well, let me know. We'll keep her until you decide. She's such a sweetheart; I might just want to keep her myself anyway. But I thought she might be just the right fit for you guys."

"I'll call you soon. Now I've got to get back to this tomato sauce."

"Don't work too hard. Take care of my nephew. Love you sis. Bye!"

Later that night, when Coop got out of the shower, Becky massaged his stiff shoulders and told him about Holly the Collie. "So what do you think? Are we ready for a new dog, and a pony, and a little baby? Think we can handle all this?"

"Sure, why not?" Coop shrugged. It felt so good to be clean, to be sitting still, and to have his wife's hands massaging him. "Go a little higher, into my neck, could you?"

Becky's hands moved up his neck, continually rubbing and squeezing his muscles. He began to relax. "Okay, I'll call Joyce tomorrow. Do you think we should get a crate for her? And a bed? Oh, and we'll need dishes for food and water, maybe some toys. Dog food too. Gee, there's a lot to get ready before she gets here."

"We had a crate for Riley. We can use that. I think it's up in the attic at the big house. The other stuff I can pick up in town." He stopped talking to fully enjoy the back rub. "Man, that feels good. You could go into business."

"Nope!" she said. "I only give massages to my husband."

"Did you feel the baby move any more today?" he asked.

"This evening, while I was lying here waiting for you to come in. I think he gets most active at night, when I want to be sleeping."

"Or maybe that's just when you are slowing down and more aware. I really wish you didn't have to work with Doc Larson at all. I would love to have you here at home all the time."

"But I do love working at the vet office. And the little income I get is good to have coming in steadily. Maybe I'll reconsider after the

baby's born, but for now, I want to keep working, at least part time."
She stopped the massage and rubbed her hands. "That's it mister. My
hands are getting stiff."

"Did Joyce say when they would be bringing Holly over? Or do
we need to go get her? It's kinda hard to leave the farm right now.
But it would be hard for Stephen to leave *his* farm too. Such a busy
time of year."

Becky gave it some thought. She let her eyes wander over his
still damp body and watched a little drop of water fall from his hair
and trickle down his back. "Well, maybe mom and I could drive over
to their place. It would be good to spend a little time together with
Joyce. We could take Jenny too. She'd love to explore Danny's farm
with him. And it would be fun for her to see the old house where I
used to live. I'd like her to get to know Joyce better too." She leaned
close to him and licked the droplet off his shoulder. Coop shivered
with delight and turned to kiss her. Another drop of water landed on
her cheek, and Coop licked it off. Becky giggled.

'Silly how these little things make me so happy,' she thought.
'Being married to Coop makes me happy every minute.' Once again
she offered up a prayer of thanksgiving. She recited the verse from
James. 'Every good gift and every perfect gift is from above, and
cometh down from the Father of lights, with whom is no variableness,
neither shadow of turning.' Silently she said 'Thank you Father, for
this perfect gift.'

Coop interrupted her thought by asking, "How do you feel
about driving the truck, and pulling the horse trailer? That way, you
could bring Jenny's pony home too."

"I've driven the truck plenty, so that's not a problem. Pulling
the trailer, that I've never done. Maybe if I practice a little around
here first, to get used to it."

"Or maybe Dana could go with you, for moral support if
nothing else. She's pulled the trailer lots of times. I bet she'd go if
you wanted her to."

"That might be a good idea. I'll ask her tomorrow, see what she
thinks." Becky rubbed her hand along Coop's strong thigh. "Are you
too tired? Or do you want to make love to me?" she asked.

"I'm tired, but never too tired. And I *always* want to make love to you," he said, grabbing her hand. "But are you sure? You're getting pretty big. I don't want to hurt you." He planted a kiss on her belly. "Don't want to hurt you either, little one."

"I will let you know if I want you to stop." She nibbled on his ear lobe and made him squirm. He laid her back on the bed and did things to make her squirm too.

Later they lay spooned side by side. Coop's arm was draped over Becky's growing baby bump. He was falling asleep cradling his wife and child. Becky was not sleeping yet, she was aware of movements within her womb. She whispered, "Coop, are you awake?"

"Hmmm? What?" Coop said, rousing slightly.

"It's all your fault," Becky teased. "You woke up the peanut."

"Huh? What do you mean?" He was a little more awake now.

Becky moved his hand around slightly and put it in just the right spot. "There. Push down just a little."

Suddenly Coop was wide awake. The movement under his hand was a certainty this time. He sat up a little, still holding his hand on the place where he had felt the kick. It was real! There really was a baby in there! His baby!

"That's amazing! I felt him. My first time!" He waited patiently for the next wiggle, but it didn't happen. "Do it again baby. Daddy wants to feel it again."

But the movement had stopped, and both parents fell asleep to dreams of hope and a happy future.

CHAPTER 27

A Chance Meeting

Craig sat in an uncomfortable chair beside JJ's hospital bed. He knew that JJ was upset. There had been a setback with his recovery, and JJ was put back into the hospital after just a few weeks at home. An infection was being treated and monitored, and JJ didn't want to be there. He was sick of hospital rooms, sick of being weak and nauseous all the time. He was sick of this needle in his arm, and he was sick of being sick. He should have been getting better, but they kept him here, running tests and taking blood and poking and prodding every chance they got. He wanted to go home.

An uneaten tray of food sat dejectedly pushed aside. "Didn't want your supper?" Craig asked. Even as he asked it, Craig knew what the answer would be. And looking at the supper offering, he couldn't fault JJ's decision to skip the meal.

JJ grumbled "I'm so sick of applesauce and mashed potatoes. I need a steak. Or even a hot dog. Something to sink my teeth into. Know what I had for breakfast?" Craig raised his eyebrows questioningly. JJ went on. "Scrambled eggs and cottage cheese! And applesauce again! Can you believe that? No bacon or sausage. Not even toast. No wonder I keep throwing up. I'm going to die of starvation before I get out of here."

"Oh, I doubt that," Craig said. You've got enough excess to last you quite a while."

"Yeah, right, you can kid about it. You probably had pot roast and vegetables and even pie. Don't tell me any more about the good food at truck stops while you're working. That's torture. Know what they give me for dessert? Pudding. Pudding!"

"You know, you really should eat what they bring you. It's something at least. You may not like it much, but you do need to build your strength up."

"You've been talking to Bev, I can tell." JJ pulled the tray closer. He lifted his spoon and stirred the applesauce. Taking one small bite, he complained, "Couldn't they at least put some cinnamon on here? Everything is so bland." He forced himself to take another spoonful. "You know what my dear wife had the nerve to do today? She tried to force feed me my breakfast! Treated me like a little baby." He laughed and mocked Bev in a sing-song voice, "Now open your mouth sweetie. Take a big bite." Good grief, she's annoying."

"She's just worried about you," Craig said. "And she's trying to help."

"Yeah, well, I don't need her hovering over me like that." He put his spoon down on the tray and reached for the Styrofoam cup containing coffee. He put the cup up to his lips and then pulled it down. "Not even hot. How can they expect me to drink cold coffee?"

"Well, you're sure in a mood today." Craig reached for the TV remote. "Maybe I can find a ball game for you to watch. Take your mind off your misery." As Craig began to scan the channels, there came a tentative knock at the door.

"Mr. James? May I come in?" Upon hearing the woman's voice, JJ sat up a little taller in the bed. His facial expression changed, and his whole demeanor improved.

Craig immediately turned his attention to the door, having recognized the voice. What luck! "Well, what do you know? Hello beautiful! Fancy meeting you here!"

Melissa had been focused on the patient in the bed, but now looked toward Craig. "Well, for goodness sakes, what are you doing here?" Then it dawned on her. The patient, Jonathan James, must be Craig's cousin, whom he called JJ.

"This is my cousin who I was telling you about. JJ, this is Melissa. Remember when I helped the police capture that woman last year? Well, this is her."

Melissa put a potted plant on the window sill and handed JJ the card that had come with it. "That was the old me," she said. "The new me works as a volunteer in the hospital gift shop. And I brought this plant up to your room." Melissa looked from one man to another. She smiled at Craig and said, "Nice to see you again, Craig. I didn't realize this patient was your cousin."

She once again looked at the man in the bed. "How are you doing, Mr. James? Is there anything I can do for you?"

"Can you get me out of here?" JJ joked. "Or at least get me a decent meal"

Melissa chuckled, "I can get you a hot cup of coffee, if you'd like. Other than that, it's up to the doctors and nurses."

"Coffee would be great," JJ said, suddenly in a much better mood. She was young and beautiful, and her presence in the room made everything seem more pleasant.

"Sure," Melissa said as she picked up the cup of cold coffee. "Be right back."

Four lust-filled eyes followed her as she left the room. JJ broke the silence. "Wow, what a looker! You know her, huh?"

"I do. I know her in every sense of the word!" He blew his breath out nosily. "Whew, she's a hot one." He puffed out his chest and shook his head. "Too bad I didn't spend a little more time with her before I called the cops on her. Could have been a lot of fun."

"Looks like you'll get a second chance with her. Work your magic, man. She'll be yours again, I just know it. Maybe tonight even. Go get her, big guy!"

"Not so sure that's going to work this time," Cash admitted. "She's changed. A lot. Says she found Jesus."

"Let me tell you something, cousin Cash. Sometimes, those righteous, holy girls are the ones that are just begging to get into bed with someone who knows what he's doing. 'Specially if she's used

144

to having her legs spread, and now it's been a while. Go for it! I bet you'll get her juices flowing in no time!'

The conversation, stimulating as it was, ended when Melissa pushed open the door. Carrying two cups of steaming coffee, she said. "I brought you some too, Craig. Hope that's okay." She put one cup on the table near JJ's bed and turned to hand one to Craig.

His fingers grazed hers as he took the cup and looked into her eyes. "Thanks, Melissa. I appreciate it."

She turned her attention to the patient. "So how are you doing, Mr. James? Feeling better every day I hope."

"Hey, none of that Mr. James stuff! Mr. James is my father, and he's long gone. I'm JJ to everybody." He held the coffee cup under his nose and inhaled with exaggerated pleasure. "Now this is some good medicine." He took a drink and sighed. "But the best medicine is you, young lady. I feel better, just looking on your beauty. Come by every day, will 'ya?"

Melissa laughed and said, "How much longer do they tell you you'll be here? I don't work tomorrow, but I could try to come by the next day, if you're still here."

"Oh, I reken I'll still be here. Nobody's told me when I get out."

"Okay, I'll plan on seeing you then. But right now I have to be one my way. I have more people to visit." Melissa turned to Craig "It was great to run into you."

Craig gulped down his coffee and threw the cup in the trash. "Hey, let me walk out with you. I'll call ya later, JJ. Take care." He put his hand on Melissa's back and ushered her out of the room. As they walked down the hall, he tried to put his arm around her. Melissa shied away saying, "Craig, I have to get back to work. See you later."

He reached for her hand as she moved past him, pulling her to a stop. Standing face to face, and close together, he asked, "When? When can I see you again? I'd really like to spend some more time with you. You know we'd have a lot of fun. We did before. We can do it again. Soon, I hope. Tomorrow?"

"Sorry, not tomorrow," she said as she pulled her hand free. "I have plans. But you have my number. Call me. We'll work something out. Maybe next week or so, whenever you're home from driving." Melissa walked quickly down the hall, turning back to look at him and wave before rounding the corner. He was watching her every move. He waved and licked his lips. He could almost taste her.

CHAPTER 28

———◆◆◆———

Puppies and Ponies and a Still Small Voice

Becky drove under the speed limit, carefully hauling the empty trailer behind Coop's truck. It hadn't taken very long to get used to the way it handled, driving up and down the road in front of their farm. The highway was smoother, that's for sure, but the traffic moved quickly around her. She decided to stick to the slow lane and let others pass her if they wanted.

She felt fairly confident that she'd be able to do all the driving, but was glad that Dana was riding shotgun. Just in case. It would normally be a two hour drive, and Becky knew she could do that under normal circumstances. Pulling the trailer made her just a little nervous and definitely a little slower. So the trip would take longer than normal. But the weather was good, the skies were clear, and her traveling companions made the journey enjoyable.

Driving home tomorrow with the pony, well, that might be a different adventure. Dana had experience driving with various livestock, so she said she was willing to drive, if Becky was unsure. That was reassuring to Becky, although she knew she wanted to at least try.

There was a lot of singing going on as they traveled down the road. They sang every hymn they could think of. Dana sang harmony with the confidence of someone who had been singing alto in church for a long time. It came naturally. Becky marveled and the sweet simplicity of her voice. She made singing harmony sound easy.

"I'm surprised you don't sing in the choir, Dana," she said. "Your voice is beautiful."

"Thanks. Mom has been saying that for years. I just never really wanted to join. No offence," she said to Elizabeth, "but everyone is a lot older than me and I just don't think I'd fit in. I'd rather fellowship with people my own age. Sorry." She shrugged her shoulders and cast her eyes down to the floor.

"Don't worry honey," said Elizabeth from the back seat. "I understand. You need to be with people your own age. Friends are important. But you do have a gift. You need to find a way to use it. God gave it to you for a purpose."

"I suppose you're right," said Dana thoughtfully. "I do have a lot of friends in the young people's Sunday school class. Maybe I should reach out to the 'choir aged' people. I mean, it's good to have friends of all ages."

Becky spoke up. "I've noticed you with some of the single girls in our class, Kathy and Cindy and Linda. And there's some single guys too, Tim and Kevin and even David, our teacher. I've heard there's talk of splitting the class and making one class for single young adults and another class for the young marrieds. What do you think about that?"

"Actually, I've heard that's a possibility and I think it's a great idea. The class has been getting bigger and bigger, and it would make sense to split it. As long as David stays on as the teacher of the singles, which I'm pretty sure he would. We were talking about it the other day. That would be his preference."

"He is a great teacher. I understand why you would hope to stay in his class. I wonder if they have thoughts on who should teach the young marrieds. There's a lot of men in the class who would be good leaders."

"Including Coop," said Dana. "He's a natural spiritual leader."

Elizabeth spoke up, "You have to turn up here, take the exit ramp and go left over the bridge. We're almost there."

"You've done great driving with the trailer," Dana said to Becky. "Like a pro."

"It wasn't bad, empty. Might be different with a pony back there!"

Jenny had been asleep in the back seat but woke when the truck slowed on the gravel road. "Benny! Benny! Here I come!"

"Here we are," said Becky as she pulled into the driveway. "Oh look, they've painted the house. Looks good."

Joyce and Danny came out of the house and met them in the driveway. Stephen and two other men made their way toward them, coming up from the outbuildings where a combine, tractor and trailer were parked. The trailer was loaded with bales of straw ready to be hoisted up to the loft of the barn.

Joyce said, "How was your trip? You're just in time for some supper. I made some fried chicken. I hope you're hungry!"

"I know I sure am!" said Stephen, putting his arm around his wife Joyce. "And you do make some good fried chicken!" He turned to the visitors and said, "Ladies, let me introduce you first. This is Todd, my oldest brother, and his son Tucker. Todd's the elder of our Davis clan, and Tucker's his oldest. They live on the next farm over, and we help each other out with harvest. Just got all the wheat in."

The ladies introduced themselves and then started to take three small suitcases from the back of the truck. "Here, let me help you with that," said Tucker, taking a bag from Dana. "I can get the others too. They're small."

"Where's Benny?" asked Jenny eagerly.

"He's out in the side barnyard." Stephen said. "You want to see him before we eat?"

"Can I mommy? Can I?"

Becky looked toward Joyce, who answered, "Make it quick. I'm about to mash the potatoes. You don't want to eat them cold."

Danny led the way to the pasture, running on ahead. Stephen walked with Jenny. "I've got some carrots you can give him. You know how?"

"Oh sure! Daddy Coop showed me a long time ago. I'm a professional!"

Becky watched her daughter head off to the pasture but said to Joyce, "I gotta get to the bathroom. I'm about to wet myself!"

Joyce laughed and said, "It's that pregnancy bladder! I remember it well! Let's get inside. You and Jenny will sleep in the guest room tonight. Mom can have Danny's room. And Dana, I hope you don't mind sleeping on the sofa bed in the family room."

"Of course, that's fine," Dana replied. Tucker had followed her into the family room, laden with suitcases. "The blue one's mine," Dana said, and he put it on the couch.

"At your service, Mam!" he said with a chuckle. "Which one is Becky's? I'll take it to the guest room." After Tucker distributed the suitcases, he came and sat down on the couch near Dana. They fell into easy conversation.

Coming out of the bathroom, Becky heard laughter in the family room and smiled to see Dana having a good time with Tucker, who was near her own age. She was about to join the conversation, but the porch door opened and Jenny and Danny burst in.

"I love him Mommy. I gave him a carrot and he ate it and then he kissed my hand. He already knows I love him."

"Silly girl," said Danny. "He didn't kiss your hand. He was just smelling it, looking for more carrots."

"Well, I know he loves me. I just know it." She turned to the collie that had followed them in, "Look mom, this is Holly. She loves me too."

Holly the collie was sniffing the visitors and getting to know them. The children sat on the floor and Holly went from one to the other for belly rubs and neck scratches. Becky could already see a connection growing between Jenny and the dog. "Of course," she thought. "Collies love kids." Becky bent down to rub the dog's head and ears. "Hello Holly. You are sure beautiful. Would you like to come live at our house?"

The dog looked at Becky with deep brown eyes and tilted her head. Then she began to lick Becky's hand. Something about her expression made everyone smile. It was like Holly actually understood what Becky had asked.

Stephen said, "You should hear the conversations Joyce has been having with Holly. They've talked about you and Jenny and Coop and moving to a new farm where there are chickens and cows and horses. Joyce has probably said your names one hundred times. I tell you this dog is *really* smart. I think she understood every word. She's happy to finally meet you."

"Everyone get cleaned up, Supper's ready." Joyce came in from the kitchen to gather the family around the table. Becky noticed that Tucker sat next to Dana. He could barely take his eyes off her, it seemed.

Stephen led the family in prayer. When Becky opened her eyes, she saw that Holly the collie was lying on the floor right at her feet. She stayed there throughout the whole meal. "Well, look at this! She's such a good girl. No begging at all, even with all the good smells here on the table. I think I love her already."

"Except for ice cream!" Danny put in. "She loves ice cream! Vanilla is her favorite." He whispered to Jenny. "Sometimes I save her some and I let her lick my bowl." Jenny giggled.

"I told you, she's really special. I knew you'd fall in love with her." Joyce looked at her sister. "She's been through so many changes, but she hasn't shown any excessive stress. I think she's just happy to be with people who want her around and have time to spend with her. She's never had an accident in the house. She isn't frightened or unsure of new things. She really only barks outside, not in the house. And I can already tell she feels comfortable around you."

After supper, Joyce and her mother worked together in the kitchen while Jenny and Becky went out to see the new pony once more. Holly followed them, happily racing ahead, only to return to Becky's side. Stephen and Danny came too; it was time to do a few evening chores. Todd offered to help before he and Tucker had to head home.

As they passed one of the outbuildings, they were met by a chorus of collie greetings. "What's that Mommy? Lots of dogs?"

"Yes honey. That's the kennel where the dogs and puppies stay. Aunt Joyce told me they have some puppies that were just born."

Stephen asked, "Want to see them? We can take a peek." He led them inside and Jenny stood on tiptoe to look over the enclosure. A beautiful sable momma lay there, surrounded by seven nursing and sleeping little puppies.

"Oh, they're so tiny," Jenny marveled. "Look, that one is almost all white. And that one has one spot of black. They're so cute." She laughed, "That one is really fat!"

"Yes, he sure likes to eat. We call him Tubby!" Stephen said.

Danny put in, "We should call him Bully. He always climbs on everybody to get to the milk first."

Jenny looked at her mother. "When Holly has puppies, I hope there's a white one. That's my favorite."

Stephen said, "Well, Jenny, Holly isn't going to have puppies. She's been spayed." Jenny looked confused so Stephen went on. "That means she's had an operation and she will not be able to have babies. Her other owners didn't want to breed her, so they took her to the vet and got the operation." He looked to Becky for approval of his explanation and she nodded.

"She'll be a great pet, and a good herder, but she won't have puppies," Becky said. "But I tell you what, we will come visit here often, and you can watch all the puppies grow and play with them. That's what I used to do when I was little. There were always lots of puppies to play with."

Satisfied, Jenny said, "Okay. Now let's go see Benny!"

Benny was at the far side of the pasture, grazing with another pony, a sandy colored Shetland. Both of them raised their heads with interest as the people approached. "That's Summer," Danny explained to Becky. "She's mine." Danny put his fingers to his mouth and gave a loud whistle. Summer trotted over quickly and nuzzled Danny's hand. "She's looking for another carrot. I didn't bring you any this time. Sorry girl."

Jenny held her hand through the fence and Benny came close. "I didn't bring carrots either. Sorry boy. Maybe tomorrow." She rubbed Benny's neck. "You're coming to my house. We will put you in the trailer and take a drive. And when we get home, you can see Nell and Slick. You'll be a family. A horse family."

Becky and Jenny returned to the house, chatting about puppies and ponies. Jenny fell silent, deep in thought. "How come Nell and Slick don't have babies? Did Nell get spayed like Holly?"

Becky smiled and decided not to get into the specifics of equine birth control. "I don't know for sure. We'll ask Daddy Coop. Or Dana. But I bet Nell and Slick will be happy to have Benny join their family."

As they approached the house Becky noticed Dana and Tucker sitting together on the front porch swing. They sure seemed to have a lot to talk about.

Later, struggling to get comfortable in the bed they shared, Becky and Jenny said their bedtime prayers. Then Jenny said, "Best part?"

"That's really hard today," Becky said. "Well, driving the truck and getting here safely. That's one. And of course, meeting Holly." She reached down to the floor, where Holly was already settled in beside her. Holly lifted her head slightly and licked Becky's hand. "What's your best part?"

"Benny. That's my best part. I can't wait to ride him." Jenny drifted off to sleep, then suddenly sat up and reached her hand to Becky's belly. "And I'm glad you didn't get spayed. I want to get a sibling."

Becky had no choice but to laugh out loud. She wrapped her arms around her daughter in a big hug. "Oh Jenny, you're going to be such a good big sister. Now let's get to sleep. Tomorrow we drive home with Benny and Holly."

But Becky didn't fall right to sleep. She lay in bed listening to the wind rustling in the trees outside her window. This was the room that she had once shared with her sister Joyce, long ago. So much had changed since then. So much was *going* to change. Suddenly, without real thought, a verse came to her mind. "Jesus Christ, the same yesterday and today and forever," she repeated it in a whisper. "Hebrews something, I think. I'll look it up in the morning." She prayed, "Thank you Jesus, for being with me back then. I didn't even really know you then. But now I do know you, and I know you are always with me and you never change. You never stop watching over me, loving me, guiding me in your path. I thank you for that. I love you for that." She drifted off to sleep.

Hours later, Becky woke with a start. Holly was sitting upright, looking intently towards the window. The wind had changed, and a tree branch was tapping against the glass. Holly was alert, and Becky was listening too. Lightening flashed in the distance, followed at length by a low rumble of thunder. There was a storm coming, but far off.

Becky reached out her arms to Holly, and pulled her close with a gently hug. "It's okay girl. Just a little rain coming. We'll be all right. Everything's fine." Holly tilted her head and looked knowingly at Becky. She nuzzled her nose into the palm of Becky's hand. Becky patted Holly's head and said, "Let's go back to sleep sweetie. We'll be fine." As if completely understanding, Holly lay back down with a trusting sigh.

With her eyes shut, Becky listened to the tapping of the tree branch. The wind was picking up and the tapping became more insistent. She tried to will herself to focus on breathing, to let sleep overtake her. Just as she was about to give in to sleep, a soft voice whispered into her thoughts. "Let Dana drive." Becky's eyes snapped open, and she looked around. Jenny was sleeping peacefully, no one else was in the room, yet the soft voice resonated within her. "Let Dana drive."

'Well, I don't know where that came from,' she thought. 'Like a still small voice.' "Was that you, Lord? Are you telling me that Dana should drive tomorrow?" She whispered, so as not to wake Jenny. It felt funny, talking to God like he was in the room. But wasn't he? After all, Becky believed he was always with her. But to ask him a question, and expect an answer, like they were having a conversation.... Sure, God had spoken to her before, through scripture, or songs, or the wisdom of other believers. But never quite like this. This was new. And yet it seems so real.

It came to her again. "Let Dana drive."

"Okay Lord, whatever you say. I'm listening." As rain began to softly pelt against the window, Becky fell into a deep and restful sleep.

CHAPTER 29

On the Road Again

Dana pulled the trailer into the pasture and parked it. She hopped out of the truck and splashed in a puddle left by last night's rain. Her footsteps fell with a soft splat in the wet grass. She went around and opened the ramp to the trailer. Stephen was there to help lead Benny up the ramp and secure him inside the trailer. Becky and Jenny watched from the fence. Jenny could hardly contain her excitement. Benny was coming to live at her house!

Tucker had come over to help with the loading, but Becky suspected he was more interested in seeing Dana again. Loading the little pony certainly didn't require more than one experienced handler. Stephen had it done in no time.

Joyce had Holly on a leash and was walking out to potty one last time before getting into the truck for the long ride home. Although she was in the business of raising and selling collies and had said goodbye to dozens over the years, this parting was particularly emotional. She came back with a mist of tears clouding her eyes. Thank goodness Holly would be remaining in the family, and this wasn't a final goodbye.

Dana got in the driver's seat and Tucker hoped into the truck next to her. Deep in conversation, Dana drove to the front of the farmhouse. She parked and waited for the rest of her family to get ready to go. She and Tucker exchanged phone numbers, and then he got out of the truck to let Becky get in. Elizabeth said goodbye to Joyce and Stephen and gave Danny a big hug. Holly's wet feet were wiped down with a towel and she was loaded into the back seat, sitting between Jenny and her grandmother.

After a parting prayer, Dana maneuvered the truck and trailer down the driveway and turned carefully onto the road. Soon they were on the highway, with a two hour trip ahead of them.

"Thanks for driving, Dana. I know I was going to try, but I think I'll just practice at home first, before I try to take a loaded trailer out on the highway. You seem really comfortable. I appreciate getting to sit back and relax!" Becky leaned back and stretched out her legs a little.

"No problem," said Dana. "You drove all the way here, I'll drive home. Unless you want to, Elizabeth." She looked into the rearview mirror to glance at Becky's mother.

Elizabeth held up her hand and laughingly said, "No thanks, dear. You're doing just fine." She patted Holly on the head. "I'll just sit back here and get to know Miss Holly."

Jenny was so excited she could hardly stop talking. "Can I ride Benny when we get home, Mommy?"

"Well Jenny, you know Daddy Coop said he would help you learn how to ride. But he is going to be pretty busy with the haying and pretty soon it'll be time to pick the corn. So you'll have to be patient. Spend a lot of time petting and brushing Benny, and letting him get used to you. That's really important. Daddy Coop will help you when he can."

"I can help too," said Dana. "I haven't spent enough time with Nell lately. I need to brush her good. I'll clean her hooves too. You can watch and see how to do it."

"Oh Dana, I want to thank you for letting me ride Nell so often," Becky said. "She's really a good horse, and I'm really enjoying riding again."

"I wish you'd be more careful about riding, Becky," said her mother. "I don't like to see you riding, in your condition."

"Thanks for your concern, mom. But times have changed, you know. Pregnant women are staying active now, doing dance and gymnastics and playing sports, even in their later months. Besides, Nell is so gentle. And I'll be careful. Pretty soon I'll be too big to get up on her anyway."

Jenny jumped into the conversation. "We can all go riding together. And when my baby brother comes, he can ride with me. And then when he gets bigger he can get his own horse. Danny's horse is Summer. She's white. But I like Benny better. He is brown and has socks. Danny said so. Dark brown socks."

Holly lay contentedly on the seat, resting her head on Jenny's lap. Jenny petted her the whole way home. "Holly likes me to pet her. Can she sleep with me, Mommy?"

"Well, she's going to sleep in a crate for awhile, in the room with Coop and me. Just until she gets used to us, and the house. She needs to learn about where the doors are, and we need to learn her signals for when she needs to go outside. But it shouldn't take long. She seems really smart, and Aunt Joyce said she's never had an accident in their house. Then we'll probably just let her sleep wherever she wants. Joyce said she doesn't sleep on the beds though. She never jumped up on beds or furniture. That makes her just about the perfect dog, if you ask me."

Before long, Jenny's eyes were closed and she was lulled to sleep by the motion of the truck. Her hand never left Holly's back.

"So, you and Tucker seemed to really hit it off," Becky said to Dana. "He seems like a nice guy."

"Oh he is." Dana was smiling. "He was telling me all about the mission trips he has gone on with his church. He's gone to Nicaragua three times already. And he's going again later this summer. They've built houses and a school and a church. He was telling me about some of the people there. How they have very little, but are so happy to share and help each other. And how appreciative they were of all the help they're getting from American churches. He's a great storyteller. I really enjoyed listening to him. He's really on fire for the work there."

"Wonderful. It's not often you find a mission minded young man these days. So many are self-absorbed. A young man with a vision for the needs of the world – that's pretty rare." Becky stretched to relieve some pressure on her back. It was getting harder and harder to sit in one position.

Dana noticed that Becky was uncomfortable. "Are you okay? Should we stop and stretch a little? I can pull off at the next exit."

"Yeah, maybe that would be a good idea. I can stretch my legs a little."

"And I can check on Benny, make sure he's doing okay back there." She drove on a little more and then said, "Look, there's a sign for a rest stop. Three miles ahead. Perfect."

Jenny woke when the truck stopped. She got out to walk around with her mother. Holly jumped down too, and Becky grabbed her leash. It was actually unnecessary, since Holly stayed right by Becky's side as they walked around the rest area. Near the restrooms, Becky asked Jenny if she needed to go. Jenny agreed and went inside the restroom. Becky stood outside waiting and Holly lay down in the grass beside her.

A family approached the restroom and Holly quickly stood up to place herself between the strangers and Becky. Holly wasn't threatening, but obviously on alert. She was ready to protect Becky if necessary. "Is it okay if I pet her?" asked a little boy about ten years old.

Becky agreed and watched carefully as Holly greeted the child. There was sniffing and exploration, but no aggression whatsoever. "Good girl, Holly" said Becky as she rubbed Holly's head. The little boy laughed when Holly licked his face.

"She's a collie, isn't she?" asked the boy's father. "I've never seen one with these colors. I usually see just the Lassie kind."

"Yes, she's a collie. She's called a tri-color. There are several different colorings, but tris are my favorite."

"We've been thinking about getting a dog. Where did you get her?"

Becky was telling the family about her sister Joyce's collie breeding program when Jenny came out of the bathroom. Holly went to Jenny and sniffed around her, then licked her hand. Jenny giggled, "I think she's licking the soap off my hand."

The boy said to his father, "I like this dog, dad. Can we get one? She's the perfect size for us. And I'll brush her everyday." Becky gave the man a slip of paper on which she had written Joyce's information and he thanked her.

A few minutes later, after Becky had used the restroom and they were back on the road, the conversation turned once again to Dana. Elizabeth asked, "So, how's school going, Dana? Have you picked a major yet?" Dana had just finished her first full year of college, and was taking only one course over the summer. She was getting her basic classes out of the way before declaring a major.

"Truthfully, no, I haven't decided on a major. I still have a semester until I have to declare, but I just don't know which direction to go. I mean, I like English and literature, but I don't see myself teaching. And what else could I do with that major?"

"Well, teaching would be the most logical use for that major, but there *are* other options," said Elizabeth. "Any business that requires writing or editing, maybe proofreading, would appreciate an English major. Have you thought about maybe office management, or administration?"

"Don't know if I could stand to be cooped up in an office all day," said Dana thoughtfully. "I need space, sunshine and fresh air. Besides, I kinda think I want a higher purpose. I mean, I want to feel like I'm making a difference in the world."

"Sounds like you need to pray that God will reveal his will for your life," said Becky.

"Yeah," said Jenny. "God has a plan for you and me and everybody. His plan is better than our plan. Daddy Coop says we might not understand but God knows best."

"I'm glad you were listening so closely," Becky said. "It's hard to be patient, but in time, God will show us his will. We will all pray for you Dana, and we can't wait to see where the Lord leads you."

"I just wish I could clearly hear God speaking to me. I mean, I want to follow his plan for my life, but I just haven't gotten the message from him yet about what I'm supposed to do. Coop always seems to know exactly what God wants him to do, but I've never really heard his voice." Dana looked at Becky. "Have you?"

"Well, you know sometimes the answers are right there in the scriptures. And sometimes you get messages from other people or even the words of a song. And sometimes, if you're really listening, you'll hear a still small voice." Becky got a warm feeling as she remembered her encounter with that type of voice the night before.

"Funny you should say that," Dana said. "Dave and I were talking about that not too long ago. He told me I need to take time to listen. I guess I better find more quiet time with God so I can sit and listen."

"Me too," piped in Jenny. "I want to listen to God too."

"Well, me too!" said Elizabeth. "We can all listen for his voice. He'll show us his plan. He'll lead us, if we listen and follow."

Elizabeth starting singing, "Where he leads me, I will follow" and the adults joined in. Jenny listened carefully to the words.

CHAPTER 30

The Best Gift

Coop and Marla Jean were waiting when Dana drove up. They greeted the travelers with hugs and questions. "So Dana drove all the way home?" Coop asked Becky as he kissed her.

"Yes, she did. I decided to wait. I just had this little nudge that said I should let Dana drive." Becky hugged Coop tightly and said quietly in his ear, "I'll tell you all about it later. It was really incredible!" She backed up and said a little more loudly, "Come, meet Holly!" They walked to the back door where Jenny was just getting out of the truck. Still on the leash, Holly jumped out and started sniffing around in her new yard. Becky took the leash and walked with her while Coop and Jenny went to the back of the trailer to check on Benny. Dana finished unloading the suitcases and then drove the trailer into the pasture, where Coop and Jenny met her. Together they lowered the ramp of the trailer and Coop untied Benny. Jenny was eagerly waiting with a carrot Coop had supplied.

"Come Benny! I've got a carrot for you!" Benny walked down the ramp and directly to Jenny and her enticing carrot. Jenny rubbed his neck and said, "Benny you are going to be my best friend. We will ride every day, and I'll show you all over the farm. We'll go to the big pasture, and see the pond and walk with the cows and look at the birds and flowers and in the winter you can pull a sleigh with me riding and we will have so much fun!"

"Whoa there sweetie! Slow down! First we will give him time to get used to us, and to Nell and Slick. Then we'll teach you to ride. And we will go together a lot first before you go riding off on your own. He's just a small pony, but he's strong and powerful, you know. You have to learn how to control him. Then you'll be safe to ride on your own."

"Okay! But we can start being best friends right now." She threw her arms around the little pony's neck and gave him a big hug. "I love you Benny!"

Then Jenny stopped and ran over to Coop. She hugged him around the neck too and said, "Thank you Daddy Coop. Thank you for getting me Benny. I'll take good care of him, and be responsible and everything. He's the best present ever. The best!"

Becky and Holly walked over just as Coop said to Jenny, "You are very welcome, honey. Your mommy and I are sure you are ready for a pony. Now you just prove us right! But I want you to remember something very important. We gave Benny to you because we love you and want to make you happy. But he's not the best present ever."

"He isn't?" asked Jenny. She looked confused and Becky smiled, knowing where the conversation was headed. Coop always had a Biblical application to everyday events and this was no exception.

"Nope!" he said. "There are some verses in the Bible that talk about fathers giving good gifts to their children. It says in Luke if a child asks for bread, what father would give him a stone? Of course, a good father would give his child bread, not a stone. And if a child asks for fish to eat, would a good father give him a snake instead? Of course not."

"That's silly!" Jenny said. "I know you wouldn't give me a snake to eat, or a stone. You and Mommy are nice. You take good care of me."

"That's right, Jenny. And if we, your earthly parents, love you and take care of you and give you good gifts, just imagine how God, your Heavenly Father, will give you even better gifts. The very best gifts possible."

Becky joined in. "Like the gift of eternal life and the gift of the Holy Spirit. Like the gift of his comfort and presence in times of trouble. Like the gift of knowing how very much he loves you." Then she remembered another verse. "It says in James 1:17 that every good gift and every perfect gift comes down from our Father in Heaven, and he never changes, he always wants to give us good things."

Coop smiled at her and marveled again at what a wonderful teammate she was for him. They complemented each other in so many ways. One more example of a good gift his Heavenly Father had given him.

"And like a plan for my life?" Jenny asked. "Like you keep saying. God loves me and has a plan for my life. So that's a gift, right?"

In unison, Coop and Becky answered, "Right." They all hugged each other and finally Coop said, "Let's get into the house. We'll let the horses get to know each other. And we have to show Holly where her crate is."

Coop noticed that Holly was off her leash, yet was still staying close to Becky. She would sniff the ground and follow the smells in the barnyard, but would not go very far from Becky, always returning to her side. He also noticed that Dana had unhitched the trailer and was waiting in the truck to drive up to the house. Coop, Becky and Jenny walked through the pasture and Coop opened the gate for Dana to drive through.

As Coop turned to close the gate, Jenny waved. "Bye Benny. You be a good boy. I'll see you again soon!" Jenny ran to walk between Becky and Coop and said, "Swing me please!" Both adults took a hand and lifted her off the ground but when they started to swing her, Becky took a deep gasping breath. She placed her other hand on her hip and tried to regain her composure, yet was still out of breath. The pain in her back caused her to stop in her tracks.

Coop noticed immediately and put Jenny's feet down on the ground. "You all right?" he asked with concern. "What's wrong?" He put his arm around Becky to steady her. Jenny stood back watching with a frightened expression.

"Oh Mommy! Did I hurt you? Are you okay?"

Becky was touched by Jenny's concern but did not want her to be upset. She tried her best to control her breathing and sound normal. "I'll be okay honey. But I guess I shouldn't be trying to lift you anymore. You are growing, and I have to be careful about lifting heavy things. I forgot. But I'm okay." They walked slowly to the house. Jenny kept looking at her mom to make sure she wasn't hurt.

Coop also kept watch over his wife. She had never reacted this way before. Hopefully the pain would subside and she would truly be all right. But he'd keep watch, just to make sure.

Holly loped along beside Becky, always staying close. She also seemed to know that Becky needed watching over.

"Looks like you've got yourself a good dog," said Coop to Becky. "Holly wants to be near you. She'll be a good protector."

"I already love her bunches," Becky said. "She's really a good girl." Becky was quiet the rest of the walk to the porch. Then she sat down and rested in a lawn chair while Coop took the suitcases inside. He came out with a tall glass of lemonade, ice cubes jingling as he walked. Becky took a long drink and sighed. "Oh, thank you Coop. This really hits the spot." She closed her eyes and leaned back in the chair. "How's everything been here?"

"We got a new calf last night. He's not eating well yet, I moved him and his momma up to the nursery in the barn." Coop pulled up another chair close to Becky. "And I contacted the guys about scheduling for the next hay mowing."

"So you've been busy." Becky took another drink and sucked an ice cube into her mouth. She rolled it around with her tongue and then dropped it back into the glass.

"Oh, and Doc Larson stopped by. He was telling me that Ed Hennessey had a seizure the other day and blacked out for a few minutes. So I told him I'd go over and check on him every couple of days, see if he needs any help with anything."

"You're a good man, dear husband."

"That's what neighbors are for. We take care of each other." Then he turned to Becky and asked, "What were you going to tell me? Something about Dana driving the truck home?"

Becky told him about the voice she had heard and excitedly explained that she thought she had actually heard the voice of God. At least it seemed like a voice that had a message for her from God. She told Coop that she really felt that God was telling her to let Dana drive. And after she acknowledged the message, she was able to go back to sleep. It seemed to bring her comfort.

"But now that I think about it, I wonder why? Like, I mean, why should I let Dana drive? Why shouldn't I be the one driving? Nothing out of the ordinary happened on the way home. We didn't have any troubles at all. Nothing happened that I couldn't have handled, really. I wonder why God wanted Dana to be driving, not me. Or maybe I was just imagining the whole thing. I have questions."

"We may never know," Coop answered. "And that's the beauty of it. You listened, you obeyed, and God took care of the details. I'm glad, because who knows what might have happened if you didn't obey. And now here you are, safe and sound, home where you belong." He took the empty glass from her hand and helped her stand up. "Now you, dear wife, are going to go in and lie down. You've been on your feet too much. You just take it easy the rest of the day."

"I guess I should," Becky said. "I have to work all day tomorrow. Doc was so nice to let me have two whole days off. I guess the new girl is working out okay, but I don't want to take advantage of Doc's kindness. Or loose my job altogether."

"I seriously want you to think abut quitting your job after the baby's born. We will get by without your income. And our children will need you. As a matter of fact, I'd like to have you around more, too. I sure did not like sleeping without you last night. The bed was way too cold. The whole house was quiet and empty. I'm really glad you're home." He bent and kissed her warmly.

"I missed you last night too. But I had Jenny to sleep with, so I wasn't lonely." She laughed and rubbed her baby bump. "But I was kicked by both kids all night long! Maybe that's why I'm feeling a little off today."

"Off to bed with you then. You and the peanut need a nap."

Jenny was romping in the yard with Holly but stopped long enough to give her mom a hug and tell her to have a good nap. She put her mouth near Becky's belly and whispered "You go to sleep too, little peanut." She blew the baby a kiss and turned back to play with Holly. She threw a stick and Holly took off on the run after it. Her beautiful long hair flowed out from around her as she ran, obviously having fun. But when she noticed that Becky was going into the house, Holly stopped immediately and walked inside behind her.

"Well, hello there girl!" Becky rubbed Holly's head and ears. "Welcome to your new home. Look, here's your food bowls and some water." Holly sniffed the food and lapped the water. Then she moved on about the house, exploring the new smells. Becky went into the bedroom and kicked off her shoes. Lying on the bed, she quickly drifted toward sleep. She was vaguely aware of the sound of Holly's nails tap tap tapping on the hardwood floor as she came down the hall and pushed her nose against the bedroom door. Next thing Becky heard was a thump as Holly settled down on the floor next to her side of the bed. Holly gave a contented sigh and Becky fell asleep.

CHAPTER 31

Testimony Time

When Melissa went back to JJ's room to visit with him, Bev was there too. JJ introduced his wife and then tried to explain how he knew Melissa. It was a little awkward. "Remember when Cash was driving his truck and helped the police catch a thief?" Bev nodded so he went on. "Well this is her."

Bev looked quickly over at Melissa, who had her eyes cast downward and was slumped uncomfortably. 'She's a pretty one,' thought Bev. 'I can see why Cash might have taken a notice to her.'

Melissa was discouraged. She did not like being referred to in this manner. JJ was talking about the old Misty. She bristled inside with anger and was about to make a sharp remark. Then she caught herself. 'Don't fall back into the old ways,' she told herself. 'You are Christ's now. Act like it. This is your chance to tell these people about the change.'

She straightened her shoulders and looked at Bev. "It's true. I'd done a lot of terrible things. Being a thief was just the tip of the iceberg. And all those bad things I did deserved punishment. But because of Jesus, my sins have been forgiven. And because of mercy, my punishment has been light. And now, thank God, my life has been changed. That old Melissa is gone. I'm a new person in Christ."

There. She had done it. Witnessed to strangers.

167

"Really now?" JJ said in a tone of condescension. "I doubt anyone can change overnight. I bet you still have what you call the old you, trying to break out. Don't you miss the fun you used to have? You can't just throw old habits away just like that." He snapped his fingers. "You know what you're missing, and I bet you want it back sometimes." He was thinking of his cousin Cash, and the relationship he and Melissa had, in the past. He knew Cash would want the old Melissa back.

Bev interrupted his thoughts. "Oh JJ, just hush. Leave her alone. She has a right to her beliefs, just like you do. And if something has happened to change her into a better person, then I say more power to her." She patted Melissa's shoulder. "Don't mind him, honey. His mind is usually in the gutter. His soul is probably there too!" Bev laughed, thinking she was pretty funny.

Melissa took a deep breath. "Thank you, Bev." Then she turned to JJ. "And you're right, the change didn't happen over night. It's been a process, and sometimes I do slip back into the old ways. But I know that God has started this work, to transform my life, even my thoughts. And I know I'm not there yet, but I also know that God won't stop working on me until the work is done. It might take heaven to transform me completely, and that's okay too. I'll just strive every day to be more Christ-like, and to give myself over to his will."

She stepped back from the bed and reached for the breakfast tray still sitting at JJ's bedside. "I'll just take these dishes now, if you're finished with breakfast. Would you like me to bring some more coffee?"

"That would be lovely, dear," Bev said and turned toward JJ. "Wouldn't it, JJ?" She asked pointedly. He nodded and grunted a yes response.

When Melissa returned with coffee, she asked, "So, how are you feeling? You seem a little better than the last time I was here." She turned to Bev to explain, "I don't know if JJ told you, but I'm a volunteer at the hospital now. I bring flower deliveries and sometime just check in to talk to patients, especially if they don't get many visitors. Seems like every time I come to this room, though, there are people here. You must have a lot of friends, or family, in the area."

"I think it's just been family," Bev answered. "JJ has always been the life of the party, but we haven't seen any of his so called friends up to visit. Fair weather friends they are, I guess." She sighed and turned to JJ. "Doctor Spollen is taking good care of you. We should be thankful."

"Yeah, well, I'm about to bust out of here." JJ looked at Melissa and said, "Doc says another day of observation, maybe two. I got an infection after my surgery, had to come back in for IVs and antibiotics. It's been a rough couple of days."

"Days?" Bev raised her voice and put her hands on her hips. "Don't you mean weeks? You were a mess at home before you finally agreed to come back to the hospital to see what was wrong. We're just lucky you got here when you did. You could have died right there at home."

Melissa smiled and said, "I'd say God is blessing you with some more time. He says you still have things to do down here."

"Well, I don't know about that. All's I know is, I want to be home and I want to eat decent food again." JJ was grumbling as he looked down at his arm, where the IV was still inserted. "And I want to get this thing out of me."

"All in good time, dear. Dr. Spollen knows best. She says you're not ready for home yet, and we'll listen to her. Just calm down." Bev paced around the bed, fidgeting with the sheets and blankets.

Melissa took a deep breath. "Would it be okay if I pray for you?" she asked.

Bev looked up and glanced over at JJ. They were not used to anyone talking about prayer. The idea of someone wanting to pray for them, well, that was just strange.

JJ spoke up. "You mean right here, right now?" When Melissa nodded, he added, "Do what you want, if you really believe in that stuff. If you want to waste your time, go right ahead." He shrugged and closed his eyes. Bev bowed her head.

"Heavenly Father, we bring JJ and Bev to you today. We pray for healing and we pray for patience. We pray for Dr. Spollen and all the nurses working with her. Give them wisdom, we ask. And give JJ peace. Thank you for listening to our prayers." Melissa wasn't accustomed to praying out loud, and hoped that she had done it right. When she said "Amen," she felt lightness come over her.

CHAPTER 32

The Lord is My Shepherd

Becky put her hands on her hips and leaned back, stretching. Her head held back, she looked up towards the ceiling and felt the tension ease slightly from her neck and shoulder muscles. A soft little pop in her spine felt good and she sighed. She lowered her arms and rolled her shoulders in slow circles. Next she dropped chin to her chest. Making circles with her head, she let her mind wander.

She'd been helping Marla Jean with the garden all afternoon. Weeding had taken its toll and she realized that she had probably overdone it. Marla Jean had wanted to stop sooner, but Becky had insisted that she was fine, and could at least finish hoeing the bean row. But now, feeling the strain in her back, Becky wondered why she hadn't listened to her mother-in-law.

Standing at the kitchen sink, scrubbing the casserole pan with baked on lasagna from last night's supper, hadn't helped either. It was beginning to feel like everything she did, or tried to do, took more effort these days. The growing baby was causing her to walk differently and otherwise normal activities were sometimes exhausting. She needed a break. She sat down at the table and stretched her legs so her feet were resting on a chair opposite her. It felt good to get those feet elevated.

Jenny had decided that Peanut was no longer the right nickname for the baby. Pumpkin was better. And Becky was inclined to agree. She rubbed the palm of her hand over her growing bulge.

"Is the pumpkin kicking you again, mommy?" Jenny asked as she walked into the kitchen. She had a basket of crayons in her hand and sat it down on the table near her coloring page. Turning back to her mother, she wagged her finger and said, "Don't you hurt my mommy. You be good."

Becky laughed and tussled Jenny's hair. "It doesn't really hurt, sweetie. And you did it too, while you were living inside me. It's what all babies do." She decided to change the subject. "What picture are you going to color?"

Jenny sat down at the table and picked out a coloring a page from her Vacation Bible School activity packet. It was a picture of a shepherd standing guard over a flock of sheep. Becky watched as Jenny carefully chose a purple crayon to color in the shepherd's robe. There was a stream running through the picture, and Jenny had already colored it blue. "The sheep are white," Jenny explained, "except for this one. He was lying in the dirt and got all dirty, so he's brownish."

"Makes sense to me!" Becky chuckled. "Hey, do you want to practice the rest of your memory first? I know you have the beginning learned but we could work on the ending."

"Okay mommy. Let's start with the table verse."

Becky shook her head with a chuckle and turned on her Bible app. on the phone. It opened right up to the twenty-third Psalm. Jenny had been working on memorizing this whole chapter and was almost finished. The 'table verse' was verse five.

Becky read the verse a couple of times out loud, and then they played the memory game. Becky started the verse, left out a word, and Jenny supplied the missing word. Soon Jenny was ready to say the entire verse by herself.

"I'm so proud of you, Jenny," beamed her mother. "You only have one more verse to learn and you will have the whole chapter. Way to go!" She gave Jenny a high five.

Jenny was prancing around the table, chanting "I did it! I did it!" when Coop came into the house. He joined in the fun, gathering her in his arms and dancing around chanting "She did it! She did it!" Jenny burst into a fit of giggles, leaning her head back and wiggling as Coop tickled her. Becky looked on with joy. It was a happy scene she wanted to remember for a long, long time.

Coop stopped tickling and looked at Jenny face to face. The giggles subsided and Jenny leaned her forehead against his. "Now tell me, little lady. What are we celebrating? What did you do?"

"My Bible verse!" Jenny exclaimed. "I learned all the verses except one. I'm almost done!"

Coop glanced over at Becky and asked playfully, "Did she really? I can't believe it!"

"It's true. The twenty-third Psalm. She's got it all except the last verse." She looked at Jenny as Coop set her down and went to the sink to wash his hands. "Why don't you tell Daddy Coop? Say the verses for him."

Without hesitation, Jenny stood tall and began. "The Lord is my shepherd, I shall not want." She completed her recitation with very few mistakes. Becky prompted her once or twice, but Jenny quickly recovered and went on.

Coop dried his hands, smiling broadly. "You really did it! That's great sweetie." He walked to Becky and planted a kiss on her forehead. "That's really terrific. Learning scripture is so important. I memorized that chapter when I was a kid too."

"Maybe after supper we can work on that last verse, okay kiddo?"

"Okay Daddy Coop! Then I'll be all done. Miss Peggy said she has prizes for anybody who can say the whole thing. I wonder what my prize will be!"

"Prizes are nice," Becky said, taking dishes out of the cabinet. "But the biggest reward is having God's word hidden in your heart." She sat three plates on the table and added, "Now please clear your coloring things away, so we can have our supper."

"Your mom is right," Coop added as he set the table. "Lots of times, a verse will pop into my head just when I need it. It happened today even." He handed the silverware to Jenny and she carefully placed it beside the plates.

"Why? What happened today? What verse popped?" Jenny folded a napkin for each place setting while Coop filled the glasses with water and ice.

"I was looking out over the corn field, and just watching the stalks move in the breeze. It's a beautiful sight to see." he said. "I was thinking that everything is growing well. The corn is over knee high already, and it's not even July yet. The wheat has had its first cut, and it was plentiful. The cattle are healthy and growing. It's all good. And then I remembered a verse in Genesis. "God saw everything that he had made, and behold, it was very good." Coop looked around the table, where his family was seated ready to eat a good supper. "And I remembered that all this goodness that I was looking at, it all came from God. And the blessings here around this table, those good things came from God too. And I was thankful."

"Amen!" said Jenny. "Was that our prayer? Can we eat now?"

Becky chuckled, "I think it was a prayer of thanksgiving."

Coop raised is eyebrows and smiled. "I think you're right. We are thankful for all the good things God has given us. Let's eat!"

Later that night, as Becky got out of the shower, she heard singing from Jenny's room. Coop and Jenny had been going over the final verse of Psalms twenty-three. "Surely goodness and mercy shall follow me all the days of my life, and I will dwell in the house of the Lord forever." Coop was teaching Jenny a song that went along with the verse. Becky smiled as she listened. The singing was interrupted from time to time with hoots and giggles, which made Becky smile even more. A sense of complete joy washed over her. God had blessed her, and she felt very good.

She wrapped her head in a towel, put on her pajamas and robe, and walked into Jenny's room. She was surprised to see Jenny and Coop sitting cross-legged on the floor, facing each other and holding hands. As they sang the verse, their bodies leaned and stretched, making a big circle. When Coop leaned far back he pulled Jenny forward and she nearly touched her nose to the floor. They continued in the circular motion, with Jenny lying almost flat on her back, and

Coop bent over her, making silly faces. Amidst bursts of laughter, they continued to repeat the Bible verse.

"Well, that's certainly a new way to memorize a verse!" Becky interrupted. "But it looks like fun!"

"Fun it is," said Coop. "And it works too. She learned the last verse."

"Wonderful. You can tell me while I comb you hair and braid it." Jenny's hair was getting long, and braiding it at night kept the tangles away. Coop stood nearby as Jenny repeated the verse.

"Good job!" he said. Looking at Jenny he saw an expression of concern come over her face. Her brows were furrowed and she was frowning slightly. "What's wrong?" he asked.

"What's mercy?" Jenny looked from her mom to Coop.

"Well, that's a really good question," Becky replied as she slipped a hair tie around the end of a braid. "It's important not to just learn the words, but to learn what they mean, too. And mercy – wow, that's a good word to understand."

Becky looked up at Coop, wondering how to best explain the concept. He took the cue.

"Well honey, it is a very important word. Mercy means someone shows a kindness or forgiveness instead of giving the punishment that is deserved. It's like if you did something that you should be punished for, but someone said, 'No, that's ok. Don't punish her. Let's forgive her instead.'"

"That would be really nice," Jenny replied. "But why would they do that? If I was bad, I should be punished."

"It's because of love, Jenny. The best kind of love there is. Love that comes from Jesus." Coop glanced at Becky. "For a person to love like Jesus loves isn't always easy, but it's what God would want us to do."

Becky nodded and raised her eyebrows. She was remembering the mercy Coop had shown when he forgave Misty and asked that charges against her be dropped. It wasn't what most people would have done, but Coop knew it was what God would have him do. And now, apparently, Misty had also come to know Jesus. Would that have happened if Coop hadn't first shown mercy?

"And of course, Jesus is the best mercy giver, isn't he?" Becky motioned for Jenny to climb into bed. She pulled the covers up to Jenny's chin and kissed her on the forehead.

"When he died on the cross, he took the punishment for all our sins. We deserved the punishment, but he made it so we didn't have to suffer the punishment of hell."

"And not only did he take away our punishment," Coop added. "He also gives us a big reward. Heaven!"

"Pretty amazing, isn't it?" Becky said. "Jesus forgave us, and gave us a reward instead of a punishment!"

"I need Marshmallow," Jenny said, looking for her favorite toy, a mother cat and her four kittens. "And the babies too." Coop gathered them up and tucked them in under the covers. "We can skip the Bible story tonight. I'm getting sleepy," she said, and yawned to prove it.

"Okay, but we won't skip prayers," said Becky.

"And best part," Jenny added though her eyes were closed and she was already drifting off to sleep. And she was asleep before they got to 'amen.'

Coop wrapped his arms around Becky and pulled her close. His strong arms enveloped her with warmth and she laid her head against his chest and sighed. "This was definitely the best part of the day for me," he said. "Time with my family. It doesn't get better than this."

"I agree," cooed Becky. "I love these times. It's what I've always dreamed of." She kissed Coop warmly, then said, "Thank you for making my dreams come true."

Arm and arm they walked out of the room, stopping at the door to turn off the light. Just as the switch clicked into the off position, Jenny sat up in bed. "Wait Mommy," she said. She was looking towards them but still seemed to be in a sleepy haze. Becky wasn't sure she was even awake.

"What honey, what's the matter?"

"Dwell. What is it?"

"Dwell?" repeated Becky.

"Dwell in the house of the Lord forever. What's dwell?" She was awake now and clearly needed an answer to her question.

"That's an easy one," Coop answered. He kept his voice low and comforting, hoping that she'd easily go back to sleep. "Dwell means to live. So the verse says you can live in the house of the Lord forever."

"Dwell means live. Like abide, like on the bird picture?" She was thinking deeper now, and putting things together in her mind. "Dwell and live and abide. It's all the same, right?"

Becky smiled down on her precious child and said, "Yes, Jenny, they are all the same. Now let's get you back to sleep." She planted a kiss on the tip of Jenny's nose, hoping that that would be the end of the conversation.

Jenny wasn't finished, however. She put her arm around Becky's neck, pulled her close, and whispered, "But where is the house?" She wasn't going back to sleep until all her questions were answered.

"The house of the Lord is in heaven,"

"Oh," Satisfied, Jenny settled her head back down on her pillow and pulled Marshmallow close. "I can live in heaven. Dwell means live. A big reward not a punishment." Her eyes were shut and a peaceful smile softened her face. Becky and Coop tip-toed out of the room, holding hands.

CHAPTER 33

◆◆◆

The Eye of the Storm

Marla Jean walked across the yard, carrying a plate of deviled eggs. There was a strong breeze blowing, and the American flag whipped around on its pole. The outside lights that Coop had strung across the porch danced around recklessly, clacking into each other and adding a rattle to the noises of laughter and joyful greetings. She put the eggs on the table, moving aside a large bowl of Becky's famous potato salad to make room.

Marla Jean wiped the corner of her apron across her forehead. It was hot, probably the hottest Fourth of July she could remember. A breeze would be nice, but this wind was ridiculous. She looked over at the grill, where Coop and his friend Greg were cooking up some hamburgers. She chuckled as the wind lifted Coop's black cowboy hat off his head and sent it rolling across the driveway. He took off on the run to catch it, then smacked it against his leg to clean the dust off. Laughing, Coop returned to the grill. Marla Jean's heart swelled with pride. Coop was certainly a fine young man.

She looked around and nodded contentedly. Everything was ready. Now if only the wind would die down, so they could enjoy themselves and not have to worry about paper plates blowing off the table and napkins flying across the yard. She looked up at the sky. Didn't seem to look like rain, but oh my goodness the wind was strong.

Marla Jean went to sit in a lawn chair near her neighbors, the Hennesseys. The elderly couple was struggling to hold on to their farm. Ever since Ed's health had starting failing a few years earlier, Marla Jean felt a kinship with Marilyn Hennessey. She thought she knew how Marilyn was feeling, having been there just a year ago herself. But the Hennessey's had gotten many more years to enjoy together than Marla Jean and Walter Smith had had. They were both in their late seventies, and had been married for over fifty years. Marla Jean and Walter had only been married thirty two years at the time of his death.

Marla Jean put her hand over her heart and closed her eyes briefly. She said a short prayer of thankfulness for the years she and Walter did have together. Was it possible that he had only been gone about a year? How had she survived without him?

Well, she had her children. And now she had a daughter-in-law and a new granddaughter, and a baby on the way. God was good. He was still with her, even in the lonely hours when she missed Walter extremely.

"Blowing in a storm," said Ed, looking up at the bright blue sky.

"Really, you think so? Except for the wind, it seems like a pretty nice day." Marla Jean replied.

Marilyn patted Ed on the hand. "Oh, Ed knows his weather. If he says it's going to storm, he'll be right. You'll see. He's never been wrong. We'll have rain before nightfall."

"They'll have to cancel the fireworks. Like they did two years ago. And two years before that. It's the pattern. Shouldn't even plan on fireworks but every other year. That's the way it goes around here." He tapped his cane for emphasis.

Jenny and Hannah came up from the barn, laughing happily. Becky and Nancy, little Andy on her hip, followed the little girls. "Hannah did great," Becky said. "She wasn't scared at all."

Nancy agreed but added, "Benny is just the right size for the girls. I did notice that Hannah wasn't too sure about the bigger horses. But she did fine with Benny."Becky called ahead, "Go get washed up, girls. Looks like we're almost ready to eat." She closed the gate, pushing against the wind, and locked it. "Goodness," she said to Nancy, "the wind is so strong. It could almost push me over, even as big as I am!"

Nancy laughed, "You aren't that big yet, Becky. Just give it a couple more months. What are you, about five months?"

"Yes, about that. My due date is November twentieth. Seems like it will never get here. And sometimes I feel like I've already gained fifty pounds."

"Well, you look great! I'm really hoping God gives you a boy. Then he and Andy can grow up together as best friends, like our girls. They will be just about a year apart." She looked down at the baby on her hip and snuggled into his neck. "Would you like to have a playmate, little man? Someone to be your best friend?" The baby cooed and then laughed as his mother tickled his neck with her hungry kisses.

"That would be nice," Becky said, smiling at the giggles. "I'm pretty sure Coop is hoping for a boy. But you know what they say. 'As long as it's healthy...' But Jenny wants a brother, that's for sure." She reached up to push some hair off her face. "I should have put my hair in a pony tail. This wind is whipping it all around."

"At least it isn't raining. Hopefully we can get to the football field for the fireworks. I guess they'll still set them off, even if it's windy, right?"

"Last I heard, Coop said they were watching the weather and would send out weather bulletins on cell phones if they decided to cancel." She looked up at the sky. "Looks all clear for now, just this wind."

Holly ran on up ahead, and her hair blew out gracefully as she raced full force in the wind. "Wow, I love that dog!" Becky said. "She's so beautiful. And you know, we haven't had her all that long, and she's just so smart and responsive. When I come home from work, there she is at the house, lying in the yard waiting for me. I think she can tell time! And oh my goodness is she excited when I get out of the car. Sometimes she brings me a toy. She wants me to play fetch a few minutes before I go into the house."

"She's really beautiful, that's for sure. Hey, I heard Jenny telling Hannah about her kitty named Mustard. So, did she finally get a yellow kitten? I know you told me how disappointed she was that Muffin didn't have a yellow kitten in her litter. So what happened?"

Becky chuckled, "Well, she suddenly decided that Mustard didn't *have* to be yellow. One of Muffin's kittens starting climbing up on Jenny every time she went out to the barn. It is a male, but black and white. Jenny decided that she loved him a lot, and *his* name could be Mustard. Until she thought about it a little more and decided to call him Oreo. Like the cookie!"

"So all's well that ends well." Nancy laughed. "I hope she will be as easily satisfied if it turns out you're having a sister for her instead of a brother!"

"Oh, I think she'll be okay. We've tried to tell her that God has a plan and even though we don't always understand, he definitely knows what's best for us."

"Look Mommy, look what Holly can do!" Jenny and Hannah ran over to their mothers, with Holly running after them. "I taught her a new trick! Watch this."

Jenny asked Holly to sit, and Holly immediately sat. Then Jenny said "Holly, go to Grammy's house!" Holly jumped up and started running to the old farmhouse. She didn't stop until she got to the porch door. Then she sat down and looked at Jenny.

"That's amazing," said Becky. "What a smart girl!"

"But wait!" said Jenny gleefully. "Keep watching." Then she called out loudly, "Holly, go home!" Holly took off on the run to the new house and stopped at the porch door. She sat and looked expectantly at Jenny. She stayed in the sit position until Jenny came over to her and offered a piece of cheese as a treat. "She'll do anything for cheese!" Jenny laughed. She rubbed Holly's head and said, "You're such a good girl!

"For goodness sakes!" marveled Nancy. "I've never seen a dog learn so quickly. That's just astonishing! You've only had her a few weeks. And how did Jenny know how to train her?"

"Dana has been helping Jenny. She used to show her collie Riley in 4-H dog shows years ago. She really knows what she's doing with the training. Of course, I would also say that Holly is really smart, and loves to please."

"Jenny's a good teacher, too. And you can tell they already have a bond." Nancy called to the girls, "Now go get washed up, girls. It's almost time to eat."

They arrived at the picnic table just as Coop and Greg sat down a huge platter of hamburgers and hot dogs. After Coop prayed, everyone enjoyed a terrific meal. While they were eating, Ed Hennessey cleared his throat and announced that he had news.

"Marilyn and I have decided to sell the farm and move into a senior living place in Atkins." Everyone was surprised. The Smiths and the Hennesseys had been neighbors for many years.

Among questions and well wishes, Marilyn spoke up. "It's going to be hard, leaving the farm where we've lived for so long. Lots of memories at the old place." There was emotion in her voice as she went on. "It's for the best though. We're getting too old to handle all that farm work. Farming is for young muscles and strong backs." She looked across the table and smiled at Coop. "You've got lots of life left in ya'. We're ready for a rest!"

Ed added, "We've been thinking about it for a while, specially since I had my spell. But a man contacted me, interested in buying my land, and it just seems like the time. Gonna be hard to leave all you fine neighbors though."

Nancy said, "I've driven past that place in Atkins on my way to do visits at the hospital. It looks really nice. Will you move into one of the houses, or an apartment?"

Marilyn answered, "We decided to go into a house first. We thought moving from four hundred acres to a two bedroom apartment might be a little drastic. So we got a two bedroom house. It has a small yard, but enough so as to give us the feeling of space."

"That sounds nice," said Marla Jean. "Then, if you need to move to an apartment later, you can, right?"

"Oh, yes. And they have assisted living, and a medical wing and even Alzheimer care. It's all there. And I like that there are activities and lots of things to do."

"Even a garden. And a woodworking shop. And a swimming pool!" Ed was glowing. "You know, all our kids have moved far away, and they won't be here to take care of us as we age. It'll be good to have people there, watching over us as we need it."

"Our kids are far away, but they do worry about us." Marilyn added. "This way, they won't have to worry as much. We're doing this move as much for them as for us."

A sudden gust of wind knocked over the paper cups and sent them flying down the length of the picnic table. Everyone jumped up and scrambled to secure things. Ed looked to the west. "Here she comes!" The sky on the horizon was darkening and clouds were rolling in. Just then, Coop had a ding on his cell phone. He read the alert and said, "Yep. Guess you were right Ed. Severe thunderstorms headed this way. Let's get this stuff all cleared up. We can move the party inside."

The dark clouds were moving in fast. Lightening flashes were seen in the distance. Holly knew something was up. She sat in the yard barking at the sky, then ran in circles frantically trying to herd her people into the house.

They were still gathering food dishes from the table when the first big drops of rain splattered down on them. Jenny had been collecting trash in a plastic trash bag, but the wind suddenly grabbed the bag and pulled it from her grip. At the same time, the American flag was torn from the pole and went flying, getting tangled in the branches of the old oak tree. "Leave the trash," Becky called to Jenny. "We'll get it later. Let's get inside, quick." A loud crash startled them all as the grill was knocked over by the wind.

Dana and Marla Jean helped the Hennesseys into the house. Greg held the door for everyone. It was no easy feat. The wind nearly pulled the door from his hand as he stood braced and holding it as best he could. When finally everyone was inside, Greg came in and the door slammed behind him.

"Oh Lordy, it's gonna be a doozy," said Marilyn. A sudden crack of lightening made everyone jump. The rain pounded loudly on the windows.

"Coop, gather a few flashlights, would you please? Just in case the power goes out?" Becky was pulling emergency candles out of the kitchen cabinet. "And why don't we all go on downstairs? Dana made some blackberry cobbler and we can eat it down there. Here Dana, would you carry the cobbler? Girls, you can help me with the bowls and spoons."

"Don't forget the ice cream," said Jenny as she headed down the steps to the basement. Soon everyone was making themselves comfortable in the lower level. The older adults sat at the card table, Nancy and the children sat on the couch, and Becky and Dana dipped cobbler and ice cream. The men stood together, checking their phones for weather updates.

"Well, no fireworks tonight," said Coop. "They might have them tomorrow, but definitely not tonight." He lit one of Becky's candles and sat it in the middle of the card table. "How's this for atmosphere? Dessert by candlelight!"

The lights flickered off for a second and then came back on. "Just in time," said Dana. I bet we're gonna loose power."

Greg looked around the room. The basement had a couple of small windows, placed up high on the east and south walls. Through them he could see the bright jagged flashes of lightening. "This is a good place to be during a storm. We don't have to worry about windows breaking. And we're mostly underground."

"Daddy Coop says we will be safe here if we have a tornado. That's why he made us a basement. He's taking care of us." Jenny scooped a spoonful of cobbler and ice cream into her mouth.

A loud *ping* sounded from Coop's phone and then immediately Greg got the same warning. The men glanced down to see the weather alert. "Okay," Coop announced, "we're under a tornado watch. High wind and hail likely. Well, we know about the wind, that's for sure."

Baby Andy was getting fussy, so Nancy pulled a blanket from her diaper bag and began to nurse him on the couch. Dana and the little girls collected the bowls and spoons and sat them on a tray on the card table. "I'll take these upstairs to the sink," Dana said. "And I'll put the ice cream back into the freezer." She carried everything up the stairs. As she climbed, the noise became almost deafening. The roar of the wind, in competition with the thundering of rain and hail on the roof, made the house almost alive with electric energy. It seemed to vibrate through her bones and made the fillings in her teeth hum. She hurried to put the dishes in the sink and was just opening the freezer when there was a loud *bang* and the whole house shook. Suddenly she was in pitch blackness.

Dana stood holding on to the handle of the refrigerator and let her eyes adjust somewhat to the darkness. He heart was pounding in her chest. "Oh Lord Jesus, please calm my nerves," she prayed. Flashes of lightening were her only light, but she made her way to the kitchen window, which was being pelted with hail the size of marbles. Looking out, she could barely see through the driving rain, but she could just make out the old oak tree in the front yard. Split down the middle, half of it was upright and dancing frantically in the wind. The other half lay on the ground. Somebody's car was barely visible under the felled portion.

Dana turned from the window and made her way cautiously down the hall towards the basement stairs. Coop met her, shining a flashlight on the steps so she could descend carefully. "Get on down here," he said. "They've up-ed the warning to a watch."

The basement was aglow with patches of light from several flashlights and a few more candles. Greg sat on the floor, holding Hannah, who was whimpering quietly. Becky sat on the couch, with Jenny cuddled against her. Holly the collie lay calmly at her feet, content to know that her family was all together and she had done her job. Marilyn and Ed were holding hands. Marla Jean had her eyes closed in prayer, her lips moving silently. Elizabeth said to Dana, "What's it look like up there?"

"Well, it's pretty dark!" Dana said, which brought a chuckle from several of them. "But our big old oak tree is half broken. That's what made the loud boom sound, I guess." She didn't mention about the car that was buried under the tree. No need for everyone to be worrying about whose car it was, and how much damage. They'd determine all that once the storm was over.

"I wish Jesus was here," announced Jenny. She stood up and moved to the center of the room. "Then he could say 'Peace be still,' and the wind would stop." She stretched her arms in a dramatic fashion and said the words 'Peace be still' in a deep voice, as if she were talking into a microphone.

"But Jesus is here," Nancy said. "Matthew 18:20 says 'Where two or three are gathered together in my name, there am I in the midst of them.' So he's here. We can't see him, of course, but we know he's here because he promised he would be. He's always around us."

"I remember Joshua 1:9B," Jenny said proudly. "It was my memory verse last year. 'God is with me wherever I go.'"

"I know that one too," said Hannah. "Let's say it together like we did in Sunday school." The girls proceeded to quote the verse in unison. All the adults applauded.

"What other verses do you know?" asked Marilyn.

Hannah looked at Jenny and smiled. "We can do the twenty-third Psalm. We learned it in Bible school." Without a fault, the little girls quoted the verses.

Marilyn was impressed. "That was wonderful girls. Just wonderful!" She hugged each girl and Ed shook hands with them.

"Well done, little ladies!" He chuckled and said, "You keep up the good work with memorizing verses. It's really important."

"It's good to know what the words mean too," Jenny said. "I know dwell means to live. And mercy is to get a reward instead of a punishment."

Ed nodded. "You're right! How very precocious of you!"

"I know what that word means too. It means I'm smart!" Everyone got a laugh out of that but Coop said "Precocious yes, humble no!" and they laughed some more.

"Well, we might as well get comfortable," Becky said. "We might be here for awhile. Does anybody need anything? I've got some blankets in the laundry room closet if anyone gets cold."

"Having these flashlights and candles makes me think of camping out, and telling stories around the campfire at night," Greg said. "Anybody know any good stories?"

Jenny sat upright and said, "If I had my Bible story book, Daddy Coop could read to us. He tells good stories."

"I bet Daddy Coop could tell you Bible stories without having to read them from your book," said Becky, looking at Coop. "What do you think, Coop? What story could you tell us?"

"Hmmm, well, I'll take requests." Coop looked around. "What do you want to hear?"

"About David and Goliath," piped in Hannah, from the shelter of her daddy's lap. Coop proceeded to tell the story of David's faith in God's desire to help him defeat the giant. Coop acted out the story, complete with a deep growling voice for Goliath, taunting cries of the Philistine soldiers, and David's humble trust in his God to bring him the victory. Coop soon had the little girls laughing, the adults smiling, and everyone focused on the faithfulness of God. Thoughts of the storm raging outside vanished as they listened closely to Coop's entertaining rendition of the familiar story.

"Do you girls know the song about David and Goliath?" asked Marla Jean. "I bet your mommies and daddies know it."

"You mean the song we used to sing in Bible school and Sunday school?" asked Dana. "The song with the motions?"

"Yes, that's the one. Let's teach the girls." Marla Jean and Dana took center stage from Coop and launched into the song. Soon the little girls were standing, singing and doing motions.

As the storm raged outside, the evening continued with more stories and songs. Marla Jean and Elizabeth led them in a rousing selection of hymns. Dana used her phone and played a new song she had heard. It was by a Southern Gospel quartet and Dana really liked the music. It talked about God being our anchor, and a shelter in the eye of the storm. She played the song twice, so everyone could get all the words. Soon they were all singing loudly enough to drown out the raging storm outside. Before long, a sense of calm settled over the basement shelter. The adults each felt the love of God surrounding them, even as the eye of the storm passed over. Despite the wind and rain, though their ships of life may be tossed and thrown about, they knew they were anchored firmly. God's word said it, and they believed it.

Coop and Becky used their phones to find verses about storms. They read and discussed several, then decided on Isaiah 4:6 as the verse that fit the day perfectly. "It will be a shelter and shade from the heat of the day, and a refuge and hiding place for the storm and rain."

Coop explained, "I know it's really talking about the pillar of smoke and flame that lead the Israelites out of Egypt, but we can apply God's name there instead of the word 'it' and it makes perfect sense for us today." They all worked to memorize the verse and even the little girls got most of it.

Greg laughed and said, "I think I'm at church."

"More like the old camp meetings back in the day," Ed said. "Worshiping outside, long into the night, by lantern-light. Singing without instruments, Testimony times. Sharing and praying as the Holy Spirit led. Ahh, those were the good ol' days."

"True," Marilyn said. "But remember there were mosquitoes and snakes and mice, too. It wasn't all good! Remember when there was a mouse on the rafters, running back and forth over the evangelist's head? The poor man, he was preaching about the second coming and he thought everybody was looking up to heaven, looking for Jesus to come down and get his people. Really everybody was watching the mouse!"

That story brought chuckles from everyone but when the laughter settled down, Jenny asked Coop, "Do you think Benny is scared out there? I wonder what he's doing."

"Oh, he's with Nell and Slick. I think he'll be all right. They may be standing in the three-sided shelter out in the pasture. They're smart animals. They've been in rainstorms before. And the cows know what to do, too. They will run away from the storm, or stand with their backs to the storm. They'll be okay."

"The babies too? Will they know what to do?"

"Their mothers will teach them. The calves will stay close to their mothers and learn. Just like you learn from your parents." Coop looked over at Becky. "Parents are good at keeping their children safe."

"And Oreo and Muffin and the other cats?"

"Where do you think they would go in a rainstorm?" Becky asked her daughter.

"The barn," answered Jenny confidently. "They are probably curled up in the hay sleeping. Muffin with Oreo and all his siblings. All together like us." She smiled and said, "And I know where the baby chicks are too. Under the wings of their mommies, keeping safe from the eye of the storm."

Marilyn chuckled and said, "This little girl of yours is sure adjusting to farm life. She's turning into a fine farm kid." She looked at her husband. "Remember how our boys used to love watching the storms move across the wheat fields?"

"I do." Ed gazed off into the darkness, as if willing to bring the memories back. "And remember that once when they all ran up from the barn in the pouring rain, and Jimmy slipped in the mud and landed kersplat in a big puddle, and the others lost their footing and fell on top of him, and they were all covered with mud?"

Everyone laughed at the thought of three mud drenched children. "Yes, I remember" said Marilyn. "And I made them stay out there in the rain to get cleaned off. They thought it was great fun."

"And then remember, every rain storm after that, Jimmy was the first one to suggest playing in the mud. And then they always wanted to take a 'rain shower shower.' That's what the boys called it."

"Well, I would rather take a real shower," Jenny said and Hannah giggled her agreement.

Greg hugged his daughter and said, "Me too, Hannah. Me too!"

The Hennessey's reminisced some more about their children. They had three sons, but all lived quite a distance away. Marilyn's eyes were misty when she talked about them.

Elizabeth looked over at Marla Jean. "I remember an old hymn about storms. I bet you know this one." She began to sing, "The Lord's our rock, in him we hide, a shelter in the time of storm." Marla Jean joined in and they harmonized beautifully. "Secure whatever ill betide, a shelter in the time of storm." Marilyn and Ed sang along on the chorus, clapping their hands and singing robustly. "Oh, Jesus is a rock in a weary land, a weary land, a weary land. Oh, Jesus is a rock in a weary land, a shelter in the time of storm."

"Nothing like the good old hymns," Marilyn said. The older people nodded in agreement.

"I agree," said Marla Jean. "There is good stuff in the newer songs, too, but I find real comfort in the familiarity of the old hymns."

Marilyn added, "There's so much good theology in the wording in the old songs, too. The hymns are often built around scripture."

Dana couldn't just sit; she had to jump into the conversation. "Oh come on now, you need to really give the new songs a chance. They have scripture too, and good theology, and they're made to resonate with young people. What's wrong with that? We need our music too, you know."

"Resonate?" Ed laughed. "It sure does! Singing the same chorus over and over! And over and over! Yep, it resonates! And how about those drums! And the instruments blaring over the sound system. It can rattle my dentures sometimes!"

Everyone had a laugh over that, but Nancy said, "Isn't it great that different types of Christian music can reach different types of people, but we can all relate and be blessed? We are all different, after all. God made us that way. So logically we all have different preferences. That variety makes the world interesting!"

Before the conversation could continue, Dana's phone lit up and played a musical ring tone. She pulled it from her pocket and moved to the side of the room to talk privately. When she returned to the group, she had a smile on her face. "Everything okay?" asked Becky.

"Oh sure. That was Tucker. He said he was watching the weather channel and saw that we are in a tornado zone, so he called to make sure we're alright. I told him we're in the basement and we'll be okay."

"That was nice of him to check on you." Elisabeth said, and smiled with a sparkle in her eyes.

"Yeah. I told him I'd call him tomorrow, after we have a chance to look around and see if there's any damage." She tucked her phone back into her pocket. Becky looked at her with a knowing smile. She offered a quick quiet prayer for this growing relationship.

Outside, the storm raged on. Occasionally, debris would be blown against the little basement windows and Holly would raise her head with interest. Andy fell asleep in Nancy's arms. Hannah was no longer upset by the storm. Those gathered in the basement felt the warmth of companionship and the protection of God. They knew they were sheltered in the arms of God. They felt him with them through the eye of the storm.

CHAPTER 34

◆ ◆ ◆

Aftermath

The power was still out, so they climbed the stairs with the aid of flashlights. Once upstairs, there was enough light coming through the windows to make walking safe. The storm had moved on, leaving in its wake a path of destruction. Coop and Becky's house had withstood the wind, but the big farmhouse had not fared so well. Shingles littered the yard, and some siding had been torn off the west side of the house. One window was broken, with a tree branch sticking into the living room.

Dana and Marla Jean went in to look around, while Greg walked to his car, which was hidden by the fallen oak tree. "Actually, it's not so bad," Greg said. A branch of the tree had landed on the back of the car and dented the trunk. "We should be able to drive it, once we cut this tree off." He got out his cell phone and snapped a few pictures.

"I'll get my chainsaw," Coop said as he headed to the tool shop. He looked toward the pasture and called to Jenny. "Look Jenny, there's the horses. They are just fine."

The ground was wet and saturated by the rain. Walking through the squishy grass, Marla Jean and Marilyn helped Ed get into the old pickup truck. "Guess we better go see to the damage at our place," Ed said. "Thanks for the picnic, and the shelter." Marilyn drove slowly down the driveway maneuvering carefully to avoid some debris.

Marla Jean waved as they turned onto the gravel road, and then called out to Coop. "Son, do we have any boards we can use to block up this window? We don't want any more rain comin' in."

"There's good lumber out in the shed," he said. "Greg, can you give me a hand? Then I'll get that tree off your car." The two men went to work and soon had the window boarded and the tree cleared. Meanwhile, Dana cleaned up broken glass in the farmhouse and Marla Jean mopped the rain-soaked floors.

Outside, Becky and Nancy supervised the little girls who, on Becky's insistence, put on gardening gloves for cleaning up debris in the yard. They filled up a hefty trash bag with soggy paper cups and plates and plastic spoons and forks. Suddenly Jenny called out, "Look what I found, Mommy! What's this?"

She handed Becky a wooden picture frame. Behind broken glass, the smiling faces of a young couple on their wedding day gazed back at her. Obviously an old picture, by the style of dress, but the people did look oddly familiar. Becky looked carefully, then lifted her head and looked off to the west, the direction the Hennesseys had driven. "Oh no," she said to herself. "Lord be with them." Then she called for Coop. "Honey look at this. I have a bad feeling."

Hannah came over, carrying a chair cushion made heavy with rain water. "I found a broken chair. Here's the cushion." She lifted it up with difficulty. "Where should I put it? It won't fit in the trash bag."

Coop took the cushion and said, "Let's just put it down here and make a pile of things that are too big for the trash bag." He looked at Becky and said, "I think I better drive over there. It might be bad." Becky nodded and said, "Be careful. Call me if you need any help."

Coop conferred with Greg, who then explained to Nancy that he was going with Coop to check on the Hennesseys. Coop threw his chainsaw into the back seat of the truck, and at the last minute, Holly jumped in. "What, you want to go along?" Coop asked Holly. The dog barked and sat facing the front. "I guess you do! Well, let's get going then!" The men left quickly in Coop's truck.

As they neared the Henessey's property, they could tell right away that trouble was ahead. Trees were down everywhere, uprooted and strewn haphazardly around the pastures. The corn crop, once strong and healthy, lay flat, stripped of ears. Some of the Hennessey's cattle ran frantically across the road. The fence must have been pulled up, and the cattle were free to run at will. "Call Sheriff Bertram, would you please?" Coop asked Greg. "Tell him the Hennessey's cattle are out, and maybe he can get some help and round them up."

As Coop neared the Hennessey farm house, he slowed to take it all in. The apple orchard was totally destroyed, trees uprooted or broken. A large maple tree lay across the yard, with its tallest branches resting on the chicken coop. A couple of hens were perched in the tree branches. They looked confused. Other chickens were pecking in the yard, already looking for their next bits of food. A few sheep wandered through the yard, unsure of what they should do or where they should go.

Coop turned his gaze toward the house, or what was left of it. The roof had been pulled off the house and lay in pieces one hundred yards away. The yard was strewn with furniture and clothing and broken dishes. Only a couple walls of the house remained upright. Picking her way through the devastation was Marilyn Hennessey, wandering as if in a daze. Every once in a while, she would bend down, pick up something from the debris and hold it close to her breast. Ed Hennessey stood leaning against his truck. He seemed to be in shock.

Coop and Greg jumped out of the truck and ran to the elderly couple. Holly jumped down too, and went immediately to the sheep. She made sure they did not wander too far. Coop smiled and marveled at the collie's herding instinct.

Coop supported Marilyn as she made her way around a tumbled china hutch. "All my beautiful dishes," she said with a sob. She bent and picked up a broken piece of a large serving platter. "This was the platter we used for our Thanksgiving turkey. It used to be my own grandmother's and now it's gone." She tossed it aside and moved on. Coop stayed near.

As Greg approached Ed, he heard the old man repeating, "Thank you Jesus. Thank you, Jesus." When he recognized Greg, Ed said, "You know, if we hadn't been at that picnic, we would have been here when the tornado hit. We probably would have been killed. Can't help but praise Jesus for his protection."

Marilyn stumbled as she tried to step over a pile of rubble. Coop caught her by the elbow and said, "Let's move over to Ed. There's not much we can do here right now. It's starting to get dark. You can stay at Mom's place tonight, and we'll take care of this in the morning. Let's get you in the truck."

Marilyn was shaking and didn't feel she could drive, so Greg took the keys from her and drove the Hennessey's truck. Ed went with him. Coop helped Marilyn into his truck, then went to find Holly and the sheep. Holly herded the sheep into the barn, which fortunately seemed untouched by the twister. Coop closed them in and turned to go back to his truck. Suddenly Holly started barking and Coop turned to see why.

Huddled amongst the roots of an upturned apple tree, Coop saw a young lamb covered with mud and shivering in the cold. He obviously had a broken leg. Holly went over to the lamb and nuzzled him with her nose. The lamb bleated pitifully. Coop bent to pick him up. He carried him to his truck and placed him gently on Marilyn's lap. Holly jumped in the back seat and sat up so she could watch the lamb.

As they left the Hennessey place, they met the sheriff and a few other men, coming out to corral the cattle. "We'll check your fence line and fix any breaks," he said and Coop waved his thanks.

Once home, Coop explained the situation to his mom and the Hennesseys got settled into his old bedroom. Coop was glad to see that the power had come back on and his sister had some hot soup cooking on the stove. Nothing like a hearty soup to calm nerves and bring back normalcy. He walked across the yard to his own house. He stopped first at the truck and lifted the lamb out of the front seat. "Thank you, Lord, for your protection. Thank you for keeping my family safe. I praise you for taking care of us, for our basement, for Holly, and for this little lamb."

Becky met him at the door, curious about what he was carrying and why. As soon as she saw the little lamb, she took over. She accessed the broken leg and made a temporary splint from two thick pieces of cardboard. Then she wrapped the little leg in gauze to hold the splint in place. She blocked off a corner of the garage, lined the area with straw from the barn, and found some fresh cow's milk to feed him from a baby bottle. Poor little fellow was so hungry, he didn't seem to care that the milk wasn't from his own mother.

Jenny was instantly interested in their newest adoption. "We'll name her Tinkerbell," she said happily.

"But it's a boy lamb," said Becky. "Tinkerbell is more a girl name, don't you think?"

Jenny thought a minute and then said, "Its okay. There's a girl in my class named Erin and there's a boy named Aaron too. So I think Tinkerbell will work for a boy or a girl. I like that name. Can we get a bell to put around his neck?"

"If you find a bell and a little ribbon, we can fix a collar, yes. But remember, this lamb isn't ours. He's from the Hennessey's farm, and we'll have to give him back. We're just taking care of him for now. The Hennessey's have a lot of things to worry about, so we'll just take care of Tinkerbell for them until they are ready for him to come back to their farm."

"Okay Mommy. I'll go look for a bell." She started skipping happily out of the garage.

"Wait Jenny," Becky called after her. "You need to get ready for bed. It's late and you need a shower. Tinkerbell will be fine for tonight, and you can get the bell for him tomorrow."

Coop came in from checking on the cattle, happy to report that everyone was accounted for and seemed healthy, though maybe a little jumpy. The horses were fine, too, and were happy to nibble at the apples Coop had taken out to them.

Later that night, in Jenny's room, it was Becky's turn to read the story. She chose the story of Paul and Silas, singing and praying in jail. "That reminds me about us singing in the basement during the storm. The music, and being together, helped to keep us calm, even though it was really dark and scary. I knew that God was with us, and even if the house blew down, he would help us deal with it."

Coop added a verse of Scripture. "Isaiah has a verse about that. I think it's in chapter twenty-six. It says that God will give us perfect peace, when we keep our minds on him and trust in him."

Jenny snuggled up against Becky's side and said, "I wasn't scared. I was with you. I might have been scared if I was by myself."

"Just remember," Coop said, "you are never alone. Jesus is with you, everywhere you go and whatever is happening around you. He loves you and will be with you."

"Best part?" Becky said. "Coop, it's your turn to go first."

He thought a second, then said, "The best part of today was helping our neighbors."

Becky said, "The best part of today was being all together and safe."

Jenny said, "I have lots of best parts. Daddy Coop telling the David and Goliath story. Getting Tinkerbell, and having a basement. And being safe with my family and my friends."

The little family bowed their heads as Coop prayed. "Dearest Lord Jesus, we praise you and thank you tonight for your protection through the storm. We thank you for sparing our home from much damage, and keeping our animals safe too. We pray for the Hennessey's and any other people who have suffered loss today from the tornado. Give them peace, and comfort them with the knowledge of your presence. Oh Lord, may we continue to be helpers for those in need. Show us how to support our friends and neighbors. Let us be the hands and feet of Jesus, bringing love and hope to a frightened world. In your precious name we pray." And they all said "Amen."

CHAPTER 35

Picking Up the Pieces

The Hennessey's house and one of their barns were a complete disaster. They were able to salvage some of their belongings before the house was totally demolished. Marilyn and Ed stood in the front yard, watching as the bulldozers were unloaded from their trailer. Some dumpsters had been dropped off earlier, and the cleanup was about to begin.

The couple held hands as the first bulldozer roared into action. Marilyn laid her head against Ed's chest and stifled tears. He patted her shoulder and said, "I know, dear. Lots of memories here, and it's sad to see it go. But it's for the best. We are ready for our next adventure."

She nodded silently and agreed. "It's really wonderful that the buyers were not concerned about loosing the house. Or even the barn."

"Yep." Ed said. "They were just gonna take it all down anyway. I guess the tornado might have even helped 'em out some."

The buyer was actually a corporation that was planning to subdivide the property into five acre lots and put in roads, electricity and water for a new housing development. So, to them, the loss of the house and outbuildings was not a problem at all. It was all going to be demolished anyway.

The cattle had been rounded up and sold at auction. The sheep had been offered to the Smith family, as thanks for all of their neighborly kindness through the years. Jenny was thrilled to have new pets, and Tinkerbell was overjoyed to see his mother unloaded off the trailer and immediately ready to nurse him. Holly the collie was happy too, and took right to herding the sheep into the pasture.

All of the farm machinery had been placed into two outbuildings and a farm auction was scheduled for next week. Coop was planning to bid on a new tractor and possibly a combine. The sale had already been advertised, and they expected quite a crowd. Coop hoped he could get some good deals, but he knew if would depend on how many other bidders there were. He had a limit as to how much he could spend.

What furniture and personal possessions could be salvaged had been put into storage. The Hennesseys would be moving into their new home in Atkins in a few weeks. The senior living facility was doing some painting to their home, cleaning the carpets, making a few minor repairs. In the meantime, they would be staying with Marla Jean, who was happy to have their company.

"I just wish the old mantle clock had survived," Marilyn said as she turned to get into the truck. "It's the one possession that really mattered to me."

"I know, I'll miss it too." The clock had been a wedding present to them, some fifty years ago. A gift passed down from his parents, it had once belonged to his grandparents. All this time in the family, and now reduced to rubble, seemingly beyond repair. The case was cracked, the face shattered, and the back was totally missing. They had written it off as a lost cause. Coop had gathered up the pieces they could find and stored them in a shoebox. He thought he might be able to get it fixed somewhere. It would make a nice house warming gift when the Hennesseys got moved into their new home.

Ed climbed slowly into the passenger seat, and Marilyn started up the truck. They turned their back on the farm that had been their home for so many years. "I know we were planning on moving anyway, but this seems to be a hard way to do it." Marilyn said.

Ed patted her arm and said, "It's just a house dear. We still have the memories, and each other, and hopefully many years ahead to enjoy together in our new home. Just think, a lot less work, and less dirty clothes, and no birthin' sheep in the middle of the night. No back-breaking weed pulling, and sore muscles from carrying milk cans. No sweating over canning and no cooking big meals for farmhands. We will be able to rest easy and put our feet up a spell."

Marilyn nodded as they pulled out of the driveway and onto the gravel road that led to the Smith's place. Ed glanced over his shoulder and watched as a bulldozer pushed over the one remaining wall of the house. "Thank you, Lord, for your protection during the storm. For the good memories and the good life we had here. For the time we have left to be together. Amen."

CHAPTER 36

◆─◆◆─◆

Thy Word Have I
Hid in my Heart

The tornado damage had been widespread, and Atkins General Hospital had been a busy place in the hours and days immediately following the touchdown. The mobile homes on the edge of Winslow had been hit hard, and several injuries came from there. Only one death had occurred, and everyone agreed that was a miracle.

Melissa was extremely busy, working overtime to help at the registration desk and answering questions from people calling in concerned about friends or relatives. Even though she wasn't a paid employee, she worked hard and tried to do her best. The job had been assigned to her as her Community Service requirement from the Courts. Right from the start, Melissa realized that the job was a blessing and she was good at it. She escorted visitors to patient rooms, delivered a lot of flowers from the gift shop, and had a few opportunities to be a comfort to frightened patients and family members. She took her job seriously and was always ready to bring some sense of hope to those she met.

Before she started her shift on the third day after the tornado, Melissa closed her Bible and prayed "Thank you Lord, for putting me in a position where I can help people. Thanks for giving me courage and words and a hope to share with others. Thank you for your comforting words in the Bible. Thank you for sending people to me, especially Nancy, and thank you for all she's done to show me the way to you. And thank you for supplying all my needs."

Nancy had told Melissa about the importance of memorizing Scripture. She called it 'hiding God's word in your heart.' She had given Melissa some little cards with special verses for her to memorize. The verse for this week was Philippians 4:19 Melissa repeated it one more time before she left her room. "My God shall supply all your need according to his riches in glory by Christ Jesus."

She turned the doorknob and prayed, "Supply my need today. I trust you."

The walk to the hospital was just two blocks, but the summer air was heavy with humidity and she was glistening with sweat before she reached the front door. She was grateful for the air conditioning and said to herself, 'There's a need you met. I'm going to count my blessings all day long.'

During her lunch break, she sat in the employee's lounge with her feet up on the folding chair across from her. She'd been on the move all morning, and this was the first time she'd had a chance to sit down. It felt good to rest a minute. Her cell phoned dinged to indicate incoming email, and she took a look. It was a short note from the HR director, with a request to come to her office before she left for the day. 'I wonder what that's about. I can't be in trouble, I haven't done anything wrong. Hmm. Well, I won't fret about it.' She remembered part of a verse she had memorized a few weeks earlier. John 14:27-Let not your heart be troubled. "Okay God I'm not worried. I know you'll take care of me, no matter what happens."

Just before her break was over, she got a text message from Craig. Seeing his name come up made her smile. The message read, 'Long road trip almost over. Should be home in 2 days. Can I see you? Hope you fared well in the tornado. Pizza on Saturday sound okay?"

"Sure," she texted back. "Call when you get home." She slipped the phone into her back pocket and prayed, "Oh God, thank you for another opportunity to share with Craig. Another blessing!"

CHAPTER 37

◆ ◆ ◆

Counting on the Collie

"You sure you don't want to go with me?" Coop asked Becky. "You might need to keep my bidding under control!" He put his black cowboy hat on and kissed Becky on her forehead. She was sitting on the couch, with her feet up on a foot stool, a cup of tea in her hand and her Bible devotional book opened on the seat beside her.

"No, you go on without me honey," she said. "I'm just going to stay here and rest today. My feet are starting to swell so I want to keep them elevated."

"That's probably best," Coop said. "There won't be any place for you to sit. And I doubt you are really interested in the farm machinery anyway. Just stay home and take care of yourself. And our little peanut." He put his hands on either side of her growing belly. "Pumpkin, I mean!" He kissed her again, this time on the lips.

"But you control yourself with the spending, right?" Becky called after him with a chuckle. "If I'm going to quit/ work in a couple of months, we have to watch our pennies."

"Don't worry, I know my limits. But hopefully I can get a good deal on that combine. I'll probably be back about three this afternoon. You rest 'til then. Love you, Becky." He grabbed his black cowboy hat off the hook on the porch. The screen door slammed behind him and Becky smiled. Some things never changed.

Becky took a slow sip of her hot tea and sighed. The house was quiet, and although it was very different from the normal Saturday morning, she was grateful for the silence. Jenny had spent the night at Hannah's and would be home about supper time. Holly was out in the yard roaming the property. 'Keeping watch by night and by day,' Becky thought as she reached for her Bible. The verses for today's reading came from Jeremiah chapter twenty-nine. The verse was familiar to Becky and she sighed and repeated it from memory. It was refreshing to sit in the quiet and focus on the words the Lord gave to Jeremiah so long ago. "For I know the plans I have for you, plans to prosper you and not to harm you, plans to give you hope and a future."

"You've protected me so many times, Lord, and I thank you. Your plans have led me on the journey that got me to where I am today. I know you've saved me from situations and dangers I wasn't even aware of. And I know you have brought me to this place, this family and this point in my life, so I can trust you to lead me through all the days ahead of me. I don't know what tomorrow holds, but I do know you are already there. I won't be alone. You will be holding my hand. And for that I thank you. Amen"

Becky took her journal and a pen and wrote some notes. She had started doing this shortly after she and Coop were married. Coop had set the example, and she thought it was a good idea and started doing it also. Sometimes they shared their written thoughts with each other. Sometimes she just read over past entries to remind herself of God's goodness and guidance throughout her life.

Becky put her Bible on the coffee table and stretched out on the couch for a nap. Feeling a little chilly, she pulled on her sweater which was lying on the arm of the couch. Then she fluffed up her pillow and lay back down. She had just gotten comfortable when she realized that Holly was barking frantically at the door. 'That's odd,' she thought. 'I wonder what that's all about.'

Becky got up and went to the door. When Holly saw her, she turned and ran toward the barnyard. Then she returned to Becky, barking insistently, and ran back toward the barn again. Becky took a few steps forward and Holly returned, nuzzling Becky's legs and pushing her out into the yard. Then Holly ran again toward the barnyard.

"Do you want me to go with you?" Becky asked, and Holly barked. Becky followed Holly to the barn and watched as Holly ran full speed and jumped over the fence. When she landed on the other side, Holly turned and barked again. Then she ran off up the hill and waited for Becky to follow.

"Well, it's obvious you want me to go out in the pasture with you," Becky said. "But I can't walk that far, in my condition." She noticed Nell grazing nearby and whistled for her. As quickly as possible, Becky saddled the horse and mounted up. It was getting harder and harder to swing her leg over the horse, and sitting in the saddle at five months pregnant took a little getting used to. But soon she had Nell headed up the hill, following Holly who kept running ahead and returning to urge them onward.

Before long, Becky found what was upsetting Holly. The first clue was the mournful bellowing of a cow. Becky heard it before she ever saw the reason for the racket. Near the pond stood one of the cows who had recently delivered a calf. But the calf was not alive. It's mangled and bloodied body lay near the edge of the water. Obviously, some larger animal had attacked the calf and killed it. A coyote maybe, or even a wolf. Becky glanced around uneasily but saw nothing threatening. Something had probably frightened it away. Maybe Holly had chased it off. The cow stood off to the side, still upset and bellowing.

Nell danced around, skitterish because of the unusual smell of blood, the noise from the cow and the sight of the calf's body. She was nervous and turned in circles, nostrils flaring and puffing. Becky reached down to stroke her neck and whisper words of comfort. She pulled the reins gently, turning Nell away from the sight of the bloodied carcass.

"Well Holly, I don't really know what you expect me to do about this situation. Thanks for letting me know, but there's nothing much I can do to help." Becky looked down at the lasso rope attached to the side of the saddle. "I've never been good with a lasso, but maybe I can get this rope around her neck and lead the momma away. But that's about all I can do. Coop will know what to do with the baby."

Becky removed a rope from the side of Nell's saddle and positioned Nell closer to the cow. She looped the rope around the cow's neck and wrapped it several times around the saddle horn. She clicked her heels into Nell's side to urge her forward. The cow was hesitant and didn't want to leave her young. Holly nipped at the cow's leg and made her move. Slowly they walked away from the pond. The cow was resistant, and Holly continued to herd her toward the barn.

Suddenly the cow planted her feet into the ground and refused to move. The rope pulled tight as Nell walked on, then was jerked to a stop. The cow threw her head in defiance, and Nell was thrown off balance. Holly barked, the cow bellowed and Nell danced left and then right. Unexpectedly, the cow charged toward Nell, and in the ensuing chaos, Becky found herself clutching the reins as she was tossed from side to side. Becky quickly decided that leading the cow wasn't working, and she tried to release the rope from around the saddle horn. The rope was slack for a few seconds, and Becky partially unwound it before it tightened again when the cow pulled away. Now at least the cow had more play in the rope, which Becky thought was good until the cow charged at them again. The rope around the saddle horn went slack, and Becky lifted it free. It stung her hand as the cow again changed direction and jerked the rope through Becky's fingers.

Holly stood between the cow and Becky and her barking was keeping the angered cow at bay. Still puffing, with her nostrils flaring, the cow stood glaring at Becky and Nell. Holly stood her ground and would not let the cow any closer.

Nell had had enough. She was upset and nervous. She turned to run away from the angered cow. Becky, hands still stinging, pulled back on the reins to slow Nell, but things were out of control. Nell took off on a gallop. Try as she would, Becky could not get her under control. She felt herself sliding to the right, her left foot slipped out of the stirrup, and time slowed. She knew she was going to fall. It felt like she was in slow motion, yet she hit the ground instantly. There was nothing she could do to stop it. She lay face down on the hard ground. The pain was instantaneous. Pain in her right leg. Pain in her abdomen. Pain in her head.

She lay on the ground, breathless and shocked. She struggled to roll over and finally got onto her back. Holly came close and sat beside her, head tilted and brown eyes fixed upon her face. Becky tried to sit up and felt a sharp pain run through her right foot and ankle. Immediately she saw that it was at an unusual angle and was already beginning to swell. "Must have caught it in the stirrup," she thought.

Nell was nowhere to be seen. Becky wasn't sure she could have stood long enough to mount her anyway. But how was she going to get back to the house? Walking was impossible. Crawling wasn't a pleasant option.

She laid back to catch her breath. Her head was spinning and she had broken out in a cold sweat. Her vision blurred and points of light swam and flashed in her eyes. She closed her eyes quickly but the flashing did not subside. She felt nauseous and turned her head to the side. The vomit surged from her uncontrollably. She wiped her mouth on her sweater sleeve and turned her head to the other side. The smell of vomit curdled her stomach and she hoped she wouldn't throw up again. She closed her eyes and prayed. Without words, Becky called on Jesus for help.

A sudden cramp from deep within her caused her to double up in pain. "Oh God. Oh God. I can't be having contractions. It's too early." The pain was intense, like being stabbed with a butcher knife, and over-shadowed the pain in her foot. It made her gasp for breath sharply.

Becky had had contractions before. She knew what contractions felt like, how they grew in intensity and duration. This was different. This was intense. This pain took her breath away. This pain frightened her.

She scrunched up her face and closed her eyes tightly. The pain was deep within her. She screamed as she felt like her inside were being torn from her. She felt a dampness between her legs and looked down. There was a damp spot on her jeans, dripping down her legs. "Oh Coop, I need you," she said, willing him to appear.

When the pain began to subside, Becky calmed slightly. She tried to gather her thoughts. She didn't know how long she had before the next wave of pain.

She needed to think. She needed clarity. She took a deep breath and opened her eyes. Holly had come up close to her and nuzzled her chin. Becky put her arms around Holly's neck and pulled herself into a sitting position. She looked down at her foot and cringed. It was already turning a purplish bruised color. There would be no walking on it.

Becky looked at Holly and said, "I'm going to need your help girl. I want you to go to Grammy's house." Holly tilted her head. "Go get help. Go to Grammy's house." Holly looked toward the house and then back at Becky. "Yes!" said Becky. "Get help. Go to Grammy's house." With one quick look of understanding, Holly took off on the run. "Get help, Holly. I'm counting on you."

Becky took her sweater off and rolled it up in a bundle. She gently placed it under her ankle, wincing as she did so. But she knew it was important to elevate it as much as she could. Then she lay back down on the grass, praying that Holly would indeed bring help. She laid her hands across her belly and said, "I'm sorry, little one. I hope you're ok. I'm so sorry." The world began to spin. Clouds in the sky swirled and twisted. Becky closed her eyes to block out the view, but still behind her eyelids everything was turning and tumbling. She threw up again but instead of wiping her mouth on her shirt sleeve, Becky passed out.

CHAPTER 38

---◆◆◆---

Intriguing

Melissa and Craig talked through their pizza like old friends, reconnected after years apart. With great excitement, she told him about her job offer. The hospital administrators had been impressed with the quality of her volunteer work and had offered her a paid position, to start as soon as her probation was over.

"It's so amazing," she said. "I had just memorized a verse about God supplying all my needs, and *bam,* this job was offered to me. It's like, ever since I turned my life over to God, good things have been happening to me. I really believe he is blessing me, and taking care of me."

"But how can you be so sure? What makes you think it's God giving you these blessings? I mean, it's you who worked hard, did a good job, made an impression on the hospital staff. God had nothing to do with that."

"Oh, but he did. The old me would never have done well with this job. I used to be nasty, lazy, and unpleasant. I talked back to my boss at the restaurant where I used to work. I robbed from him. I pretty much did whatever I wanted, and I didn't care about how it affected others." She slid another piece of pizza onto her plate. "But now, I have a whole new attitude, a respect for people, and a desire to be a good worker, to prove I am a new woman in Christ. I have no fear of slipping back into the old ways. I pray and I know God will be with me, and help me. Whatever temptations come my way, I know he will be there to give me a way of escape. That's another verse I memorized. It's in First Corinthians." That verse would be permanently etched in her mind, always connected to memories of Coop Smith and a phone call that interrupted the evil plans she had for him. That was a long time ago, when she was a whole different person. But the verse stuck in her mind, along with several other seeds he had planted.

She chewed on pizza and silently counted Coop as another blessing. She'd been finding blessings in every day, and was always thankful. 'And I've got to talk to Nancy,' she thought. 'She'll be so glad to hear about the changes in my thinking, and my conversations with Craig. Testifying isn't as hard as I thought it would be. Nancy's prayers must be helping.'

Craig asked, "I can't deny that you have changed since I first met you. And your story about seeing hell has given me a lot to think about over the past few weeks. I'm not sure I'm ready to swallow everything you've said, but neither will I just dismiss it as hogwash. You've got me thinking."

"That's all I can ask, isn't it? Give it some thought. We can talk about it more whenever you want. Now let's talk about you. Where were you when the tornados were hitting us?"

"About two hundred miles away. We had some heavy rain but nothing like the storm you had here. I heard about it on the news and right away I thought about you and wondered if you were okay."

"Oh, I was fine. I was volunteering at the hospital that day, and the sky got all black and then the rain started. But we didn't have any wind damage, like Winslow and a couple other towns had. Kids were not at the high school, fortunately. And the fireworks had already been cancelled. I heard that the roof was torn off part of the school. I haven't been over there yet, but I guess it's quite a mess. But they expect to have all the repairs made before school starts in the fall."

They fell into a comfortable silence as they ate their pizza. Craig watched Melissa, especially noticing how her tongue flicked across her lips as she tried to reclaim an errant trail of melted cheese. She noticed and quickly asked, "Have you seen your cousin since he got out of the hospital?"

"Talked to him on the phone a time or two. Sounds like he's doing better day by day. Bev says he's driving her crazy. So, I guess he's getting back to normal."

They laughed and Melissa said, "They're good people. Maybe we could go over and visit them together sometime. And bring your sister Pat. I'd like to meet her too."

"Hey, I've been wondering why they call you Cash instead of Craig," Melissa asked as she stood to clear away the paper plates.

"It's a nickname because of my last name. All the Cashman cousins had nicknames. That's how Jonathan James became JJ. I was the oldest boy with the actual Cashman last name, so I got to be Cash."

"I get it! I'm ashamed to say I don't think I actually remembered your last name! But if you don't mind, you'll always be Craig to me! Fits you better!"

The evening wore on, with more conversation and plans to meet again. Before Craig dropped her off at her rooming house, Melissa thanked him for the pizza and spending time with her. She said, "I thank God for your friendship. I'm so glad he brought you back into my life. I'm glad for this opportunity to share my story with you, and tell you about my salvation."

"I'm glad we re-connected, too," Craig said. "But you sure are different than I expected. Call it intriguing, I guess!" He reached for her hand. "I'd like to know more."

"Good!" Melissa answered, pulling her hand away. "We'll talk more next time. There's lots more to tell you."

He'd been hoping for a goodnight kiss, or maybe more, but saw now that it wasn't going to happen. It was another surprise. As he drove home to his little apartment in Catonsville, he shook his head and thought to himself, 'Man, maybe there really is something to this God thing. To make a drastic change like that, something sure has gotten ahold of her. Intriguing, that's the word for sure! It's a lot to think about.'

And think about it, he did. But every time he imagined a conversation with Melissa, his mind would focus on her lips, and the memory of her in the sleeper compartment of his rig. He couldn't get that picture out of his mind. He wanted her that way again. No doubt about it, he wanted the old Misty back. She was wild and hot, just his type. But this Melissa, she was a different story. Maybe JJ was right. Maybe she was just waiting for him to bring out the wild side again. Maybe she needed him as much as he needed her.

CHAPTER 39

———◆◆◆———

At the Auction

Coop's cell phone rang and he dug it out of his back pocket. His hands were full but he juggled things around as best he could. The auctioneer's paddle with number seventeen written in large dark blue lettering was tucked precariously under his arm pit. He had his wallet and credit card out, and he hurried to slip the credit card into its proper spot. He was thankful he had already procured a loan from the bank and the funds were available for this purchase. What a deal he had gotten!

The combine wasn't new, by any means, but was running just fine. It needed some maintenance, but would be well worth the investment. Coop thought the price he had paid was a fair one, and was content that the Hennesseys would be satisfied with the negotiations. Coop didn't want to feel like he had cheated them out of a fair price, yet he was hoping for a good deal for himself, too. This transaction seemed about right.

He stepped away from the table and answered the call. He immediately discerned that Dana was upset, though he could tell that she was trying hard to control her emotions. Trying and failing, he realized, as she said, "Coop, come home right away. It's Becky."

"What do you mean, it's Becky? She can't be in labor yet. Its months too soon. What's going on?" Coop was already making his way through the crowd to his truck parked out on the road.

"She fell. I think her ankle is broken. We called the ambulance. But get here quick, Coop. She's asking for you." Dana hesitated but went on, "We're worried about the baby, Coop. She's having a lot of cramping."

He sprinted toward the truck and said, "Five minutes. Tell her I'll be there in five minutes." He made it in four.

CHAPTER 40

Pray Without Ceasing

The ambulance siren whined as it sped ahead, throwing up dust as it maneuvered along the gravel road. Coop drove a little slower, but still didn't want to lose sight of the flashing red lights. He had wanted to ride in the ambulance with Becky, but then realized it would be better if he took the truck. Being apart from her, though, was hard. He wanted to hold her, sooth her with his words, at least hold her hand. But the EMTs had her hooked up to monitors and were watching her vitals and he knew he'd just be in their way. Once they got to the hospital, he'd be able to comfort her.

All he could do now was pray, and that he did. He prayed for Becky, that she would be brave and strong. He prayed for the techs working with her now in the back of the ambulance. He prayed for the doctors and nurses who would be helping them soon in the emergency room. As tears slipped down his cheeks, Coop prayed for their unborn child, who was apparently struggling to survive.

Even when he wasn't consciously forming words and praying in complete sentences and thoughts, Coop's mind was in a state of frantic prayer. 'It's a good thing God knows the desires of my heart, because I can't even seem to speak them right now,' Coop thought. He took a deep breath and said out loud, "I trust you Lord. It's in your hands."

By the time Coop had found a parking space and hurried to the ER registration desk, Becky was already in an exam room. He filled out the necessary paperwork and was asked to have a seat in the waiting room. Someone would call him when they were ready for him to go back into Becky's room.

Coop took a seat and looked around. Atkins General wasn't a really big hospital, but was always busy. The waiting room was pretty crowded this afternoon. Coop looked around quickly and prayed for each person there. Worry was evident on so many faces. Coop himself was worried. Yet he had a peace too, knowing that God was with him, was with Becky, and was with the baby. His plan was a good plan. Coop could find comfort in that. They were not alone. God was with them. "Oh God," he whispered. "Help us."

The doors to the ER ward opened and a nurse called his name. He stood, took a deep breath, and followed her down the hall. Finally, they came to a sliding door labeled with a big number seven. The nurse slid the door open, moved the curtain, and he saw Becky. He walked to her quickly and took her hand. Becky was pale, had been crying, and smelled slightly of vomit. Her hair was damp because a nurse had tried to clean her up, but the smell lingered.

Becky was hooked up to an IV. The bag hung on a pole over her shoulder and something was dripping slowly down the tubing. She was wearing a blood pressure sleeve on her upper arm and a pulse oxygen meter was clipped onto her finger. Ice was packed around her elevated right leg. She looked so small in that bed, so helpless. Coop wanted to take her in his arms and hold her. He wished he could be lying there in her place. He wished more than anything he hadn't gone to that auction.

Becky made a weak attempt at a smile and looked up at him. "I'm so glad you are here. I'm so scared."

"I'm here, Becky, my love. Don't be afraid." He leaned over and kissed her forehead. "What happened? How did you fall?" He hadn't gotten any details at the farm before Becky had been whisked away by the ambulance. He had lots of questions.

What came out of Becky was a jumble of memories, which didn't make a lot of sense at first. "It was my fault. I shouldn't have tried to rope that cow. The baby was dead. She didn't want to leave it. Holly tried to help, nipping and herding. But she was angry. Nell ran off. I hurt my leg. Vomit in my hair, I smelled it in the ambulance." She made a face. "Disgusting." Then she started to cry again. "I'm so sorry. I was so stupid." She broke down and sobbed. "So sorry."

Coop rubbed her hands and said, "Shhh now. Just rest." She calmed a little and Coop dried her tears with a tissue. "You were riding Nell?" he asked. "Why?"

"Holly was barking and she told me to go out in the pasture. So, I took Nell. I couldn't walk all that way."

Coop had more questions but was interrupted when the nurse came in to check Becky's vitals once more. "Hi Becky. My name's Carole and I'll be your nurse here in the ER." Becky looked up at the nurse, who seemed vaguely familiar. She'd seen her somewhere before. Carole adjusted the blood pressure cuff on Becky's arm and started the machine. "How's that pain level now?" she asked. "A little better?"

Becky pulled herself together and answered as calmly as she could. "Oh yes, it's better. I'd say it's a seven. I still feel the cramping in my uterus, though, but it doesn't hurt as much. My foot feels better too."

"Okay. That's what we want to hear. The toredal is working." She closed down the computer and turned to Coop. "Dr. Rosencrantz has examined Becky and did an ultrasound. He will be back in shortly to talk with you. Then we'll get her down to X-ray and start fixing up that ankle." She turned back to the bed and asked, "Do you need anything, Becky? Maybe another warm blanket?"

"Oh, yes, that would be nice. This ice is making me cold all over!" Becky smiled but then burst into tears. "Thank you. You're being so nice. I'm sorry."

Nurse Carole patted her hand and said, "That's okay honey. You've been through a lot. Tears are understandable. Now let me go get that blanket for you." She turned to leave but Coop stopped her.

"That medicine won't hurt the baby, will it?" he asked.

"You can talk with the doctor about it," said Carole. "I'm sure it will be fine or he would not have prescribed it."

"I think I know that nurse," Becky commented to Coop after she had left the room.

"You do. She goes to our church. I think she goes mostly to the early service, but you've probably seen her around."

"Oh, that's it. I knew she looked familiar."

Before Carole could come back with the blanket, Dr. Carl Rosencrantz pulled open the door and walked in. He took Becky's hand and looked at her kindly. He gave Coop a nod of recognition. Dr. Rosencrantz had been Becky's obstetrician during this pregnancy, and had met Coop a couple of times in his office. He remembered Coop's look of complete joy when he had heard the baby's heartbeat for the first time. And the ultrasound pictures that he had watched on the computer screen had been such a thrill for Coop that he could hardly stop looking.

Sadly, the news Dr. Rosencrantz had to give the couple now was not so happy.

CHAPTER 41

———◆◆◆———

Empty

Hours later, Becky lay in the hospital bed, staring blankly at the ceiling. Her eyes were swollen and red from crying so hard. She placed her hands over her belly and pushed hard, willing to find proof. The doctor was surely wrong. He must have made a mistake. Surely this didn't really happen. But her probing fingers felt nothing. The skin on her abdomen was loose and floppy. It was not stretched tightly over her child. There was no child.

Empty. She felt empty. Not only was her uterus empty, but her arms were empty. Her heart felt empty too. She was numb. She felt dead. She wished she *was* dead.

"Why God? Why?" she muttered. Her voice startled Coop, who had fallen asleep in a chair in the corner. Becky instantly stifled her voice and Coop settled back to sleep. "I'm so sorry," she whispered. And she didn't know if she was talking to Coop, or to the little one who had been taken from them.

The past hours had been a whirlwind. No wonder Coop was exhausted. Dr. Rosencrantz had been kind, as kind as he could be. He was obviously touched by the circumstances. After all, he went into obstetrics so he could deliver healthy, thriving babies and present them to their overjoyed families. But the baby boy he delivered last night was different.

He was so small. One pound ten ounces. And quiet. He didn't make a sound. But he was perfect. Ten fingers and toes, wrinkled from floating in amniotic fluid. A little fuzz of hair. His skin seemed reddish and translucent at the same time. And tiny, so very tiny.

The delivery nurse cleaned him up a little and wrapped him in a soft blanket. They put a tiny knit cap on his head. They had put a hospital band around his wrist, and Becky noticed that his arm was barely bigger than a drinking straw. His eyes were closed, but his little mouth was slightly opened. It was easy to imagine he was smiling.

Becky groaned and let out a sob. Coop woke completely now and came immediately to her side. He slid his strong arm under her shoulders and whispered, "I know, sweetheart. I know."

Suddenly Becky's emotions dipped to a new low. She turned away from him and spoke with frustration. "You don't know. How could you know how I feel? Our baby should be inside me, kicking and rolling and growing and living. But he's gone. You can't know how empty I feel." She wouldn't meet his gaze.

"You're right, Becky," Coop wished she would turn her face toward him, but he wouldn't force her. "I don't know that emptiness. But Becky, he was my son too, and I feel the loss. My heart is breaking as well. But we are not alone, honey. Jesus is here. Let's put our trust in his plan. Let's rest in the knowledge of his love."

"What kind of a plan is this? Surely not a good one. Why would a good God plan to let my baby die? Why? How could this plan of his be to prosper me and give me hope and a future? All this plan has done is take away my hope and the future of our son." Becky was angry. All the pent-up wrath came pouring out.

Coop was taken aback. He wasn't used to Becky talking like this. Usually, she was all into praising God in all circumstances, looking for the good in whatever was happening around her, trusting that God's ways were higher than hers. This anger was uncharacteristic. Yet he could understand how her faith could have been shaken. This was a big blow. It might take a while for her to accept and trust God again.

"Why don't you just go on home? You don't need to be here. I'm sure there's work to do at the farm." She paused. "What are you going to do about that dead calf?" Dead. She already hated that word.

"I'll take care of it. Don't you worry. And I'll take Jenny over to your mother's place. She'll know best how to tell her what happened."

"No!" Becky shouted insistently. "I want to tell her. Take her to mom's but tell mom I want to be the one to talk to Jenny. She's *my* daughter."

That stung like a slap in the face, but Coop didn't retaliate. He just said, "Well, okay, if that's the way you want to do it. Maybe when you get discharged and come home...?"

"Yeah, then. Just tell her my foot is broken and I'll be home in a couple of days."

"Maybe the nurses will help you get up and take a shower this morning," Coop suggested. "I'm sure you'll feel better then."

"And what if I don't want to feel better?" Becky snapped.

Coop was surprised by her curtness. This wasn't his Becky. He tried again. "A shower always makes me feel better. You can get your hair really cleaned. It'll help you to get up and around. Maybe tomorrow you can."

"I don't want to get up. I don't want a shower. I just want more pain medicine and I want to go to sleep. And sleep forever. I'll never forgive myself for this. So go home. Leave me. I don't deserve for you to be here. Just go."

Coop tried to be comforting. He rubbed her forehead and tried to kiss her. She turned further away and closed her eyes. "Just go," she said, voice muffled in the pillow.

"Okay," Coop said and hesitated. "I love you."

"Maybe you shouldn't. I don't deserve to be loved. Just go"

"Becky, please don't talk like that. I do love you. And I always will, no matter what."

"Coop, stop. Just stop. I don't want to talk. I don't want to think. I don't want to live. Just go. Get out."

Coop left. He was shaken by her words and didn't know what else to do. He made his way down the hall and took the elevator to the first floor. He found directions to the chapel and entered quietly. The room was empty so he walked slowly to a row of seats near the front. He sat facing an altar rail with a kneeling pad covered with a deep burgundy fabric. A wooden table was centered in the front, adorned with a cross and candles on either side. On each side wall there was a smaller table, laden with dozens of candles, some of which had been lit earlier when petitioners had come to pray in the night. The room was dimly lit by sconces along the wall and the flickering light from the candles. It was a peaceful place, and Coop felt the presence of the Lord.

Coop sat in silence. He drooped his head and his shoulders sagged. He felt heavy. This was a terrible burden to bear alone. His heart was broken from the loss of his son. He longed to take his wife in his arms, to swear to help her through this pain. He felt the distance between them grow as she struggled to process the events of the past day on her own. He wanted so badly to help her, to comfort her, to assure her of his love. But she was pushing him away. That pain hurt as badly as the loss of their son.

Coop put his head into his hands and began to sob. He poured out his sorrows to the Lord. He wept and pleaded with God for the words to comfort Becky. He begged for his strength to be her strength until she could muster strength from within herself. He cried to the Lord for wisdom to understand and to know how to bring her to a place of acceptance and peace. He prayed with words until he ran out of words. He sat in silence and let the spirit of God intercede for him.

Then Coop's emotions were lifted and he began to praise God. He celebrated his marriage and the gift of Becky in his life. He worshiped the Lord and thanked him for salvation, eternal life, and the hope of heaven. He praised God for sending the Comforter who would be with them through this low point in their lives.

With his head still bowed into his hands, Coop sat in the quiet room. The candles flickered and danced as someone else entered the room and stirred the air. Coop heard the clicking of a woman's heels and someone walked down the center aisle and stopped near his chair. He looked up and smiled.

"Hello, Coop. I thought I might find you here." The hospital chaplain, Barb Olsen, put her hand on his shoulder. "Would you mind if I sit with you?"

Coop straightened in his chair and slid over a bit. "That's fine, have a seat."

"Thank you. I came looking for you. Wanted to see how you're doing and if there's anything I can do for you."

"I'll be okay. I've just spent some time with my Savior. I know his plan is perfect, and even though I don't understand and I wish it wasn't this way, I will rest in his promise to never leave me or forsake me." He hesitated but went on, "It's Becky I'm worried about. She's not herself right now. She's angry. She's blaming herself, and she doesn't want to talk with me about it. That's not like her. She's closing me off."

"That's not unusual. She has a lot to process. Give her some time. Let her know that you're here, when she's ready to talk. You know, a woman's emotions are often all over the place. And a pregnant woman can be especially emotional. Now add the loss of the baby, and an abrupt change in hormone levels, well, I think you can see that emotional swings are to be expected. Be patient with her. I know your love is founded on the solid rock and will not be shattered by this storm."

Coop nodded. "I don't understand why she's blaming herself. It was just an accident."

"Maybe because she's processing. Maybe she's angry at God, that would be a normal reaction too, even for a strong Christian. It's often the first, most basic reaction. But she knows that God has a plan, a good plan, and she can't find it in herself to blame him. So, she blames herself. She may even move on and find blame in other places too. She just has to work through it." She paused. "You know, God sometimes uses the bitter to make the sweet sweeter. It may take her some time, but she'll come to understand that."

Coop was silent as he considered her words. "Have you talked to her?"

"No, I went to her room a few minutes ago but she was asleep. Or at least, her head was turned away from the door, and she didn't respond when I called her name. Sometimes people just aren't ready to talk yet. I'll go back later this afternoon."

"I was thinking I'd come back about supper time, and maybe get something to eat with her." Coop checked the time on his phone. It was time to get going. He also saw that there were several text messages. Lots of people wanted to see how Becky was doing. He didn't know how to answer them, so he put his phone away and stood up.

"I want to thank you for your help after the delivery last night," he went on. "The photographer, the special blanket, the time we had to hold him and name him and look at his perfect little fingers." His voice caught but he managed to go on. "It was hard, but I'm sure it was helpful to have that time, and the special memories. Becky's hurting now, but I think she'll really appreciate the pictures and the memory box. So, thank you."

Chaplain Olsen stood too. "My prayers are with you, Coop. You and Becky are strong and you have the assurance of God's presence with you, through whatever comes your way. You will get through this, with the Lord's help, and a lot of prayers."

"Thank you, Ms. Olsen. I appreciate your prayers. Becky does too, I know."

Back in her room, Becky tried to sleep. She thought if she could only sleep, maybe she could forget. If her conscious mind would let go of reality, then she wouldn't have to think. She wouldn't have to feel. She could just float in oblivion.

But she couldn't get comfortable. No matter how she tried to position herself, there was just no way to ease the pain in her leg. No way to get the kinks out of her back. No way to put her mind at ease. 'Maybe I need more pain meds?' she wondered. She reached for the call button but it was just out of reach. Her arm stretched awkwardly, fingers wiggling, but she couldn't pull the cord or will it to come to her.

"Great," she said in disgust. She banged her hand down on the bed and turned her head towards the window. "And look at that – dark and cloudy, probably a storm coming. Just the right weather to match my mood. Gloomy and depressing. It figures. I'll have flashes of lightening keeping me awake when all I want to do is sleep. Sleep and forget."

The remote for the TV was within reach, even if the nurses' call button was not. She flipped the TV on and a beautiful scene of a waterfall flashed on the screen. There was soothing music playing softly and Becky's attention was drawn to the peaceful movement of water. The picture faded out and brought up a bright orange butterfly flitting across a meadow of colorful flowers. Becky thought back to the meadow where Coop had proposed to her. There were flowers blooming that day too, and Jenny had gathered an armload. Tears flowed easily down Becky's cheek as she remembered the joy of that moment. It seemed so distant. Yet it was barely a year ago.

The soft soothing music worked its magic and Becky drifted off to sleep. Tears on her cheek dried in a salty trail.

CHAPTER 42

—◆ ◆ ◆—

Missing Mommy

"But when will Mommy come home?" Jenny asked Coop.

'He looks so tired,' Marla Jean thought. 'Lord please give him strength. And the right words to help Jenny.'

Coop got Jenny's little overnight bag down from the top shelf of her closet. "It's going to be a few more days, maybe a week. Her broken foot is in a big cast to help it heal. The doctor wants her to rest a little more before she comes home." He hated to hide the truth from Jenny, but that's what Becky wanted. And it's not like he was lying, it just wasn't the whole truth. "So, you get to have a sleepover at Grandma Emerson's house tonight."

"Here," said Marla Jean. "I'll help you pack. I did you-all's laundry today, so you have plenty of clean clothes. What do you want to take?"

"Thanks, Mom," said Coop. "Thanks for keeping Jenny with you last night. And thanks for everything else you've done to help." He looked at the laundry basket piled high with folded clothes. "I stayed at Hannah's one night, and Grammy's one night, and now I'm going to Grandma Emerson's house tonight. That's a lot of sleepovers." Jenny took her clean pajamas out of the laundry basket and put them into her bag. "I need to pack Marshmallow and the kittens. And I better feed Oreo before I go. And I promised Benny I'd bring him an apple today."

"You have plenty of time for all that," said Coop. "I have some farm work to do, and your Grandma Emerson said she has some errands to run too, so we won't be going to her house until later this afternoon. Close to supper time." He turned to his mom and said, "I'll be out in the pasture. Back in a couple of hours."

Marla Jean nodded, gave him a hug and a knowing look, and turned back to Jenny. "Be sure to pack your toothbrush too."

"I don't need to. Grandma has a toothbrush for me at her house. She has my hairbrush too." Jenny picked up her stuffed cat, Marshmallow, and looked around for all the kittens. She knew they all needed to be with their mommy. She didn't want to leave any behind.

Coop went out the front door and practically had to step over Holly. The collie looked up at him forlornly and Coop bent down to rub the top of her head. "You miss her, don't you girl? I know. I miss her too." Coop made a sudden turn and went back into the house, coming out a minute later with a piece of cheese. He sat on the steps and called Holly over for a conversation.

"I wanted to thank you, Holly. You are such a good girl. Have some cheese." He tore off a bite and offered it to Holly, who took it greedily. "You were such a good help. I heard how you came to Grammy's's house and barked and barked. And then you showed Aunt Dana where Becky was. You were such a good girl." He gave Holly more cheese and hugged her tightly. "I'm so glad you love your mommy so much. And you're so smart." Holly tilted her head at the word 'mommy.' Coop had no doubt but that Holly understood his every word. "She'll be home in a couple of days. I'm sure she misses you. Here, one more bite of cheese. Then I've got to get to work."

Before going out to the pasture to find the dead calf, Coop climbed the steep ladder into the haymow. He opened the loading door to get a little breeze and hoped it would cool the loft somewhat. Then he sat down on a bale of hay and talked to God, a practice he had learned from his father so long ago.

"Lord, you tell us not to worry about anything. You tell us that we should pray and petition you with thanksgiving. You tell us that you will give us peace. You tell us you will guard our hearts and minds. So I come to you now, thankful for your presence in my life. Thankful for my family. Especially right now I am thankful for my wife. The woman I believe with all my heart was chosen by you to be my partner forever. But Lord, she's hurting now. And I don't know how to help her."

He paused to think, then continued. "Please give her your peace, the kind of peace that passes all understanding. Because God, we don't understand. So we trust. We ask for your perfect peace in this far from perfect situation. Please God, keep our minds focused on you. Grow our trust. And God, please send someone to talk with Becky, someone who can give her hope."

As Coop sat in the peace of the haymow, a motion in the corner of the barn caught his eye. It was a barn swallow, flying into the barn. He watched as the swallow flew, swooping and dipping near the peak of the barn roof. A second bird rose from a nest in the corner and the first one took its place, settling in the nest comfortably. 'They must have eggs there. Maybe babies. Teamwork,' he thought. 'Just like Becky and me.'

"God," he prayed, "I know you care about us. You even care about sparrows or swallows. You love us even more, because we're made in your image. You know what we're going through right now. Cover us with your love, we ask. Thank you."

Coop stood up. He closed the loading door and went down the ladder. There were chores to be done. Then he'd drop Jenny of at Grandma Emerson's house before he headed for the hospital. He felt better, knowing that they would get through this somehow, and their faith in God would grow because of it. God promised it.

Later, as Marla Jean sat alone in the quiet living room, looking across at Walter's empty chair, she spoke to her husband as if he were actually there with her. "Oh Walt, our family is hurting. This is so hard. I wish you were here to help us through it. I wish I could cry with you and you would wipe my tears. You were always so strong. I need you now. I can't carry this burden alone."

She reached for Walter's old Bible, still sitting on the side-table where he always had kept it. Lovingly she stroked her fingers across the leather cover, worn and shiny from years of use. "You could always find the right verses for every situation. I need to hear from you now, Walt. Find me a verse of comfort. Something I can share with the children."

She sighed deeply and closed her eyes. 'Try Psalms,' came to her, whispered softly. She looked down at the Bible and opened it to a page near the center. A quick glance showed her that she had indeed opened the book to Psalms, and she smiled. "Thank you, Walter," she breathed and then inhaled quickly. 'Not me. Thank the Lord.' The words were insistent and she knew, without a doubt, what Walter meant.

"It's from God, of course, I know He's the one sending me the message. But Walter, I'm so used to having you lead me, following the Lord's prompting, and being the spiritual head of the house. I don't think I hear from God like you used to. So when I hear a word, I think it's coming from you. I'll have to try harder to realize it's God, not you, who is talking to me! Anyway, Lord, help me pick a Psalm. Something I can share with the kids and bring them comfort."

She rifled through a few pages and her eyes settled on Psalm 34:18. "The Lord is close to the brokenhearted and saves those that are crushed in spirit." She repeated it several times, to commit it to memory.

Closing the Bible, she returned it to the side-table. She patted the worn leather cover and said, "Thank you Lord. That's the perfect verse to share with Coop and Becky,"

CHAPTER 43

Close Encounters

Elizabeth walked into Becky's room and placed a vase of flowers on the movable tray beside the bed. Becky was asleep, or so it seemed. Elizabeth noticed that her hair had been washed. She sure looked better than she had the night before. Smelled better too.

It had been a difficult day for everyone, but Elizabeth was taking it especially. To see her daughter struggling with this tragedy, well, it was more than any mother would want to deal with. But deal they must. She offered up another quick prayer for strength, for Becky and the whole family. This wasn't easy, that's for sure.

When Marla Jean had called that afternoon to say that Becky had fallen off a horse, the nightmare began. Elizabeth hurried over to the farm as quickly as possible, but the ambulance had already left with Becky, and Coop was right behind in his truck. Elizabeth stayed to talk with Marla Jean and Dana and learned some of the details.

Dana had told her how Holly had come running up to the house, barking and whining at the door. When Holly made it obvious that she wanted to be followed, Dana had jumped into the four-wheeler and found Becky out near the pond. It was obvious right away that her foot had been broken. It was difficult, but Dana had somehow managed to lift Becky and put her into the four-wheeler. Then she called her mom and told her to get some ice ready and to call the ambulance.

Dana tried to drive as quickly and yet carefully as she could, but every bump in the pasture made Becky wince with pain. Dana apologized but Becky was pretty out of it. But when Dana stopped the four-wheeler to open the gate, Becky gave the most frightening scream of pain. Dana reached for her hand and Becky gripped it so tightly she left fingernail prints oh the back of Dana's hand. Becky's eyes widened and she cried, "Oh God." She arched her back as the pain tore through her abdomen.

When Dana asked "What is it, Becky? Your foot?" Becky had answered breathlessly. "The baby. Something's wrong." That's when Dana called Coop.

Marla Jean brought ice packs and they tried to calm Becky while they waited what seemed like an eternity until Coop arrived. Soon after that, the ambulance pulled in, and the EMT's got Becky inside and headed to the hospital. No one knew at that point what the outlook was.

Elizabeth decided to drive right over to the hospital in Atkins to be with Becky. Jenny was due to return from her sleepover with her friend, Hannah, so Marla Jean and Dana said they would stay at the farm and wait for her. They all agreed not to tell Jenny anything to upset her. They would say that her mommy fell and hurt her foot and needed to be checked at the hospital. That would suffice.

She hadn't been allowed to go into the ER examining room while Coop was there; only one visitor was allowed at a time. When he came out into the waiting room to get her, Elizabeth could see that something was terribly wrong. He hugged her tight and then choked out the words. The baby didn't make it. Dr. Rosencrantz was taking Becky up to surgery. They would do a C-section to remove the baby. The baby who would never come home with them.

Elizabeth walked in a daze to room seven. She didn't know what she was going to say. When she saw her daughter, hooked up to IV bags and monitors, with her leg elevated and iced, she wanted to break down and cry. Her daughter, her baby girl, was facing the challenge of a lifetime. Oh, how Elizabeth wished she could take all this pain onto herself. Anything to spare her daughter from this anguish.

There had been only a minute before Nurse Carole came into the room and said it was time to leave for the operating room. A quick hug and a kiss on the forehead and Becky was whisked out of the room. "This should take about an hour," Carole said. "Then she'll be moved to room 318. You and Mr. Smith can wait for her there, if you'd like."

So Coop and Elizabeth waited. They sat in the dimly lit room, drinking coffee they had gotten from a vending machine, and waited. They talked a little, cried a little, prayed a lot, and waited. When Becky was brought into the room later, she was still a bit groggy from the anesthesia. Elizabeth stood near the hospital bed, holding Becky's hand and gently stroking her hair. Coop watched as his mother-in-law lovingly tended her daughter. Then Elizabeth hugged her gently and said she was going home. Coop had stayed the night, sleeping restlessly in the chair at the side of the bed.

Elizabeth hadn't slept well that night either. Concern for her daughter kept gnawing at her mind. She roamed the house in a state of numbness, unable to stop thinking about what Becky was going through. A little after midnight, her phone rang. Kaye from the church choir was calling. She said she felt led of the Spirit to call and pray with Elizabeth. That conversation and prayer time helped Elizabeth calm her mind and eventually the words from John 14 lulled her to sleep. "Do not let your hearts be troubled." She prayed that those words would also bring comfort to Becky.

While getting ready for this visit, Elizabeth had been surprised at how rested she felt. "Thank you Lord," she prayed. "Please help me know what to say to Becky to help her through this."

Now Elizabeth pulled a chair up close to Becky's bed and sat quietly for a moment. Then she reached for Becky's arm and rubbed it softly. Becky stirred and opened her eyes. "Oh, I didn't mean to wake you," Elizabeth said. "You need your rest. How are you feeling this afternoon?"

Becky turned to look towards the door. "My foot hurts when the pain meds wear off. I asked for more, and the nurse said she'd bring it, but it's taking forever."

"Take some deep breaths honey, nice and slow. I'm sure they'll be in soon."

"Seems like they are in here all the time, poking me and asking me questions and hooking me up to machines. And then when I need something, they just disappear."

She stifled a sob. "Like my baby. Gone."

"Oh sweetie, I'm so sorry. I know this is hard." Elizabeth stood there, rubbing Becky's arm and praying silently. She didn't know what else to do.

Becky shook her shoulders as if trying to shake away the pain of loss. "Will you take Jenny to your house tonight? But don't tell her about the baby. I'll do that later."

"I talked to Coop earlier and we arranged that already. Don't worry, you just rest and get your strength back. I'll keep her as long as you need me to."

"Marla Jean had her last night, but I think she should be with you."

"That's fine. I'll make her macaroni and cheese for supper. That's her favorite." Elizabeth pointed toward the flowers on the table. "I brought these for you. Aren't they lovely?" It was a beautiful bouquet of daisies in a variety of colors.

"They're pretty, but you shouldn't have. I don't deserve flowers."

"Becky! Now why would you say that? Of course you deserve flowers."

Becky pulled her hand free and glared at her mother. "No, I don't. My baby is dead. Dead. And I killed him."

Elizabeth caught her breath and said softly, "It was an accident, Becky. You did not kill your baby. It just happened. You can not blame yourself."

"But if I hadn't been on that horse, if I hadn't tried to rope the cow and pull her away from her dead baby, then *my* baby would still be alive. It's my fault.

Elizabeth was confused. "What's this about a cow and a dead calf? I don't understand." So Becky began to tell the whole story. All while she was talking, her hands lay protectively across her stomach.

"But honey, you didn't do it on purpose, You can't say it's your fault. It was an accident. Please honey. Don't blame yourself."

The door opened and a nurse came in with her next dose of pain medication.

"Finally," said Becky with a sharp tone to her voice.

"Doctor's orders are every six hours. I'm sorry, but we'll need to talk to the Orthopedist on call before we change up your meds. He should be making his rounds between now and supper time. We'll talk with him then,"

Elizabeth stepped back and let the nurse take Becky's vitals and record everything into the computer. Then she emptied the catheter bag and made a note as well.

"How long will I need to have the catheter?" Becky asked. "It makes me feel like an invalid."

"It's for you own convenience right now. You won't need to get up out of bed and try to walk to the bathroom. You'll probably have it for another day or two." The nurse closed down the computer and asked, "You need anything else?"

Becky just shook her head no. Elizabeth thanked the nurse as she left the room. Then she turned to Becky and said, "You were a little short with her. That's not like you."

"Maybe that's because I don't feel like me. Part of me just died." The room echoed with the words.

Elizabeth tried another tactic to get Becky's mind off her loss. "Have you ordered your supper yet? What are you going to have?"

"I ordered it, but I doubt I'll eat. I didn't eat lunch. I just don't feel hungry."

"Maybe not, but you should try to eat something. You need to build up your strength."

Becky shrugged. That put an end to the conversation. Elizabeth looked out the window. Becky's room was on the third floor and there was a pretty good view of the town below. Elizabeth watched traffic moving in the streets and people going about their business, totally unaware of the dramas unfolding all throughout the hospital. Elizabeth sighed and turned back to Becky.

"I guess Coop will come see you after he drops Jenny off at my place. So I better go. I need to get to the grocery store before they arrive." She bent to kiss her daughter on the cheek. "Try to get some rest honey. And eat a good supper."

As she waited for the elevator doors to open, Elizabeth prayed again. She smiled and thought. 'You sure are hearing from me a lot, Lord. I'm so glad you are always listening!'

The doors opened and several people stepped out. From the back of the elevator, a tall thin girl exited carrying a vase of purple flowers and a helium balloon that said "Get Well Soon" Elizabeth caught the door as it was about to close and held it open for the girl. The girl smiled and said, "Thank you so much. Have a nice day."

The girl checked the room number on the card and walked down the hall. Her black hair hung just to the collar of her volunteer uniform shirt. She walked with a slight limp.

CHAPTER 44

Sowing and Reaping

She knew who the delivery was for and she took a deep breath before knocking on the door. She whispered, "Lord, help me with the words." Sometimes, dropping off flowers for patients was quick and easy, but this delivery, well, it might be difficult. In fact, it could be down right uncomfortable. She tapped on the door and pushed it open. "Hi! I have a delivery for you. Where would you like me to put this?" She looked at the woman in the bed and was surprised to see how small and pale she looked.

Becky pointed to the window sill and said, "Over there I guess." The volunteer put the flowers down on the sill and arranged the balloon so it cleared the curtains.

"Is there a card? Who's it from?" Becky asked.

"Yes, there's a card." The girl took the envelope over to Becky who opened it and pulled out a beautiful hand made get well card. As she did so, a smaller inserted three by five note card fluttered out and skittered under the bed. "Oh, I'll get that for you," the volunteer said as she bent to recover the card. She held it while Becky opened and read the get-well card.

When Becky was done reading the card, the girl commented, "Oh my goodness, that's a beautiful card. Did somebody make it? I've sure never seen anything so pretty in the stores."

"Yes, my friend Nancy makes all occasion cards. They're really special." Becky sighed and gazed at the cheery card. Her heart relaxed a little as she fondly remembered her friend.

The volunteer smiled. She knew Nancy. And though she knew a lot about her, she didn't know she made unique cards like this. She would have to get some of these special cards to send to people. There were a few people in the hospital that didn't get visitors. A nice card might cheer them up. Maybe Chaplain Olsen could help her know who to give the cards to.

"Oh, here, this fell under the bed." The girl reached out her right arm to give the note card to Becky. Becky noticed a long flowery tattoo on the girl's arm and took a second glance. Something about that tattoo seemed familiar.

"Um, will you read that for me? I just had a pain pill and I'm getting really groggy." She rubbed her eyes and laid her arm across her forehead.

"Sure thing," said the girl. "You keep him in perfect peace whose mind is stayed on you, because he trusts in you. Isaiah 26:3." She looked at Becky and said, "That's a great verse. I think I'll try to memorize it. It could really help to remind me that God can get me through tough times." She nodded toward the cast on Becky's leg. "I had an accident and major trauma to my leg. Thought I might not ever walk again. But Jesus worked a miracle. First, he forgave me and healed my soul. Then he worked through the surgeons and therapists and my leg was healed. Well, almost, I still have some pain and walk with a little limp. But God is not done with me yet. I have peace. I know I can trust him, like that verse says."

Becky grumbled, "Yeah, well right now I'm not feeling much peace or trust."

"But wait, you're a believer, aren't you?" The girl already knew the answer. She knew a lot about this woman lying in the hospital bed. But she didn't let on. Now wasn't the time. "If you have Jesus as your savior, you know you can trust him to keep his promises. He said 'Come unto me, all you who are weary and burdened, and I will give you rest.' He will give you rest, Becky. He will. He did for me." Becky didn't respond so Melissa went on. "And you know, I bet if

237

you think back, you'll remember lots of times when he was with you, to carry your burdens. Just think back on those times, and thank him and be grateful. You'll get your joy back!"

The girl could see that Becky was drifting off to sleep, relaxed by the medication and maybe, hopefully, by the comforting words she had shared. As she walked toward the door, she thought, 'I really need to call Nancy tonight. She's been praying that I'd feel comfortable telling my testimony. I've got a lot to tell her. And when I tell her *who* I just talked with – my goodness, it's a small world.'

She paused at the door, turned and said, "I can see you're getting sleepy. I hope you can get a good nap this afternoon. And remember, Jesus hasn't left you. He's here to help you through all this." Becky's eyes were closed, but the girl thought she saw a little smile on her face.

Becky slept for a couple of hours, waking only when the evening shift nurse came in to take vitals. She felt much better after the rest, and was actually a little hungry.

She sat quietly in her room, looking at the flower bouquet her mother had set on the rolling table. Zinnias of yellow and red stood proudly among white chrysanthemums. The colors cheered her up. Purple irises brightened the window sill. She thought about her friendship with the Martins. They were good people.

As she leaned back against her pillow, Becky relaxed a little. Some of the tension of the past days was slightly lifting. "I know you're here, Lord," she prayed. "I know you haven't left me. You've helped me and comforted me so many times in the past. But God, this is hard. I feel so defeated, so frightened. I know I shouldn't be angry, but right now that's where I am. I'm just stuck in anger."

Becky reached for her cell phone, which was on the table. She went to her Bible app. and searched for a devotional plan. She passed over several suggestions before settling on a plan about anxiety. The verse that jumped out at her was Psalm 121:5 "Those who sow with tears will reap with songs of joy."

"Well, I've sure got the tears right now, Lord. And I don't feel like singing songs of joy. But I'll step out in faith, because I do believe you keep your promises." Her eyes filled with tears once again. As the tears trickled down her cheeks, Becky remembered something Nancy had taught her. It was a way of praying, a simple phrase repeated with every breath in and out. 'Breath Prayers,' she had called it. No particular words were necessary. Just a meaningful phrase. 'I guess I'll give it a try,' Becky thought.

"Jesus I am yours." She breathed out, whispering softly. "Jesus you are mine," she said as she inhaled. With the first phrase, Becky imagined standing before God in total surrender. She laid her arms out on the bed before her, palms up, releasing all the fear and anger that had filled her in the last few days. With the inhale, she felt God filling her, taking over her struggles, removing her doubts, carrying all her burdens. She repeated the phrases over and over. Her depression lifted and she felt the comfort of her loving Savior, drawing her close under the protective safety of his wings.

Out in the hallway, she could hear the food trays being taken into rooms. She adjusted her bed so she could sit a little upright and pulled the table over across her lap. She was ready to eat whenever the food arrived.

CHAPTER 45

---◆◆◆---

Bringing It Back to Romans

And arrive it did. The food service lady brought in a tray with the evening meal. Turkey, mashed potatoes, green beans and a Jell-O salad. It all smelled really good. Before she could unwrap her silver ware, Coop came into the room. He was carrying his own tray of food, purchased from the cafeteria. He sat the tray on the counter space and went to give Becky a kiss. He was relieved when she smiled at him and didn't turn away from his affection. He'd been praying that she would be in a calmer state of mind. Apparently, she was. Whatever caused the change, he was grateful.

Coop took Becky's hand and offered up a prayer, thanking God for the food and those who had prepared it. He also gave thanks for the doctors and nurses and the medications that were providing pain relief. When he said 'Amen' he squeezed Becky's hand, and she squeezed his back. They ate their supper together, enjoying each other's company and catching up on things around the farm.

"I know Holly misses you," Coop said. "Last night, she just wandered around the house like she was looking for you. When I told her you'd be gone for a few days, she went to your side of the bed and plopped down like she was pouting. When I left this afternoon to take Jenny to your mom's, Holly followed us to the truck and wanted to get in. Mom said she spent most of yesterday sitting at the front door, waiting for you to come home."

"I'll be glad to see her too. I have to thank her for being my hero. I think she is just the best, smartest dog I've ever known. I don't know how I could have managed without her help that day." *That day* was just yesterday. How could so much have happened in just one day's time?

Becky thoughts drifted back, and a darkness came over her. She'd been trying so hard to face this evening with a positive attitude, but she was slipping back into a depression. She shook it off and said to herself, 'No. I will not dwell on that. I will look to the future. My life is ahead of me, not behind.' It was going to be a constant battle, but she was determined to win, with God's help. She remembered her breath prayer. 'Jesus I am yours. Jesus you are mine.' She felt peace returning.

"And how's Jenny? Did you take her to moms?"

"I did. She was looking forward to Grandma's macaroni and cheese. Of course, *your* mom doesn't know that *my* mom made her macaroni and cheese for supper *last* night!"

"That girl! She does like her mac and cheese." Becky's thoughts drifted off and she whispered, "I wonder if Matthew Peter would have liked it too." Her voice caught slightly at the mention of the baby's name and she looked away. "Sorry," she said apologetically.

"You don't have to apologize, sweetie. It's perfectly natural to think about him, wonder about him. I've been doing that today too. We'll never forget about him. He will always be a part of our family."

Coop reached into a small paper sack he had brought in with him. "Here" he said. "Jenny made cookies with Dana this afternoon. She sent these to you." He pulled out a plastic sandwich bag, stuffed full with chocolate chip cookies.

"They smell good!" Becky said as she reached for one. "Tell her thanks."

"Why don't you call your mom tonight and talk to Jenny?" Coop suggested. "I know she'd love that."

Becky swallowed a bit of cookie and said thoughtfully, "I don't think I can talk to her yet. I need a little more time."

"Time, we have," said Coop encouragingly. "You'll know when you're ready." He decided to change the subject slightly. "How is your foot feeling? What did the doctor say about it today?"

"He was here for a minute this morning, but I was still pretty drugged. I don't really know what he said. I guess he'll be back tomorrow. I know I have to keep this catheter for a couple more days, because they don't think I'm ready to walk to the bathroom yet. And they're probably right about that, but man, it's annoying."

Coop chuckled. His old Becky was coming back to him.

"You just rest and do what they tell you. You'll be home and moving around soon enough." He took a second cookie from the bag and handed it to Becky. "These are really good! Between chocolate chip cookies and blueberry muffins, Jenny's a great little baker." He took another cookie for himself and said thoughtfully, "You seem to be in a little better mood. I know this loss has been hard on you. On all of us. But honey, we'll get through this. We're not alone. We have each other, and we have the Lord."

"I know that, I really do," said Becky. "But I feel like, oh, I don't know how to explain it. I feel like God is punishing me. Like maybe he planned for me to have one pregnancy, and I messed it up by having Jenny without a husband. Like I blew my one chance and now I have to live with the mistake I made."

"But Becky, you know God doesn't punish his children. He allows us to live with our choices, good or bad, but he doesn't punish us. He is a god of love, He *is* love. And he's going to love us through this."

"But I can't stop thinking that this is all my fault. Not just for the mistakes of my past, but I mean for how stupid I was yesterday." She took a big breath and shuddered in memory. "I mean, I should never have thought I could rope that cow and bring her up to the barn. I should have known that wouldn't end right. I acted impulsively, and ended up causing this disaster. I'm so sorry." Becky couldn't help herself. The tears were flowing now, and she couldn't stop. All her resolve to be positive had disappeared. Was she going to fight with these emotions forever? Ups and downs, like a roller coaster, but not as much fun.

"Don't you do that," Coop insisted. "You are not responsible for this. It was an accident. That's all. I mean, I've spent some self-pitying moments thinking it was all *my* fault. If I hadn't gone to that auction, I would have been home, and I would have been the one following Holly and taking care of the problem." He sighed and went on. "But remember that Romans verse? God doesn't condemn us. And we should not condemn ourselves."

Becky dabbed her eyes with the corner of her bed sheet. She took a deep breath and let it out slowly. "It comes back to that again, doesn't it?

"It does." Coop said. "That verse is applicable in so many circumstances." He put his arm around Becky's shoulder and pulled her close. "Mom reminded me of another verse today. Psalm 34:18, do you know it?"

"I'm not sure. I know there's a lot of comforting verses in Psalms. Do you have it memorized? Or do you want to look it up?"

"I've got it." Coop recited the verse. "The Lord is close to the brokenhearted and saves those who are crushed in spirit."

"Well, I sure do want Him close to me, and I need him to save me because I do feel crushed in spirit. It's a perfect verse. I'll try to focus on it. I know I can't stay in this dark place forever."

"Let's pray about it," Coop said and took her hands in his. "Lord Jesus, we are struggling. We are discouraged. We need you to come close, to heal our broken spirit, to save us from depression and despair. We do trust you and we are assured of your love for us. But we're hurting and sad. Please Lord, bring us back into joy. Lift us into your arms and hold us close. Comfort us, as only you, our creator, can do. We thank you and praise you, for you have already provided for our needs. You have been with us every step, and you will never leave us. Your love brings us comfort. And we will never stop loving you. Amen."

He squeezed Becky's hand and they sat alone in silence. Coop was breathing deeply and slowly and soon Becky realized that her own breathing was keeping pace with his. She snuggled against his chest and relaxed for the first time in days.

CHAPTER 46

Finding Closure

Coop and Becky were comforting each other when there was a tap on the door and Chaplain Olsen peaked in. "Hello friends, may I come in?"

Coop looked at Becky, who nodded. "Sure, come on in," he said and offered her the only chair in the room.

Chaplin Olsen waved him off saying "No, no, I don't need a seat." She looked at Becky and asked, "How are you doing today?"

Becky wiped her lips with a napkin and said, "Just had a great supper, topped off by chocolate chip cookies baked by our daughter. There's some left. Would you like one?"

"Chocolate chip is my favorite," she said. She really didn't need a cookie but knew that sharing food was often a great way to make people feel comfortable. She sat a package down on the foot of the bed, being careful not to jar Becky's leg. "Mmm, these are really good. Please congratulate the baker!"

"I will," said Coop. "She makes good muffins too. Pretty soon she'll be baking cakes and pies for all our special occasions."

The chaplain finished her cookie and reached for the package. "I've brought your memory box. It's been put together with prayer and love by some of the volunteers here at the hospital. It's a service we provide for grieving parents and we hope you will cherish it always." She handed the box to Becky and Coop came to stand near her.

Becky took the box and moved her hand lovingly across the top. It was a wooden box, with inlaid details along the edge of the lid. Across the top, carved in neat block letters, was the baby's name – Matthew Peter Smith - with yesterday's date.

Becky looked up at Coop, who nodded encouragingly. Slowly she lifted the lid. She took a hesitant breath before reaching in. Not sure she was ready for this, she took a moment to collect herself. She closed her eyes for a brief second, asking Jesus to be near her. This was hard.

Becky took out a small knitted hat, blue and soft. Their baby had worn it during the short time he had been with them. She held it to her face and inhaled the sweet baby smell that seemed to linger. Was that even possible? How long would it last? Tears welled up in Becky's eyes but she put the hat aside and looked deeper into the box.

There was a small lock of baby hair, captured in a thin blue ribbon. She rubbed it gently against her cheek, then laid it on top of the cap. She looked up at Coop, whose eyes were beginning to water. She handed the hat and lock of hair to Coop and he took them tenderly.

Becky reached into the box and removed a small white silk gown; the one Matthew had been dressed in after he had been cleaned up. "It's so beautiful," she said softly. "I guess I didn't really look at it closely before."

Chaplin Olsen smiled. "We have some wonderful women who make these baby gowns out of donated wedding gowns. They are a real blessing. We call them Angel Gowns." She reached out and touched the silky material. "If you choose to have a funeral service, you might want to dress him in this. Or if not, you can just keep it here in the memory box."

Becky turned to Coop. "I guess we have to decide what we want to do." Her voice was raspy with emotion. He took her hand and nodded. Becky squeezed his hand and said, "We'll talk about it later."

Becky carefully folded the gown and reached for the next item in the box. A tiny infant wrist band, with the hospital's name and doctor's name, came next. "So tiny," she whispered. She slipped the band over her little finger and it fit tightly. "His arms and legs were so tiny."

Fingerprints and foot prints were inked on a card. Again, she marveled at the smallness. Then she removed the official Death Certificate and handed it to Coop. "I can't look at this yet." He took it without comment.

A small photo album lay at the bottom of the box. Becky lifted it and hesitated before opening the cover to view the pictures.

"Many parents find it very comforting to have these photos," said Chaplain Olsen. "It helps bring closure and healing."

Coop took the album from her hands and held it out as he opened the book. The first picture was a close-up of Matthew's face, eyes closed, mouth slightly open. He was wearing the silky gown and looked like an angle. "He was beautiful," Coop said and Becky nodded. She couldn't bring herself to speak.

The next picture was one of Becky holding Matthew across her chest. Her lips rested on the top of his head and her eyes were shut like his. It was almost like she had been photographed praying over him. Maybe she had been.

There was a picture of Coop cradling the little bundle in his big strong arms. There was a picture of the two of them together, Becky holding the baby and Coop standing beside her, with the baby's hand grasping his finger. "I love this one," Becky said.

They looked through the book and then closed the cover reverently. They gently re-packed the box and Chaplain Olsen said, "You will need to decide what you want to do about a service. I'll be back tomorrow to go over the arrangements with you. But it's really whatever you want. The state requires either burial or cremation, but it's up to you. I'll help you with whatever you decide."

"Thank you for the memory box," said Coop. "We appreciate it."

"Yes, it's very special. Thank you. And please express our gratefulness to the volunteers who put it together. It's a real treasure."

"I will," said the chaplain. "I also want to tell you about a parents support group we have here at the hospital." She handed Becky a brochure and explained, "It's a PRIDE group. That stands for Parents Responding to Infant Death Experience. There are several options for meeting times and even an online zoom group you could attend. It's completely voluntary, of course, but we've found that the support of other parents going through the same things as you can be very helpful." She smiled at Becky and Coop. "Just think about it, and I can get you enrolled if you're interested."

Becky looked up and Coop and nodded. "I think it might be a good idea. Let's talk about it later." Coop smiled down at her, happy that things seemed to be headed in a positive direction.

"Now, before I leave, could I have prayer with you?" the chaplain asked.

"Of course," they answered in unison.

Chaplain Olsen took a book of prayers from her sweater pocket. She turned to a marked page and read. "Abba Father. We long to be with our dearly beloved child. Our hearts are heavy with sorrow, and our breath is shallow. Please carry us, for we are overwhelmed by the pain of our grief. Words cannot express the depths of our loss or the heartache we feel.

We know you are with our dearly loved son; your heart is overjoyed by him. His breath is new life in Heaven. Please come and nurture our precious one. Thank you for the hope of eternal life that he has now received.

Lord, you will keep him safe until we meet. We entrust him into your care now.

And now dear father, I ask that you encircle my dear friends in their grief. Cocoon them within your arms of love, whisper heavenly truths into their souls, and keep each fragment of their broken hearts safe.

May they come to know that their beloved child is safe with you. Not lost, but found, known and cherished. Amen."

"That was lovely," Becky said. "Could you make a copy of that prayer? I'd like to keep it in the memory box."

"Certainly," said Chaplain Olsen. "I'll have it ready for you tomorrow."

"Thanks again," said Coop as the chaplain turned to leave. He walked with her to the door. "Becky and I will talk about the arrangements and have a decision for you tomorrow. Goodnight."

When Coop looked back at the bed, Becky was holding the memory box close to her heart. Tears were streaming down her face. His heart broke. He went and sat on the bed, careful not to disturb her leg or jostle her in any way. He didn't know what to say, so he just sat. Minutes passed and he watched as her shoulders sagged and her grip on the box relaxed. Eventually she looked up at him and said, "I'm so sorry. I know how much you wanted this baby. You wanted a son. And now he's gone."

"Becky," he said soothingly, "Becky, my love, yes, I did want a son. And I still hope to get one some day. I'm grieving like you are, only a little differently. But honey, the Lord is good. He will supply all our needs. We need to put this all in his capable hands. We may not understand the mystery of his ways. But we can trust that his ways are perfect. I love you. I hate to see you cry. But I do understand. And I'm here for you."

She leaned her head against his chest and sighed deeply. The tears dried on her face, tiny almost invisible streaks of saltiness left on her cheeks. He kissed one cheek, then the other, then sought her mouth. For the first time since the accident, she felt like kissing him back. She was safe in his arms. He was her strength. He loved her despite what had happened. And slowly it dawned on Becky that the characteristics she was accrediting to Coop also applied to her Heavenly Father. It brought her a comfort she could barely endure. The tears that fell now were ones of praise and gratefulness. Maybe she would eventually be able to sing songs of joy, after all.

They sat cuddled together, with the memory box between them, and rested in the assurance of their love for each other and God's unfailing love for them. A sense of peace settled around them. They sat that way, wrapped in each other's arms, drawing strength from each other and their trust in their Savior. Becky pictured Jesus, surrounded by little children like in a picture she had seen often with the verse "Bring the little children unto me." And she pictured Matthew, perfect in every way, sitting on his lap, smiling at Jesus with great joy. Becky's eyes imagined an even bigger smile on Jesus' face, and he gazed upon their little boy with an intense love that make Becky's heart swell. Her baby was in good hands.

Later that evening, after they had discussed and decided on cremation, Coop left for home. The nurses came in to give her pain meds and take her vitals and Becky settled into her bed to try and get to sleep. She was tired of lying on her back but because of her leg being elevated, she had to. Soft voices in the hallway began to lull her to sleep. In the dim light of the room, a reflection caught on the Mylar of the balloon bouncing gently near the window.

'I forgot to show Coop the card and flowers from Nancy and Greg' she thought. She recalled the events and conversations of the day. She pictured that girl, the volunteer who brought the flowers. There was something familiar about her. She was really tall. And thin. And the black hair, well, lots of women have black hair. But that tattoo. That was very unique. Becky was pretty sure she had seen it before.

Becky's evening pain medicine had kicked in and she fell asleep. Her subconscious dealt with the haunting vision of the tall girl with the flowery tattoo. In Becky's dream, she saw the girl, wearing short shorts, riding a motorcycle and wearing a black cowboy hat. Coop's hat.

Becky's eyes flew open. All the pieces fit into place. She knew who the girl was. And she was completely surprised to see her here. Yet even more surprising was the way she talked about her Savior. Was it possible for someone to change so completely, so suddenly? Becky thought, 'Could it be real? Or some other trick she's pulling to get what she wants?'

Nancy had told her about the girl's conversion and baptism. But it had been easy to put all that in the back of her mind and not really think about it. Now here it was, right in front of her. The girl was real, the past brought up, old emotions stirred. Becky was surprised as jealousy, anger, disgust and doubt rolled over her. She didn't like this girl; she had put Coop through unthinkable danger. How could she really forgive and forget that? Becky noticed that her hands were clenched into fists. She was aware of tension all throughout her body. Could this girl be trusted? Becky signed and tried to relax.

Nancy seemed to believe it was genuine. And maybe it was. This girl, Melissa, did seem to know the right words to say. But was it real? Or maybe just an act?

'Old things are passed away, behold all things have become new.' The verse popped into her mind. She fell back to sleep, repeating the verse.

CHAPTER 47

———◆◆◆———

Nurse's Aid

Early the next morning, even before breakfast arrived, there came a tentative tapping on Becky's door. A woman's head peeked hesitantly into the room and whispered, "Becky, are you awake?"

Becky turned her head to look towards the door. "Yes, I'm awake." She was surprised when Nurse Carole walked into the room. She was wearing light blue hospital scrubs and had her hair pulled back and, like most nurses Becky had met, she was smiling.

"I came in early today to see how you're doing. My shift starts in fifteen minutes, but I wanted to see you first."

"Oh hi, Carole. That's so nice of you." Becky grabbed the controls and adjusted her bed so she could sit up a little. "I'm doing okay. Slept pretty good, so that helps."

Carole moved closer to the bed. "I don't know if you remember, but I was working in the ER when you came in the other day."

"I do remember. It's kind of a blur, but I remember your smile and your kindness. That was a difficult day. It was nice to see a familiar face, even though I didn't really recognize you at the time. Coop reminded me that you go to our church. I knew I'd seen you somewhere before!"

"I'm sorry to hear about the baby, honey. You know, there are lots of people at church praying for you. We want you to know that

251

if there's anything you need, you just let me know and I'll see what I can arrange. Food brought in, cleaning help, or just some company. You call me. Number is in the church directory."

"Thank you, Carole, that's so nice of you. I don't know yet when I'll be going home, but I'll probably need a little help at first. What with the cesarean, and then having to deal with this huge cast, I suppose a little help would be nice.

"I know you have family nearby to help, but don't forget that your church family is here for you too." She patted Becky's hand. "Your name is on the prayer chain and lots of us have been praying for you."

Becky looked Carole in the eye, smiled sincerely, and said, "Thank you. I can honestly say I have felt your prayers. It's been hard, but I've felt Jesus right beside me."

"Holding you by his mighty right hand," Carole added. "Is there anything I can do for you right now?"

"Well, actually, there is something I need," Becky said. "There's a girl, a volunteer. I'm pretty sure her name is Melissa and she might be in the gift shop. Could you get a note to her? I'd like to talk with her."

Carole nodded, "I think I know who you mean. Real tall skinny girl? Walks with a limp?" She went on as Becky nodded. "Yes, she does work out of the gift shop. I'll stop by there on my way to the ER and leave her a message to come see you." After a brief prayer, Carole left.

Becky sat back onto her pillows and whispered, "Dear God. Give me words. Give me wisdom. Help me discern the truth."

CHAPTER 48

———◆◆◆———

Visiting Hours

Jenny waited in her grandma's kitchen, watching out the window for Daddy Coop. He was going to pick her up and take her to the hospital to visit her mommy. Other than face-time calls, she hadn't seen her mom in over a week. It had been fun at first, staying at Grandma Emerson's house. They had made cookies and done jigsaw puzzles. They had gone hiking and fishing at the lake. They had gone to a movie theater in Atkins and had lasagna for supper at Olive Garden. It was a special time for the two of them, but Jenny was anxious to see her mother and get back home, where she could play with Holly and Muffin and Oreo, and maybe Daddy Coop would let her ride Benny around the barnyard.

Every night, at prayer time, Grandma had encouraged her to pray for the healing of Becky's leg. As far as Jenny knew, her mother's broken leg was the reason for the hospital stay. Becky and Coop wanted to tell her about the baby together. That was the reason Coop was coming to take her to the hospital. They had prayed that the Lord would give them the words, help with the explanation, and comfort Jenny's heart as he had brought comfort to them. How do you explain a miscarriage to a six-year-old?

Coop pulled up to the house and Jenny met him at the door. She had made a card for her mother, covered with hearts and flowers and butterflies. As she showed it proudly to Coop, he glanced up at Elizabeth and she gave him a comforting smile. She made a sign with her hands as if praying, and he understood her meaning. Lots of people were praying.

The drive to the hospital took half an hour. Jenny talked the whole time. Coop was grateful for her excitement, as it meant he had less chance to say the wrong thing. He did tell her that Becky's leg was elevated and in a big cast, and that she needed to be careful when she sat on the bed. "And no jumping on the bed, of course!" he said, and Jenny laughed.

Coop listened as Jenny talked about wanting to get home to the farm. She said she missed her animal friends. She wanted to play with Oreo and give Benny a carrot. She wanted to see how Tinkerbell was doing with his broken leg. And she had a new trick to teach Holly. On and on she chattered, until they finally arrived at the hospital.

Inside, the sterile halls and quiet atmosphere subdued her somewhat. She held Coop's hand in the elevator and stared at the floor numbers as they went up to the third floor. When the doors opened and Coop led the way to Becky's room, Jenny looked around and took it all in. At the nurse's station, one of the nurses said, "So this must be Jenny! Your mother told me you were coming to visit today."

Jenny smiled politely and said, "I made mommy a card. It has hearts on it, because I love her."

The nurse said, "That was very sweet of you. I'm sure she's going to love it."

Coop nodded and said, "Let's go find her. She's in room 318. Think you can find it yourself, Jenny?" He showed her the numbered directional signs on the wall and she figured out which way to go. Soon they were standing outside Becky's door.

Coop pushed the door open slowly and Jenny went inside.

CHAPTER 49

——◆◆◆——

Truth Be Told

"Jenny!" exclaimed Becky, with a big smile on her face. "I'm so happy to see you. I've missed you so much!"

"I missed you too, mommy! I made you this." Jenny handed the heart card to her mother. She stood to the side, looking at the cast on her mother's leg.

Becky took the card, looked at it and said, "Come give me a hug."

"I don't want to hurt your leg." Jenny was hesitant but took a step closer.

"A hug won't hurt my leg! In fact, it will make me feel so much better." Becky spread her arms wide and Jenny walked right in. The hug lasted a long time, and when they finally parted, Becky had tears in her eyes.

"Why are you crying, mommy?" ask Jenny when she stepped back and looked at her mom's face. "I didn't hurt you, did I?"

"No honey. I'm crying because I missed you so much, and hugging you feels so good."

Coop put his hands on Jenny's shoulders. "You won't hurt her unless you jump on the bed, or pull on her leg. See the big cast?" He pulled the blanket off Becky's leg to expose the cast, which covered her entire foot and went up to her knee.

"Can you walk mommy? When can you come home? I want to go back to the farm and be a family again."

"I'm learning how to walk with this cast, but mostly I get to use this rolling cart to hold my leg so I don't put weight on my foot." She pointed to the apparatus sitting under the window. "When I get back home, I'll have to take it easy for a month or so. Pretty soon they will make the cast smaller, and then give me a boot and eventually I'll be fine."

"Eventually?" asked Jenny. "How soon is eventually?"

"I don't know for sure honey. It will be a while. I won't be able to walk and run and do everything normally for a long time. Maybe when you start school. Or maybe Thanksgiving time. We'll just have to wait and see."

"I'll help you, Mommy. I can set the table, and carry the food to the table. And I can put the dishes in the dishwasher. You can rest. I'll do everything."

"Thank you, Jenny. I know you'll be a big help. And before the summer is over, I'll be much better. When you go to first grade, I should be able to walk you to your class the first day." She stopped and looked at Coop. He nodded, knowing what was coming next.

"Jenny, I have to tell you something." Becky paused to gather her thoughts. "Jenny, when I fell off the horse and hurt my foot, something else happened. I'm sorry to say that the baby inside me got hurt too. Really bad. And he was hurt so bad, he died. I'm so sorry honey, but we won't be having a baby brother for you."

"The baby got hurt? Couldn't the doctor fix him?"

"No, I'm sorry honey. He was hurt too bad. There was nothing the doctor could do."

"So I won't get a sibling?" Jenny looked sad and puzzled at the same time.

"Well, maybe sometime in the future, but not soon. We have to wait for my body to heal, and then maybe God will bless us with another baby. But we don't know God's plan, and we will just have to wait and see what happens. This baby, your brother, is with Jesus now. And he'll be waiting up in heaven for all of us to come and find him someday." Becky took a deep breath and asked, "Would you like to see pictures of him?" Jenny quietly nodded her head. Coop reached for the memory box and opened it reverently. "We have this little box with some precious memories. The people at the hospital took some pictures for us. Here, this is your brother Matthew Peter." He handed Jenny a picture of the baby.

"Hello, Matthew Peter. I'm Jennifer Hope. I love you." She had tears in her eyes. "He looks so tiny. Like a little tiny baby kitten."

"He was very tiny. Just fit in the palm of my hand." Coop held out his hand to demonstrate. He took the picture and put it back in the box. "We'll take this box home with us, and we will put it somewhere special. Matthew will always be a part of our family. And maybe someday we will get another chance to give you a brother or a sister.

But for now, we'll go home and get your mommy all better, and we will keep on loving our little family. And we'll never forget that God's plans are good, and better than we can understand right now."

Becky added, "Sometimes we go through hard times, things that we don't understand, but God is always with us, whatever comes our way. And he'll never leave us alone in the hard times. He's always with us. And believe it or not, we can rejoice, even in the hard times, because we know our faith can grow through it."

"So Matthew Peter is in heaven with Jesus? And with your daddy?" Jenny looked at Coop as he returned the picture to the memory box.

Coop knelt down beside her and took her in his arms. "That's right, Jenny. And your mommy and I can go there too, because we have asked Jesus to come into our hearts. We know Jesus has forgiven our sins and promised us a forever home in heaven."

"I want to go to heaven too. I want to be with you all forever. I want to see Jesus there."

Becky asked, "Would you like to ask Jesus to come into your heart?" Jenny nodded her head with determination. Becky smiled through her tears and said, "Daddy Coop and I will help you pray."

"You need to tell Jesus you are sorry for your sins and ask him to forgive you and come live in your heart. Can you do that, or do you want me to say it, and you can copy me?" Coop had led others to Christ before, but never a child, and never with such a lump in his throat. This was such a special moment.

"I can do it." Jenny said and immediately bowed her head. "Dear God, I have done sins and lots of bad things. I am sorry. I wish I never did those things, and I don't ever want to do them again. I hope you can forgive me, and then help me be a good girl. And I can't wait to see you and my brother in heaven so we can all be a family. Amen." She looked up to see both her mother and Daddy Coop beaming with joy.

Becky was overcome with a sense of the presence of Jesus in the room. She couldn't help but think that, through the tragedy of the loss of her baby, there was now rejoicing in heaven as one more child came to the foot of the cross. Jennifer Hope was now a redeemed child of God. Like the verses in Romans said, tribulation had ultimately led to hope. Her heart was full. She knew without a doubt that God himself was with them and would always be with them.

Becky had a sudden urge to sing. It was an old song she remembered from her early years of Sunday school. She began softly, "My Jesus, I love thee, I know thou are mine." Coop smiled and joined his voice with hers. "For thee all the follies of sin I resign."

Coop gathered Jenny onto his lab as he and Becky continued to song. "My gracious redeemer, my Savior art thou. If ever I loved thee, my Jesus is now." Coop reached for Becky's hand and they repeated the final words. "If ever I loved thee, my Jesus is now."

With complete contentment, Becky squeezed Coop's hand. Jenny snuggled against Coop's chest and sighed, "I love Jesus too!"

CHAPTER 50

◆—◆◆—◆

Reconciliation

Becky napped until late afternoon. Her therapy sessions had worn her out. Learning how to maneuver with her foot in a long cast was tiring. She was frustrated with the slowness of her recovery, and knew that there was a long road ahead.

As she slowly roused from sleep, she let her thought drift. 'What next?' she wondered. 'I know my leg will heal. I'll work hard in therapy, and I'll be okay. And even if I'm not completely back to normal, I'm sure I can cope. It might slow me down but I won't let it stop me from doing the best I can for my family.' Her orthopedic surgeon, Dr. Scott, had been optimistic about her recovery, and Becky was hopeful.

And Dr. Rosencrantz was also reassuring. He said her reproductive system should heal completely and she'd be perfectly fine in just a short time. The cesarean scar was healing already, and she'd just have to rest and take it easy for a couple of months. 'That's not going to be a problem, considering my leg.' Becky shrugged and smiled. 'No lifting and no strenuous exercise. Fine by me, for now.'

'And at least he says I'll be able to have more children.' She remembered Coop's sign of relief when he'd heard that. She took a deep breath and whispered, "God is good." She exhaled and said,

"All the time." She repeated the breath prayer until she heard a gentle tapping at her door.

"Come on in." Becky said, straining her head to see who was there.

It was Melissa. She entered hesitantly. "Hi Becky. I got a message that you wanted to see me?" It was more a question than a statement. She wasn't sure what Becky might have in mind.

"Oh good. Yes, I was hoping you would be able to stop by before I get discharged." She pointed to the chair. "Sit down, would you please? I just want to talk to you. Come close."

Melissa pulled the chair to the side of the bed and sat facing Becky. "So you'll be going home soon? That's great."

Becky nodded yes. "Probably the day after tomorrow. And I'm ready. Everybody here has been great, but I need to be home."

Melissa sat quietly, holding her hands in her lap so she wouldn't fidget. She was a little confused about why she was here. "I'm glad you're getting better," she said. She couldn't think of anything else to say.

Becky looked intently at Melissa and leaned forward. "I've heard from Nancy that you've become a Christian, and I wanted to talk with you about it, if that's okay with you?"

Melissa immediately relaxed. "Sure," she said eagerly. "I'd love to talk with you about my salvation, and my growing love for Jesus."

What unfolded was a comfortable conversation between two believers. Melissa spoke of her vision of hell and how she had learned, from Nancy, Pastor Green, and Chaplain Olsen, about God's gift of eternal life, offered through the death of Jesus on the cross. She told Becky that she had prayed asking forgiveness for her sins, and knew that her heart now belonged to Jesus. "And I want to ask your forgiveness, too, Becky. I know I caused all kinds of trouble for Coop, and I'm sorry for it. And sorry I involved you and your little girl too. Can you ever forgive me?"

Becky sensed Melissa's sincerity. She'd been reassured; Melissa really had changed. Becky trusted her and reached for her hand. "God sure has worked a miracle in your life. You seem to have left that old life behind you. And yes, I can forgive you. Jesus is working on my heart too. I want to be Christ-like in every way. I can't hold grudges. Jesus forgave you, and I forgive you too."

"Thank you! God is good!"

"All the time," Becky added and they both smiled.

"Hey, can I tell you about what I was reading this morning? Nancy gave me this little book." Melissa reached into her smock pocket. "It's got a verse for every day, and then a couple sentences to explain what it means."

"A devotional," Becky said.

"Yes, that's what Nancy called it." She found the page and read, "But Jesus, turning and seeing her, said, "Take courage daughter." That's Matthew 9:22.

"I think that's from the story of the woman who touched Jesus' robe and was healed."

"Right. And that's cool. She just knew Jesus had this amazing power. But what really got me was the word seeing. It hit me. Jesus sees me. He saw all the terrible thing I used to do. But he still loved me enough to help me. He died for me, even though he saw all the bad I'd done. He sees me. He is a God who sees. And he sees how I'm trying to live for him now. And it's not easy. But he says he'll give me courage. I just love that!"

Becky sat in amazement. Here was this woman who had a life so different from her own, yet they had a common bond. Jesus Christ, who died for all, regardless of their pasts. They both had been redeemed and loved, changed from the old nature into the image of Christ.

Tears came to Becky's eyes and Melissa reached for the tissue box, getting one for herself as well. They each dabbed at their eyes and chuckled. "I'm so glad we had this chance to talk," Melissa said. "When I came in the other day, I wasn't sure you knew who I was. And you weren't really in any condition to get into a deep conversation. I didn't really know what to say, anyway."

"It took a while for me to remember where I'd seen you. Then I remembered seeing your arm tattoo in the pictures." She cast her eyes down onto Melissa's arm, which was covered with the long sleeves of her smock.

"I'm so sorry about those pictures. You do know it was all fake, right? Coop wasn't awake. He had no part in that."

"Oh, yes, I know. I was upset at first, but then I just knew that Coop was not that kind of man. You drugged him, and he was not a willing participant. And that's all in the past now. Forgiven and forgotten."

"I'm so glad you feel that way. And I'm glad we can move past it. I mean, we might not be best friends in the future. We each have our own lives and other friends and I wouldn't imagine you and Coop would ever want to hang with me much for just fun. But at least now I think I won't be filled with guilt and self-loathing every time I see your family. We can move on without fear of running into each other. That's good."

"It is good," Becky agreed. "But let's not totally discredit the friendship possibility. Jesus is a miracle worker, you know!"

"You're right about that," Melissa said as she stood. "I need to get going now. Your supper's coming soon. And I have a date for pizza." She turned at the door. "Thanks Becky. This has been good."

"Very" said Becky. "Bye Melissa. See you around."

Later that evening, Melissa sat cross-legged on Craig's sofa, pizza in hand. She told him about her conversation with Becky. She was animated and joyful. Craig recognized a peace as she spoke. She was glowing with happiness and kept repeating, "God is so good. He sees me and he still loves me and forgives me. He is *so* good!"

After driving her home, Craig sat in his car and thought about the evening. 'Maybe there really is something to this salvation stuff. She sure believes it. And look at how she's changed. Guess I better think about this some more.' Then, totally out of character, he said out loud, "God if you are really real, you're gonna have to make it clear to me."

As he headed back to Catonsville, he rounded a curve and drove over a little hill. Before him, a full moon was rising over the tree tops. It was a spectacular sight. An orange ball of moonlight was glowing right in front of him. It was almost as if he could reach out and touch it. "Wow!" he said. "Wow!" He pulled his car off to the shoulder and sat there, staring at the amazing view. He was overwhelmed by the magnitude and beauty of the sight. He'd never thought of it before, but maybe this world had been created by a God. A God who saw him and loved him and wanted to forgive his sins. "Oh man, what's happening here?" he questioned out loud. "All these thoughts about God. Maybe Melissa is getting to me." He paused and thought a bit more. "Maybe her God is getting to me." He shook his head and shrugged his shoulders, as if trying to dislodge the thought from his mind. It didn't work.

CHAPTER 51

Swallows and Signs

Dana walked in from the barn, with Holly close behind her. They had been checking on the sheep and especially looking over little Tinkerbell. Doc Larson had been out to cast the lamb's broken leg and Dana was happy to see that the little guy was up and moving. He was nursing well and showing signs of improvement. Dana breathed a prayer of thankfulness, then stopped and turned abruptly back to the barn. Holly looked confused but turned and walked with her toward the barn.

"You stay outside," Dana said to the collie. "I'm going up to the haymow and you can't come. Go find Jenny. She'll play fetch with you." Holly sat and tilted her head with an expression that indicated she was trying to understand. "Go find Jenny," Dana repeated. She rubbed the dog's head and Holly took off on a run.

Dana climbed the ladder to the haymow and found a bale to sit on. As she settled in and got comfortable, Dana looked up to the rafters and saw that a couple of barn swallows had built a nest in the corner. There was a flutter of movement and some cheeping noises when an adult flew in to feed the babies. Dana watched as the parent fed the chicks and then settled herself down to cover them all with her wings.

With a sigh, Dana closed her eyes. She let the silence enfold her as the barn smells comforted her and brought her peace. 'Coop says this is a good place to pray.' she thought. She let her mind wander a little. She thought about her brother and his wife. She prayed briefly for them, and for little Jenny too. This was a difficult time for them and Dana couldn't imagine the pain. But she told God she trusted his wisdom, and asked him to show her how to comfort and help them. Then she thought about the neighbors, the Hennesseys, who were getting ready to move into the senior living place in Atkins. Aging and ailing, they were nice people facing many changes. Dana prayed for them too, and threw in a prayer for her mother as well, and even Becky's mother Elizabeth. Both were getting up in age, and slowing down. Dana wondered what her life would be like when she reached their age.

"And now for the real reason for this prayer time," she said and took a deep breath. "I need direction, Lord. It's time to figure out what I want to do with my life. I need to decide about college, a career, a purpose. And then, there's the issue of a husband. God, I know I can put it all into your hands. And I know you have a plan for my life. And I know you love me and will lead me. But God, I just don't *see* your hand or *feel* your presence or *hear* your voice. I mean, I know you're here, and I really do trust you. But I've never really heard you, even when I ask you to speak and make your way clear. Why can't I hear you? Why do others know without a doubt when you are giving them directions, but I never do? I'm just so confused."

Dana paused and sat quietly. She leaned back against the stack of hay bales and let her gaze fall on the swallow's nest. The adult in the nest raised its head and soon took off and flew out of the barn. Within seconds, another adult flew in with food for the hungry babies. After the excitement of his arrival, he settled down and covered the young with his wings. Dana marveled at the smooth cooperation and teamwork between the parents. Her mind wandered back to her younger years and remembered observing teamwork between her parents.

Mom was always supportive of dad's farming endeavors; fixing meals for the hired help, assisting with emergency calving and bottle feeding the young when needed. Even in his later years, after Coop had taken over more strenuous farm work, their dad would help mom with gardening and canning when he could. They were a team. And not just with the work. Mom and Dad had shared in the fun too. Horseback riding as a family, swimming and fishing together in the farm pond, and venturing out to national parks for overnight camping trips – they did it all as a team.

And they had shared child rearing responsibilities, too. Dad had been the spiritual leader of the family, with family devotions every evening and prayers at bedtime. But mom had shown the children the softer side of Jesus' love. With a heart for missions and outreach, Mom was always looking for ways to help those in need. She had demonstrated the hands and feet of Jesus. Dana's mom had led many to Christ by her loving and caring example. People were drawn to her compassionate nature, and soon learned that Jesus was the source of her joy and peace.

"That's what I want too, Lord. I want to be on a team, where we are both focused on working together, doing your will, helping others, showing the path to eternal life. Please God, show me the way. I wish I had a clear vision of how to reach that goal." Dana sighed and paused a moment. "But for now, I guess I'll just go about being me, doing what I do, and waiting for a sign of some sort. Help me be patient!" Dana stood and made her way to the ladder. She took another glance at the nest in the corner and saw that everyone seemed comfortably settled. The babies were quiet, resting under the wings of the loving and protecting parent. They didn't have a worry in the world.

Holly was resting in the barnyard and stood up when Dana came out of the barn. With her tail up, she trotted over to Dana and barked a welcome. "I told you I'd be back," Dana chuckled, leaning down to rub her hand down the collie's back. "You're such a good girl, to wait for me. Did Jenny play with you?" Holly barked and ran to get the ball that was lying in the grass near the porch steps.

"Oh okay, I'll throw it a few times, but then we have to get ready. I want to give you a good brushing before your family comes home." They played fetch for a few minutes, Holly's long hair flowing gracefully as she ran chasing the ball. Dana threw the ball again and told Holly, "Last time girl. We've got stuff to do."

Before she could go to the porch and find Holly's brush, her cell phone rang. The ring tone told her immediately who was calling – Tucker. She smiled as she pushed the 'accept' button and said hello.

"Hi Dana." His voice was deep and had a bit of a southern drawl, which Dana found delightful. She had often wondered where the drawl came from. Certainly not his father. Dana had met Todd Davis, and there wasn't a hint of southern to his voice. Maybe Tucker got it from his mother. Dana hadn't met her yet. Didn't even know her name.

"Hi Tucker! What's up?"

"Well, I was just thinking about you and thought I'd call and see how things are going at your place."

Dana caught her breath in a quick inhale and said, "You were thinking about me? Really?"

"Yeah, well, I was walking out by the corn crib, and I nearly got my head cut off by a bird dive-bombing me."

"And that made you think of me?" Dana questioned laughingly. "I don't know how I feel about that. I hope you don't think I'd ever cut your head off."

"No, no, not that. It's just that, well, this is kinda silly." Tucker hesitated. He was feeling a little embarrassed. "Maybe I better explain." He took a deep breath. "See, the birds, I think they were barn swallows, had a nest in the rafters of the corn crib, and when I walked too close, they got upset and started flying at my head to scare me off. So I moved away and sat down on an old wagon and just watched them. There was a mom and a dad, and they took turns feeding the nest-full of babies. It was just so peaceful and perfect, I just thought, 'Call Dana and tell her about this.' So I did."

Dana stopped in her tracks and sat down on the top step of the big house. "You're kidding. You'll never believe this. I was up in the haymow this afternoon, and saw a barn swallow nest, and watched the parents come and go and feed the babies. I sat watching them, and praying about stuff, for about half an hour. Maybe it was at the same time you were watching your birds. Isn't that something?"

"It sure is. Maybe it's a sign or something."

Dana was stunned. A sign! Hadn't she just been asking God for a sign? Was he trying to tell her something? Could this have a deeper meaning than just a coincidence of nature?

They talked on and on, but Dana never got over the feeling that something very special had just happened.

Looking across the yard, Dana saw her mother and Marilyn Hennessey coming out of Coop and Becky's house. Marilyn took the porch steps slowly, holding to the rail for security. Marla Jean walked casually along beside her, ready to offer support if needed. Marilyn's gray head was bent to watch her faltering footsteps.

Dana waved at the older women and they waved back. "Hey, Tucker, I need to go. We're getting ready for Coop and Becky to come home from the hospital. They should be here pretty soon, and I've got some things to do to get ready."

They said their goodbyes, and Tucker said he'd call her again in a day or two, to see how things were going with the family. "I've been prayin for y'all," he said before he hung up, and Dana got a warm fuzzy feeling. She put her phone away, grabbed the brush, and started working on Holly's thick coat.

The older women had been cleaning at the new house, getting ready for the family's return. They knew it would be hard for Becky to do much when she got home from the hospital because she was still pretty immobile. They wanted to make everything as easy for Becky as possible. The two had worked hard to have the housework done, and now Marilyn's back was bent and Marla Jean was feeling a strain in her knees. "You know what they say," said Marilyn.

Marla Jean looked over and asked, "What?"

"They say aging is not a job for sissies!" Marilyn laughed.

"They also say aging is a privilege not granted to all," Marla Jean put it. "I guess we should just count our blessings and take one day at a time." Marilyn chuckled and nodded in agreement.

Coop had already dismantled the nursery and turned it back into a guest room. The crib was returned to the attic. The old double bed was set up, and clean linens put on. The baby blue curtains with animal characters had been removed from the window and folded neatly, packed away with baby clothes and diapers waiting for the day when, hopefully, they would once again be placed back into the nursery. Until then, they would stay in the attic with the crib and rocking chair.

Marla Jean looked over at her daughter, who was brushing Holly. Jenny was with her now, holding Holly's head still as Dana worked on a particularly tangled area. Marla Jean marveled at the dog who had fit so naturally into their family. She was thankful for the collie's devotion and understanding. Without it, who knows how long Becky would have lain in the pasture. 'Thank you, Lord, for bringing Holly to our family. May she always watch over her people,' she prayed in her thoughts. 'And Lord, again I ask for your touch on Becky and Coop. Give them peace and help them trust in you to comfort them through this hard time.'

Marilyn seemed to read Marla Jean's mind. "May God bless the young people as they start again to build a family in this house. Amen."

Marla Jean looked again at her daughter. Dana had stopped her grooming, and was gazing off down the road. "Here they come," she called out. Coop's truck was making its way slowly down the dirt road. As it turned into the driveway Jenny stood waving wildly while Holly jumped up and ran barking excitedly, happy to have her family back home.

CHAPTER 52

—◆◆◆—

A Fall of New Beginnings

The air was crisp with the fragrances of fall. Corn fields were ripening and drying. The stalks were yellowing and almost ready to harvest. Coop and his hired hands had cut and baled the hay and filled the haymow with fresh bales, with more bales stacked in the storage shed. It was a good yield. It had been a good year on the farm, despite a few setbacks along the way. His family was safe and healthy, with a promising outlook for the future. As he drove toward town, he listened to the chatter between his wife and daughter. Yes, his daughter. The paperwork had come in the mail. Just this week, the three of them had met with the judge at the Atkins courthouse. Jenny was now officially his daughter.

Coop pulled the truck up under the church portico to drop off Becky and Jenny. Becky was still using a cane to help her walk, but was doing much better. A few more weeks of therapy and she would be free. One day at a time, that was their motto now. And each day showed improvement and brought hope for the future. He smiled to himself. The future was looking bright, in so many ways.

He parked the truck, gathered his Bible and other Sunday school materials, and prayed. 'God, I thank you for each new day. I thank you for this opportunity to open your word and share with others. I pray that you will use my words and they will be pleasing to you.' He looked across the parking lot and smiled as he watched Jenny pull the door open and hold it for her mother. 'And thank you, once again, for my family. You've been with us through so much. And I know you'll continue to protect and lead us. All of us.'

Coop was thankful for the progress Becky had made, both in her physical therapy and her mental state. The days of anger and regret were well past them, and although there were times of sadness and weeping, he knew that was normal and understandable. He had those moments, too. They would never forget the little boy that didn't get to grow up in their home. But the grief that had at first consumed Becky was part of the healing process. It hadn't been easy, but day by day, with the Lord's help, they were working through it.

Coop was also thankful for the good report from Dr. Rosencrantz, Becky's OB/GYN. She had been released from his care, for now. Her internal organs had healed and she was cleared for normal activities. "That includes resuming intercourse," he had said, with a wink in Coop's direction. And resume they had, cautiously at first, but with a newfound wonder and complete enjoyment. Coop smiled at the memory. Just last night they had shared an intimacy that they had been missing for months. First advanced pregnancy, then the accident had interrupted their love making. But last night, well, last night made up for all the lost time.

'Oh God, I do love that woman. Thank you for every day you have given us together. Thank you for healing her. I praise you for blessing me with Becky as my wife. I can't thank you enough.' Coop's mind was focused on praise, and he was overcome with joy.

He crossed the church parking lot with a smile on his face, radiating peace. Greg Martin met him at the door and noticed his demeanor. He looked confident and prepared. "You ready for this? I've been praying for you."

"Oh sure, I'm ready. I'm all prayed up! I'll just let God lead as he will. I'm just the facilitator. My prayer has been that the Lord will enter me, and my words will be his."

The young adult class had grown steadily in the past year, and had now been divided into two classes. Coop and Becky would be leading the married young adult class. Greg and Nancy would be assistant teachers. Dave Cole would still be teaching the class of single young adults. Today was the first time the classes had been split.

Today was also the first day of Jenny's first grade Sunday school class, but she walked confidently down the hall to her classroom. It was a new class, with a new teacher, but most of her classmates were her friends and she wasn't the least bit concerned about the change of classrooms. Becky walked slowly beside her daughter, and Coop quickly caught up with them.

As they got to the children's wing and registered at the front desk, Jill Hawkins was there to greet them. Jill looked at her attendance sheet and said "Jennifer Hope Emerson, here's your name." She put a checkmark behind Jenny's name on her list.

"You need to fix that," Jenny said. "That's my old name. I have a new name now."

Jill looked up from her paperwork and caught the smile on Coop's face. She looked to Becky questioningly. Becky nodded and said, "It's true. Jenny has a new last name now."

Jenny proudly announced, "I'm a Smith now. Jennifer Hope Smith. My parents are Coop and Becky Smith. We all have a Smith name now. I was adopted." She smiled up at Coop. "This is my daddy!"

"That's wonderful Jenny! Congratulations! I'm so happy for you." Jill looked between Coop and Becky and said, "I'm happy for all of you!" She put her arm around Jenny and said, "Come on, Jenny Smith. Let's go find your classroom!"

Coop and Becky walked hand in hand toward their new classroom. Nancy and Greg joined them. Nancy was carrying a tray of donuts to share with the members of their class. They passed by Dave Cole's room, where the singles were gathering. Coop stopped at the door to have a quick word with Dave. While they were talking, Dana and a group of young friends filed past them. Coop was glad to see that Dana went immediately to welcome two visitors to the class. Nancy had told him that she expected the visitors to be there today. He was so proud of Dana, to put the past behind her and to extend a hand of friendship to one she once considered a servant of the devil.

He recalled the conversation they had had a few months ago. Nancy and Greg had told him about the changes God had brought to Misty's life, how she had been saved and baptized, how she was not the same person he had encountered last summer. She had even changed her name back to Melissa, putting her old life behind her. She was studying Scripture and sharing her testimony. It was a marvelous story of redemption and transformation.

Dana had been a little hesitant to believe it at first, but Nancy had encouraged her to believe in the power of God to change a person's heart completely. And Becky had spoken about her encounter with Melissa in the hospital, and shared about the changes she had observed and believed to be sincere. So when Dana caught sight of the tall newcomer to class, she knew immediately who it was and went to re-introduce herself.

"Hi! Welcome to our class! I don't know if you remember me, my name is Dana Smith. We're glad to have you with us today. Melissa, right?"

"Yes, thank you. And this is my friend Craig. It's his first time here too. Nancy Martin told me this would be a great class for us, and we'll both learn a lot about the Bible and God's love for us. We're both pretty new at this and want to learn as much as we can." Melissa glanced at Craig and smiled.

Craig said, "Well, Melissa's been religious for a little while, but this is all new stuff to me. She's been telling me about what happened to her and how meeting Jesus changed her life. So I'm here to see what it's all about. I just bought this Bible." He held up a brand new Bible. "I don't know where to begin."

Dana waved her arm toward Dave, who was mingling with others in the class. He came over to stand beside her. "This is our class leader, Dave Cole. Dave, this is Melissa and Craig. It's their first time in our church."

Craig jokingly said, "Correction. It's my first time in *any* church!"

Melissa added, "Nancy Martin invited us. But she goes to the married people's class."

"Well, if you're not married, then this is the class for you. Let me introduce you to some others in the class." Dana took the visitors around to meet several other members, then they all took their seats and Dave began the class with prayer.

Across the hall, in the young married's class, Coop stood in front of his class, with Becky at his side. He held her hand and encouraged the couples in the class to do so also. "Dear heavenly Father," he began. "We come to you this morning, thankful for our spouses, grateful for bringing us together, excited about what we are going to learn today, and how you are going to lead our families in the months ahead. Bless us now in our time of fellowship and sharing. Bring new understanding to your Word. In your name we pray. Amen." He squeezed Becky's hand and she beamed up at him.

An hour later, seated near the choir loft, Coop looked up to see his mother at the piano. He looked to the choir and saw his mother-in-law sitting with the sopranos and his sister sitting right behind her in the alto section. Dana looked a little nervous; this was her first time to sing with the choir. He winked at her and she smiled back. Coop noticed that Dave Cole was singing with the basses. It was his first time singing with the choir too.

The congregation rose to sing the call to worship song together. Marla Jean played the introduction and everyone sang, "Turn you eyes upon Jesus, look full in his wonderful face, and the things of earth will grow strangely dim in the light of his glory and grace."

Coop took Becky's hand in his and together they raised their arms, united in an act of worship. Once more, Coop thanked the Lord for his family. He praised the Lord for the constant presence and protection he felt. Despite everything he and Becky had been through in the last year, he believed with all his heart that God was guiding them. And without him, they would be lost. He felt confident that his Savior, *their* Savior, would be with them always. An overwhelming sense of peace settled on him.

The congregation stirred in anticipation as the young children took the stage. Jenny and Hannah stood side by side, looking out into the audience. When Jenny found her parents, she waved and smiled.

She nudged Hannah and pointed in their direction. Hannah's parents were sitting right behind Coop and Becky. Hannah waved too.

The Sunday school director took the microphone and explained to the congregation that the first, second and third graders had been learning the twenty-third Psalm in both Vacation Bible School and during the summer Sunday school classes. The children looked confident as they began in unison. "The Lord is my shepherd, I shall not want." Then one by one, each child recited a phrase. For the last verse, Hannah stepped forward and said, "Surely goodness and mercy shall follow me all the days of my life." Then Jenny took the mic and said loud and clear, "And I will dwell in the house of the Lord forever." Unexpectedly she added, "That means I'll live with Jesus in heaven. Forever!"

A chuckle went up from the congregation and several members turned to look for Becky and Coop. Some were smiling with approval; a few gave the thumbs up sign. Becky caught sight of her mother in the choir loft. She was one proud grandma. She smiled when Dana nudged her shoulder. Both beamed at the little girl who had relayed a new meaning to Psalm twenty-three.

The children came down to sit with their parents. As Jenny snuggled in between her parents, Coop bent down to whisper, "You did great kiddo!" A big smile lit up Jenny's face.

The choir rose to sing and everyone in the congregation settled down to listen. The anthem for the day was "Under His Wings", an old hymn beautifully arranged with a blend of the traditional hymn with modern phrasing at times. The words were not changed, however, and Jenny was listening carefully. "Under his wings I am safely abiding." She pulled on her mother's elbow and mouthed the word 'abiding.' Becky nodded and smiled. The song went on, "Under his wings my soul shall abide." This time Jenny poked Coop. "Abide," she whispered.

Over her head. the two grown-ups looked at each other. The family circle, such as it was right now, was secure in the future heaven offered them. That knowledge brought a smile to each face and tears to Becky's eyes. She dabbed at the moisture with a tissue and turned her attention back to the choir. The harmony was close and tight, and Dana seemed comfortable singing with the older people. It was a beautiful song, and the words spoke to Becky.

> *"Under His wings, what a refuge in sorrow!*
> *How the heart yearningly turns to His rest.*
> *Often when earth has no balm for my healing,*
> *There I find comfort, and there I am blest."*

Once again the tears welled. Becky was overcome with emotion. Jenny noticed and took her hand. Coop put his arm across the back of the pew and stroked her arm. He was in tune with her thoughts and amazed that it had happened so quickly. They'd been married less than a year, but already he knew her moods and could predict her thoughts and sometimes even knew what she was about to say.

He knew she was thinking about Matthew Peter, the baby they had lost, just a few months ago. He knew she was remembering the sorrow, the pain. He was feeling it too, but knew that his comfort came when he was under the Savior's wings. Nothing the world offered could compare to the safety and peace he found in Jesus.

Becky wiped her eyes with her free hand, then looked over at her husband. Their eyes met in understanding. The look that passed between them was one of strength and empathy. Becky knew that their home, founded on the Lord Jesus Christ, could withstand any storms. The two of them could sail safely through any troubled waters, as long as Jesus was at the helm. Coop and Becky were becoming a team, a force to be reckoned with. 'And the two shall become one,' thought Becky. Coop squeezed her shoulder and she relaxed.

'But it's more than two,' Becky remembered. 'We have three, a cord of three. Jesus is here with us, keeping us safe, leading us through all kinds of dangers and fears. Even losses and disappointments.'

The chorus rose and Becky's thought returned to the music.

> *"Under His wings, under His wings,*
> *Who from His love can sever?*

Under His wings my soul shall abide,
Safely abide forever.

When the choir song ended, the choir members went to sit with families in the congregation. Coop watched as his mother and mother-in law chose seats together near the front. He noticed that his sister and Dave Cole went to sit with Misty and her friend. 'What was his name? I don't think I know him.' Coop pondered the problem of names as he remembered that Misty now wanted to be called Melissa. That was going to be strange, although he supported the name change almost as much as the lifestyle change he had witnessed. 'The Lord works in mysterious ways," he thought

During the sermon, Jenny drew pictures in the notebook she always brought to church. Becky glanced down now and then and watched as the picture unfolded. There was a big fluffy cloud with a house sitting on it. The house was a bright yellow color, with streaks of yellow coming off it, much like Jenny drew sunbeams on every sun she colored. Next to the house Jenny drew a stick figure man and added clothes. She made a long brown robe and a shepherd staff. Then Jenny added yellow sunbeams to the man. Next came three little sheep. One of them was looking out the window of the yellow house. Jenny wrote letters under each sheep. J. M. and D. The sheep in the window had the J. under it.

She showed the picture to her mommy, then whispered, "J for Jenny, M for Mommy and D for Daddy." Becky smiled and nodded, putting her finger up to her lips to remind Jenny not to talk during church.

As she thought about the picture a little longer, Jenny decided that she wanted a white dove, with its wings spread out over the house. She struggled to make it just right, drawing first with a pencil and erasing until she was satisfied. Then she colored it in with a white crayon and added black dots for eyes.

Jenny sat back to admire her work, then leaned over the paper again. She added a shiny yellow crown on top of the man's head, with yellow sunbeams of course. Finally she added words. In childish six-year-old printing she wrote: *DWL=ABID=LIV*

The spelling was phonetic and the letters danced around on the page, but Becky understood the meaning. She smiled at her daughter and patted her hand. Jenny decided to add more letters. Using a purple crayon she wrote *JESUS*. Pleased with herself because she knew how to spell it, she showed her mother once again, and then passed the notebook over to Coop for his inspection. Coop leaned close to whisper, "Nice job! Let's hang it up when we get home." Jenny looked up and him and smiled brightly, bobbing her head up and down in agreement.

The picture was placed on the front of the refrigerator in the Smith's kitchen. It was a daily reminder that the family was safely abiding in the house of the Lord, under the protection of Christ's comforting wings, where they would dwell forever.

CHAPTER 53

———◆◆◆———

A Change in the Weather

A chill wind whistled around the corners of the house, and Becky, napping in her bedroom, pulled the blanket up close around her chin. She heard giggling coming from the kitchen and smiled. Jenny and Coop were up to something.

She lay in the bed, listening to the comforting sounds of family. She stretched her injured leg, flexing the calf muscle and pushing her knee down flat onto the mattress. Although she was no longer going to physical therapy, Becky knew the importance of continuing to do her exercises. She turned her foot in a circle ten times to the right, ten times to the left. She felt strength returning to her foot and ankle. She wasn't one hundred percent yet, but that was okay. Every day she felt a little stronger.

Coop's deep laugh rumbled from the kitchen and Becky decided to get up and see what was going on. She sat on the side of the bed, being careful with her foot placement on the floor. Holly was sleeping there, cuddled against the wall, with her feet up in the air and belly exposed. This position always made Becky smile. How the collie could be comfortable like that was beyond her imagination. Coop called it 'the dying cockroach position.' Holly slept that way often.

Ever since Becky had returned from the hospital, Holly had stayed close to Becky's side. Always a loyal companion, Holly now seemed to know that her job was to protect Becky and give comfort. Holly was not disturbed by the walking assists that Becky had needed at first. She respected the equipment but was not afraid of it. The wheelchair, the leg brace, the knee roller, even the walker and cane were all put away now, no longer needed. Aside from a little stiffness in the mornings, Becky was almost her old self. Holly had been a big part of her recovery.

Jenny had worked hard, teaching Holly some new tricks. Holly could now pick up things that Becky had dropped, carry pieces of mail to Becky, and even pick up her dog toys off the floor and put them into the toy basket. Every day Holly amazed Becky and others in the family with her understanding and intuition.

From time to time in the past months, Holly had sensed a sadness come over Becky and had always known when Becky needed a friend. She would make herself available for some cuddle time, or lick Becky's hand. Sometimes Holly would just go over to Becky and sit next to her, as if to say, 'I'm here, Becky. You are not alone.'

"Ewww, that's gross!" Jenny's laughter carried from the kitchen.

"What in the world are they doing, Holly?" Becky asked the collie, who had rolled over and raised her head, curious about the noise. "Let's go see." She slid her feet into slippers and pushed her arms into a sweater. Holly stood, stretched herself and pranced down the hall ahead of Becky.

Newspapers were spread out over the kitchen table and pumpkin seeds and slimy strands of pulp littered the area. Jenny was kneeling on a kitchen chair, bending over a big pumpkin. She was elbow deep and giggling. "Look mommy," she laughed as she lifted her hand from the pumpkin. "Pumpkin guts!" Her fist was clutching gobs of slippery seeds, which scattered onto the table as she wiggled her fingers.

"Sorry we woke you," Coop said with a grin. "But we thought it was time to make a jack-o-lantern. It's almost Halloween so we need to get some decorations up. We thought we'd have a little fun with carving this one into a cat face. Maybe call it Pumpkin Kitty, right Jenny?"

"Yup! And that little pumpkin can just be a normal face with triangle eyes." She dropped another handful of guts on the newspaper. "It's yucky slimy though. Wanna help?"

"I think I'll leave the pumpkin carving up to you two. You seem to have it well under control. I was thinking I'd make potato soup for supper. How's that sound?"

"Yummy!" Jenny replied. She went back to work on the pumpkin.

"Mom brought over a loaf of sourdough bread she just baked," Coop said. "It's over there on the counter."

"I thought I smelled something wonderful!" Becky said. "Couldn't imagine pumpkin guts smelled this good!" She lifted the loaf of fresh bread to her nose and inhaled deeply. "This is the best smell in the world. I can't believe your mom is still baking bread. Maybe she better teach me how. That's something I've never done before."

"I know she'd love to teach you. She did say her arthritis is bothering her today. Maybe because it's getting colder. She said it was hard to knead the bread because her hands were hurting."

Becky got potatoes from the pantry and started peeling them. "I'll ask her to let me help her next time. Then I'll learn how, and she won't have to do all the kneading herself."

"Mom used to make kolaches a lot when we were little, but she hasn't done them in a long time. Ask her to teach you how to make them, too. They're really good."

"Now that I haven't gone back to work with Doc Larson, I'll have more time to spend with your mom. And since I can actually stand and walk and lift much better now, I'll be able to do more around the house. And help you out on the farm, too."

"Well, don't go rushing into all this activity too fast. You need to take it slow, or you might have a setback." Coop cut the top off the small pumpkin and handed the squash to Jenny. She started scooping seeds. Coop took the carving tool and started making the large pumpkin turn into a cat face.

"Do you know that a Christian is like this pumpkin?" Coop asked as he carefully cut the ears of the cat. He was following lines from a stencil he had traced onto the orange pumpkin skin.

"Huh?" Jenny asked. "That's silly! I'm not like a pumpkin."

"You are," Coop replied. "And mommy and daddy too." He looked up at Becky and winked. She smiled back in understanding.

"What do you mean?" Jenny asked.

"Well, let's think back about this pumpkin. You went out to the pumpkin field and picked it out, right? You brought it in and cleaned it off. Then you scooped out all the bad yuckyness that was inside. Now you're making it smile. And you're going to put a light in it, right? So everyone can see."

"Yeah," Jenny agreed with skepticism. "But how does that make *me* a pumpkin?"

"It's because Jesus chose you. He thought you were exactly the one he wanted. He cleaned you off and then scooped out all the yucky sin from your heart." Coop had put down his carving tool and was looking directly at Jenny.

Becky pulled up a chair and sat close to her daughter. "And when he did that, when he cleaned out your heart, you were happy. You were smiling because Jesus had forgiven your sins."

"Ohhh, I get it!" Jenny said excitedly. "Jesus loved me and died for my sins and forgave me, so now I'm happy!"

"Right!" said Coop proudly. "So tonight we'll put a candle inside the pumpkin. What do you think that means?"

"I know! I know!" Jenny exclaimed. "It's like my other verse from Bible club. About the light under the bushel. The one that says to let your light shine."

"Let your light shine before others, that they may see your good deeds and glorify your Father in heaven." Becky completed the verse for her.

Coop finished with "Matthew five sixteen. So see, you are like a pumpkin!"

Jenny giggled, "Wait till I tell Hannah!"

The family worked on their own projects and soon the table was cleaned off in preparation for supper. The jack-o-lanterns were placed outside on either side of the porch steps. Holly went outside to sniff the creations and approved of their location. She trotted on out to the barnyard to check on the chickens and sheep. Tinkerbell let out an excited 'baaa' when Holly got close. They had become great friends and were often found napping near each other.

After prayer, Becky scooped potato soup into three bowls and set them on the table. The soup was hot and steaming, potatoes, carrots and celery blended into a milky, creamy broth. Bread and butter topped off the meal, with fried apples for dessert.

"It was fun having no school today," Jenny said as she put her dishes into the sink after supper. "Teachers had to work on report cards. I hope I get a good one."

"As long as you have tried your best, we will be proud of you," Coop encouraged. "What's your favorite thing to do in school?"

"That's easy," Jenny said enthusiastically. "It's art! That's my favorite!"

Coop went to the hall closet and got his flannel lined jacket. It was time to do evening chores and the temperatures had dropped steadily through the day. Now with the wind picking up, it was going to be a chilly evening. He walked through the kitchen as the conversation continued.

"You have always liked coloring and drawing," Becky replied. "I have a big box of your art work I've been saving for years." She rinsed the dishes and handed them to Jenny to be placed into the dishwasher. "How are you doing with your math? You were working hard on counting money, and I know you understand that. What are you learning now?"

Jenny's head went down and she didn't answer. She took a plate from her mother and busied herself putting it just so in the dish rack, then re-arranged the cups on the top shelf. Anything to keep from facing her mother.

Becky dried her hands on a dishtowel and lowered herself to Jenny's eye level. "Jenny…," she started. "What's going on?" Coop stood near the door, waiting to hear Jenny's answer before he went outside.

Jenny's eyes were brimming with unshed tears when she finally answered. "Its factors, Mommy. I have a worksheet I was supposed to do today. But I can't do it. I don't get it."

"Factors, huh?" said Coop from the doorway. "I think I can help you with that, after I get my chores done." He looked over at Becky and asked, "Didn't I see you had a bag of candy corn somewhere?"

Surprised, Becky nodded her head slowly. "Yes, I got a bag when I was at the store the other day. But I'm not sure what candy corn has to do with math factors."

"Just wait, you'll see." Coop turned to Jenny. "You finish helping mommy with the dishes, and when I come back in, we'll work on math factors. Deal?"

Jenny was puzzled too, but replied, "Deal!" She hurried to finish loading the dishwasher, then wiped off the table. She got her backpack from her bedroom and looked through the papers to find her math page. She ran back to her room to get a pencil and when she returned, Becky was sitting at the table, studying the worksheet.

Becky lowered the paper to the table and turned to Jenny. "You know, honey, Daddy and I are always here to help you. Never be afraid to ask us for help."

Jenny wiggled in her chair and lowered her head. Barely above a whisper, she mumbled, "But I didn't want you to think I'm stupid."

Becky put her arm around the girl and pulled her close. "First of all, we would never think you are stupid. That's a word I don't even like to say." Becky lifted Jenny's chin gently. "God gave each of us a brain, and everybody's brains work a little differently. Some people are really good at math, and others are good at art. Some can read big words and some can solve hard problems. Everybody is important, and everybody is special."

Coop stood on the porch, removing his boots and coat. He hung his hat on the peg and came into the kitchen to wash his hands. Becky continued, "If you need help to understand something, just ask. Your teachers want to help, and so do we." She looked towards Coop, who was picking the bag of candy corn off the counter. "The thing is, if you don't tell us you need help, we won't know. Don't ever be afraid to ask. We will never get mad at you for asking for help. We might be upset if you hide your homework again, though. Now let's see what Daddy plans to do with candy corn!"

CHAPTER 54

———◆◆◆———

Factors of Ten

By the time Becky got out of the shower, Jenny had mastered the factors of ten. "Look Mommy, I'll show you," Jenny said with a big smile. She dug into the bag of candy corn and carefully counted out ten pieces, laying them in a straight line on the table.

"See, here's ten corns. And there's zero corns over here." She patted the table to the side of the corn line. "So ten plus zero is ten." Jenny moved one piece of corn over to the empty space and said, "Now there's nine corns here, and one corn here. So nine plus one is ten." She slid another piece of candy. "And now eight plus two is ten."

Jenny moved another piece and said, "And now, seven plus three is ten!" She smiled up proudly at her mother. "Get it? It's easy!"

Coop rustled his daughter's hair and said, "You learned quick. But show your mom what else you learned." He was having as much fun with this lesson as the little girl was, and he smiled up at Becky with delight. "Once she learned all the factors of ten, we moved on."

"Moved on? I can't wait to see what you mean!" She caught the gleam in Coop's eye and knew he was up to some mischief.

"Show her, Jenny." Coop nudged Jenny and she giggled as she arranged all the candies in a straight line again.

"Okay, ready," she said expectantly as she looked at Coop, waiting for his signal. Before he could say anything, she turned to her mom and said, "I learned takeaway!"

Becky raised her eyebrows and caught Coop's attention. "Take away?" she asked.

"Yeah, she's really good at it too. Watch this." Coop tapped his forehead with his finger as if thinking, then said, "Ten take away four."

Without hesitation, Jenny called out "Ten take away four is six!"

"Correct! You may take away four!" As Jenny removed four candy corns and ate them, Coop reached into the bag and reconstructed the line."

"Ten take away two."

"Eight! Ten take away two is eight!" She reached her hand, poised for the removal upon Coop's signal.

"Correct! You may take away two!"

Becky was laughing as she asked, "And I wonder how many pieces of candy you have actually eaten this evening?"

"Not too much mommy. Daddy will only let me eat them if I get the take away right." Then she sheepishly added, "But I am pretty good at it!"

"One more problem, then it's time to get ready for bed," Coop said as he straightened out the candy line. "Ten take away ten."

"That's easy," Jenny piped up. "Ten take away ten is zero."

"Correct! You make take all ten. Then be sure to brush your teeth really good tonight."

"No, wait. Here." Jenny carefully separated the line into two equal lengths. "Five for Mommy, five for Daddy. Five plus five makes ten."

As Coop and Becky enjoyed their snack, Jenny put her papers away into her backpack. She turned to Coop and gave him a big hug. "Thank you for helping me, Daddy. Tomorrow can we do factors of one hundred?"

Coop laughed and looked at Becky. "I think you better go buy more candy corn!"

Later that night, after prayers (Jenny's request was to always remember to ask for help, and Becky's thankful response was remembering that Jesus is our strength and help in times of trouble) and Best Part, which of course included factors of ten, and take aways, Becky and Coop lay wrapped in each other's arms. "You really are a good father," Becky whispered into the soft flesh of his neck.

Coop slowly ran his hands over Becky's flesh, resting on the gentle rise of her hips. He kissed her softly and said, "She's a great kid. All credit to you."

"And mom. And prayer. And now you and your family, and the church. They say it takes a village. Guess that's true." Becky put her arms around Coop's neck and pulled him close. Her kiss was warm and inviting. "I love you Coop." She shifted her body and he raised himself up on his hands.

Coop tilted his head and asked in a husky voice, "You sure?"

She giggled and squirmed under him. "Yes, I'm sure I love you! And I'm sure I want you, too.

Holly the collie rose from her sleeping spot on the floor near Becky's side of the bed. She stretched full length and yawned, then left the room, to give them some privacy.

CHAPTER 55

Festive Plans

The group of young people gathered around a table in their Sunday school classroom. Dave Cole called the meeting to order and thanked everyone for coming. "Our purpose here this afternoon is two-fold. First, we're going to plan our winter fellowship bash. We'll need to come up with a theme, some decorations, and plan the food. It's a good thing Dana and some of you other girls are here, because party planning is not my thing. I'm counting on you for all that!"

"We can handle it," Dana said, and the other girls nodded in agreement.

"And second, we're going to have a time of prayer. Our focus is going to be on inviting and encouraging. We've had several visitors to our class in the past couple of months, and I want to cover them in prayer. I think we have done a good job of making them feel welcome, and now we want to move towards discipleship. That starts with prayer." Dave opened the meeting with prayer, and the work began.

An hour later, the party planning well on its way. The focus of the meeting changed to an atmosphere of prayer. Dave mentioned all of the visitors by name and prayer was offered for each one. The group prayed for all those in the class to feel the nudging of the Holy Spirit as they were drawn closer and closer to the Savior. Members, occasional visitors, and visitors yet to come – all were covered as Dave prayed for a crowd of witnesses to surround them, encourage them, and show them the way of the cross.

The young people left the meeting with a new sense of empowerment. They were invigorated and inspired, committed to making an impact on the world, one soul at a time.

Dana waved goodbye to her friends and walked to her car. The semester break was still two weeks away and she had some research to do for a paper in contemporary literature. She'd have to work on her computer at home before supper.

A vibration in her back jeans pocket took her mind off schoolwork. She pulled the phone out and smiled. Tucker. It was always good to talk to him. She leaned against the car and enjoyed the feel of the late fall sun on her head and shoulders. "Hi! What are you doing on this beautiful day?" she asked cheerfully. It was a cheerful kind of day.

"Hi Dana. Sounds like you are in a good mood. It's beautiful here too, but it will be better if you say yes." Tucker paused, knowing what her response would probably be.

Dana laughed. "How can I say yes when I don't know what you're asking?"

"Oh trust me, you're going to want to say yes. Do you have a passport?"

"A passport? No, I've never seen a reason to get one."

"Well," Tucker paused for effect.

"Well what?" Dana asked with a hint of impatience in her voice. "Don't leave me hanging. What's going on?"

"Here's the deal." Tucker took a big breath. "Our church mission team is going to Central America next summer, and I want you to come along! You'll need a passport for the trip. And some money for travel. But it will be so worth it. I can't wait to show you the school we helped build last year. And this year, we're going to put a new roof on the hospital. Think about it Dana. We'd be doing good in the name of Jesus. We'd be sharing the gospel by lending a helping hand. And the people, you can't believe how great the people are until you see them for yourself."

"I don't know, Tucker. I've never done anything like that before. I don't know anything about roofing. How long would we be gone? And what's the cost? I don't know how to speak much Spanish either. I'm not so sure this is a good idea." She was hesitant, yet somehow excited as well.

"Aw, come on. It's a great idea. It would be a month, and we could really get to know each other. And don't worry about the work, or the language. There's lots of people to teach you what you need to know. Just think, a month to see each other every day. It would be so good. Besides, look at all the good we could do for those people, who have so little. But despite their poverty, they are the most happy people you could ever find. They want to hear more about Jesus, but they teach me every time I go."

Dana was intrigued but cautious. She wished her dad was alive; she'd love to get his opinion about this. But it had been over a year since he had passed. She had lots of questions, but she'd have to talk with her mom about the opportunity. And Coop - she wanted to get his advice too.

"Okay, I'll think about it. We'll talk more about it tomorrow. I have a paper I have to finish tonight. But I do want to know more. Thanks for thinking of me."

"I think about you a lot. I would love to see you more, and this would be a good chance. Besides, there's one more thing you have to know."

"What's that?" Dana asked. Her eyes were following the dipping and diving of a bird flying low over the church yard. From its movements, she recognized it was some kind of swift or swallow. It reminded her of the birds at the nest in the hay mow.

Tucker's words brought her back to attention. She caught the excitement in his voice as he said, "It's just that, you aren't going to believe this, the team leader this year is Tom Swift! And when I heard his name, I just thought about the birds we were talking about, that time when you were in the barn and I was getting dive bombed. They were swifts, or swallows, and I just knew it was a sign. I don't often get a sign from God, but I really think this is one. It's meant to be!"

Dana's heart swelled with joy and she smiled. Tucker had been thinking of her. Tucker wanted to get to know her better. Tucker loved the Lord and wanted to share this mission opportunity with her. Tucker thought swifts and swallows were their sign. And how could she argue about a sign from God?

Dana watched as the swift in front of her skimmed across the grass, looking for insects. Her eyes widened when it was joined by another swift. Together the two of them flew in circles over the yard, first dipping low, then climbing to dive again in unison. Together.

Maybe it *was* a sign.

CHAPTER 56

---◆◆◆---

'Twas the Night
Before Christmas

Becky rose early on Christmas Eve morning. Coop was enjoying a bit of much needed sleep. He'd been up late last night, working on the thermostat that controlled the temperature of the water in the animal's trough. The weather had taken a sudden turn, and water in the trough had frozen. It had to get fixed, which required a drive into town for a new regulator, and then time working in the cold and dark, installing it. When Coop finally got to bed, it was after midnight. But he was satisfied. The animals would have fresh water.

There were still a few presents that needed wrapping, and Becky was planning to make a breakfast casserole for Christmas morning. But first she wanted to prepare a gift for Coop.

The home pregnancy test packaging was in the trash can. She left the white testing tube on the bathroom counter, where Coop would see it when he got up. Two pink lines were clearly visible through the little window. She looked over at her sleeping husband and smiled. "Surprise! And Merry Christmas!" she whispered as she headed to the kitchen.

An hour later, she was sprinkling the top layer of cheese on her casserole when she heard a *whoop* from the bedroom. Coop came bounding into the kitchen, scooped her up in his arms, and swung her around the kitchen. He covered her face with kisses, he whispered "I love you Becky" into her ear, and he placed his hand over her still flat belly. "Grow little baby, grow and grow. Welcome to our family."

Becky could barely catch her breath, but when she finally did she said, "It's not official yet, of course, just a home test. But I'm pretty sure anyway. My breasts are extra sensitive, and I feel bloated. Just like before. Oh Coop, I'm so happy."

He reached up under her sweatshirt and gently massaged her breast. "It feels bigger too! Yep, you're pregnant!"

Over his shoulder, Becky saw a sleepy Jenny coming down the hall, clutching one of her stuffed kittens. She pushed Coop's hand down and whispered "Should we tell her?"

Coop turned to watch Jenny stumble into the kitchen. "You're making too much noise. You woke me up," she mumbled, rubbing her eyes.

He looked at Becky and nodded. Then he picked Jenny up and held her close. "Sorry we woke you, but we have some good news."

Suddenly awake, Jenny pushed her hair out of her eyes and waited expectantly.

Becky was the one to break the news. Jenny clapped and shouted "Hurrah! My sibling is coming!" She wiggled out of Coop's grasp and ran off down the hall to her bedroom. Becky and Coop hugged each other and were standing wrapped in each other's arms when Jenny ran back into the kitchen.

She pushed a chair up to the refrigerator and began to draw on the picture that was hanging there. A tiny little white blob, with blue eyes, appeared in one of the windows of the house. It was a lamb, very small, but a lamb just the same.

Jenny looked from one grown-up to another with a puzzled expression. "What's the baby's name going to be?" she asked.

"Well, we will have to think of a good name for him. Or her. We don't even know if it's a girl or a boy yet."

"Then I'll put a question mark. I learned how to make it at school." Carefully Jenny drew a question mark under the little lamb. She climbed down off the chair and stood with her parents, looking at the picture. "Let's call the baby Lambie," she said. "We called Matthew Peter 'Peanut.' This baby can be Lambie."

"Lambie it is!" Coop said, and Becky added, "For now!"

The growing family stood, wrapped in thought, gazing at the picture on the refrigerator. Becky was grateful to God for this opportunity to mother another child. Coop was thanking the Lord for his growing family, and praying for guidance as he fathered them all. Jenny was excited about a sibling.

In one quick movement, Jenny was back up on the chair. She added a big smile on the face of the shepherd. "He's so happy," she said, "Because we are all safely abiding in the house of the Lord forever!"

"Amen!" Coop said and Becky and Jenny echoed him.

"Can I tell Grandma and Grammy and Aunt Dana?" Jenny was so excited she was jumping up and down. "I want to tell them I'm going to be a sibling!"

Becky knelt down beside her and put her hands on her shoulders. "I've got an idea. Let's not tell them right away. Let's leave the picture up on the refrigerator and see if anyone notices. Then it will be our little secret for awhile."

Jenny was all for it. "It's like a game!" To see if anyone can figure it out! But won't they know, when your tummy starts growing?"

"How about, if no one guesses our secret, we tell them on New Year's Day? That's just a week away. Do you think you can wait that long?" Coop asked Jenny and she nodded.

"Now I have to get outside and do the morning chores," Coop said as he headed back to the bedroom. "Then we'll have breakfast and head out to deliver some presents. I can't wait to see the look on Marilyn and Ed's faces when they see we were able to get their clock fixed!" He turned around quickly and planted another kiss on Becky's lips. "I love you, Mommy," he said to her.

"I love you too, Mommy," Jenny echoed as she skipped off to her bedroom to dress.

Becky stood looking at the picture a bit longer. "Thank you, Jesus," she said out loud. "Thank you for my family. Thank you for this new life you're blessing us with. Thank you for being our shepherd, always keeping us safe. Thank you for our heavenly home, where we can abide with you forever."

From down the hall, Becky could hear her husband singing. "Under his wings, I am safely abiding." She took some bacon from the refrigerator and placed slices into the frying pan. When Coop got to the chorus, Becky joined in. "Under his wings my soul shall abide."

Jenny, in her own bedroom sang out in her loudest voice. "Safely abide forever."

Watch for book three in

THE WHITE DOVE SERIES

Heaven's Waiting Room